Cousins
A Sequel to The Family

J. Andrews Smith

J. Andrews Smith, MSW

Dear Laura and Curtis,
2017
"Merry Christmas"
I love you,
Aunt Edith

This book is dedicated to

Susan, my friend, soul mate, and wife:
you have endured many lonely hours and have been
my strongest support in bringing this book to fruition.

Jerry, Jr. and Mark, my wonderful sons:
you have always been respectful, supportive, and loving,
even when I've left you alone to travel that dirt road of my childhood.
You've touched my heart and soul more than you'll ever know.

I will always tell our stories.

~ J. Andrews Smith

Table of Contents

◇◇◇◇◇◇◇◇◇ JERRY SMITH PAPERS ◇◇◇◇◇◇◇◇◇

Foreword

Charles Warren, MBA
Board President
KidsTLC
Olathe, Kansas

As a member of the Board of Directors of KidsTLC in Olathe, Kansas for the past thirteen years and board President for the past four years, I have participated in extraordinary organizational growth for KidsLTC (www.kidstlc.org). The good news is that the 35-member board, comprised of some of the most talented and extraordinary leaders in the Greater Kansas City Metro Area, has successfully anticipated change and adapted as required. The not so good news is that our community, and indeed our society in general, continues to face a growing demand for services designed to assist children and families in crisis. With ever present budget pressures from federal, state and local sources, health and human services (HHS) organizations across the country and around the world will continue to confront an array of challenges within their respective operating environments. Residential treatment for youth and families will remain a viable component of a comprehensive approach.

The history of care for children outside the traditional family, two-parent home goes back to the use of orphanages and Children's Homes as long term residential care. Foster care, smaller group homes, and emergency shelters were established to help fill the gaps left by parents missing in action. Surrogate parents can today take many forms, with short term temporary programs helping to fill gaps across a continuum of care. An interesting trend beginning to gain traction with HHS professionals around the country is a return to long term care options that include Children's Homes with residents expected to stay for years, not just weeks and months.

This trend will likely have support from an unlikely social demographic—those who were raised in orphanages and Children's Homes. This group generally looks back on their experiences as residents of long term care with overall positive recollections and favorable impacts from the quality and kind of care provided. Independent surveys and children's homes alumni interviews bear this out as former residents recall experiences that impacted their lives while living in institutional childcare.

In my own childhood experience at the Free Will Baptist Children's Home in Middlesex, North Carolina, (from 2/1967 to 8/1973), I remain convinced that my nuclear family circumstances were so fragile and untenable that without the intervention of social services I would not be here today. Furthermore, if I had managed to survive the chaos that was my life at age eleven, the age at which I entered the Free Will Baptist Children's Home, I would today be a diminished person relative to my current lot in life.

There exists a special relationship between those who have lived in orphanages or children's homes. This is most apparent when upon chance discovery of a childhood history that includes time in orphanages, the kinship of shared experience is immediate, even when orphanages are different or the time of stay is separated by years. Sharing stories from different circumstances with this common factor immediately reveals shared feelings and an alignment of perspectives on childhood. For much of my life I have celebrated these relationships of strong affiliation and genuine love, most of which began under desperate or dire circumstances. In many cases strong bonds develop and are often shared for lifetimes.

I have known Jerry Smith since my early adolescence. My first encounter was not with Jerry directly but rather I learned of Jerry through my Aunt Ora Bell, with whom I and three of my sisters were living following the sudden separation from our Mother and death of our Father. My aunt was talking to us about the Free Will Baptist Children's Home as a place where kids like us go to live with lots of other kids from similar circumstances. Jerry Smith was a parole officer in Williamston, North Carolina and sometimes attended the Doodle Hill Free Will Baptist Church, where my aunt was a member. One Sunday Jerry was in attendance and my aunt pointed him out as the nice young man who grew up at the Free Will Baptist Children's Home (1949-60).

My sisters and I, along with my brother, found ourselves living at The Home with a total population of 103 children and youth from various counties around the state. Most kids, like my family, had found their way to the Home through Free Will Baptist churches or were sponsored by a Free Will Baptist Church somewhere in Eastern North Carolina.

Some years later through the Free Will Baptist Children's Home Alumni Association and while attending the annual children's home "homecoming" event, I met Jerry Smith and we became friends over time. From that initial meeting a lifelong friendship has grown. Over the years, I have attended school and athletic events for his two boys. In addition to reciprocal attendance at childhood events while living in the same town, Jerry and his family traveled cross country to attend the wedding of my daughter. Through the years, Jerry together with our mutual friends and family have vacationed together, supported each other as family, and despite distance and age, remained steadfast in our mutual love and respect.

First as a Social Services Director in the State of North Carolina and later following his retirement, working from a self-appointed position a child welfare advocate Jerry has written about, publicly spoken about, and lived an exemplary example of advocacy on behalf of those who have no public voice. While camping in state parks, hiking rim to rim the Grand Canyon and backpacking in the Great Smokey National Park, through many nighttime campfire dialogs, Jerry and I and other like-minded "orphans" have pondered together, "With so much working against them, why do kids from a children's home background make it in this world?" We orphan have first-hand knowledge of hundreds of orphan kids going on to become intelligent, successful, socially responsible, high achieving citizens from all walks of life: University Presidents, doctors, lawyers, bricklayers, business owners, business managers, distinguished professors and ordinary citizens—all no longer dependent upon public or private agency assistance for support.

In the individual accounts provided within this book, there is strong testimony for institutional childcare, congregate childcare, residential childcare—all euphemisms for children's homes or orphanages Exactly why it is so is not fully understood, but it is an undeniable fact that kids from this challenging background are successful at a rate equal to or greater than children and youth in society at large.

As you read and consider the accounts shared within this book, you can do so knowing that each story is unique and each is a story of relative success. As he did with his first account of young lives in peril on their life journey at the Free Will Baptist Children's Home (*The Family*, 2010, Lulu Press and Amazon Press), Jerry Smith has gathered in the sequel compelling life stories of children, youth, and families beating the odds from other Homes in our country. In the sequel, Jerry has too included reflections from professionals working with children in residential and foster care.

Whatever the future of children's homes, the history of this form of child rescue is a matter of record and success. And although successful outcomes are apparent, it is the stories that remain most fascinating. As you read the pages of this book, know that the words represent much more than an accounting of events. Each story represents major, life forming, life changing, imprints on the hearts, minds and souls of those who lived them.

About Charles Warren

Over the past nine years Charles Warren has built a successful and thriving consulting practice with Expense Reduction Analysts (ERA). Prior to joining ERA, Charles spent 33 years in the corporate world of telecommunications with Sprint. During his telecom career Charles held numerous management and executive positions encompassing responsibilities across the entire value chain, from Network Operations to Research and Development.

Charles's career has been marked by results oriented Quality Management. He has experience in Total Quality Management (TQM), Malcolm Baldrige National Quality Award (MBNQA) and Capability Maturity Model (CMM) for software development. He led team projects resulting in millions of dollars in annual savings from business process improvement efforts.

Charles' Continuous Quality Improvement experience dates back to 1985 when Quality Circles were being adopted. As a trained facilitator he led quality improvement efforts across Coastal and Eastern North Carolina, using the model put in place by award winning Florida Power and Light. In 1988 Charles joined the Sprint Long Distance Division and moved to Kansas City where he began his work with Business Process Improvement. Following two years in the San Francisco Bay area working with Silicon Valley companies as a part of Sprint's technology labs, Charles returned to Kansas City as Director of Concept Realization Center (CRC). He was responsible for the development of new product prototypes and lab service validations for major corporate accounts.

Together with his wife and business partner, Charles enjoys spending time with his daughter and family, which includes two grandchildren. He serves on the board of KidsTLC in Olathe, KS where he has been a board member since 2003, and board chair since 2013. He holds an M.B.A. from the University of Kansas and is an American Society for Quality (ASQ) Certified Quality Manager (CQM).

Introduction

My interests in residential care began early in my childhood and has continued for more than sixty years. This is the third book I've authored with history and stories from those who spent their childhoods in residential care, as well as stories from staff who provided care to these children. Since 1996, I've written numerous newspaper columns about adults who did not live with their biological parents in childhood and adults who provided temporary parenting care to children in orphanages and children's homes.

My first book, *I Have Hope* (1978, ERA Press) is the study of a children's home and was written to partially fulfill requirements for my Masters degree in Social Work from the University of North Carolina, Chapel Hill, North Carolina.

My second book, *The Family* (2010, Lulu Press and Amazon.com) is the history of the Free Will Baptist Orphanage where I spent my childhood in Middlesex, North Carolina (known today as the Free Will Baptist Children's Home). *The Family* is a compilation of essays written by those who lived at the home from 1920–2010, and these memoirs give a first hand account of life in residential care throughout many decades. The chronicles include not only writings from the children who lived there, but also from staff and the children of staff who grew up on campus with us.

More than 2,400 children have lived at the Free Will Baptist Children's Home since it opened in 1920. My intent in this book was not only to provide a history of my home, but to offer readers the experience of how we felt growing up in residential care, and to vicariously live that life through us. I'm happy to say that my objective has been affirmed by many readers.

Cousins is my third book, and is a sequel to *The Family*. It includes writings from children and staff from more than a dozen children homes and orphanages across the U.S., and one from an orphanage in Africa. One section of the book is written by child care advocates and offers a professional viewpoint on the current status of residential care. Another section includes my writings about former residential children and staff written for the *Tazewell County Free Press* in Richlands, Virginia, where I've contributed monthly columns since 1996.

Cousins will be my last book on residential care. Other books should be written about the status of residential care across this nation, specifically about caring for children of color and LGBT kids, and drug use. We also need to share more about the positive outcomes from residential care.

Residential care homes and foster care homes are the two primary safety nets for children when biological families break down. Residential care, especially if long term, provides a stronger path for lifetime "family" bonding and support for those of us missing blood connections and emotional support. Unlike those children with placements only in foster care, our networking creates a truly supportive, non-judgmental "family" for those who grew up in the same residential home—and when we meet others from different children's homes, they quickly become "cousins" as we share our undoubtely similar experiences. My hope for this book is that it will inspire more "cousins" to get to know one another.

Of the many paths you will walk in life, select one that is dirt. Without asphalt or concrete, that path will not be well traveled, and you will feel every bump and dip in the road. Many of us who came to residential care traveled a dirt path, and many were able to find their way to the pavement of their future. Others got lost along the way and wandered much too long in life. Some are still wandering.

I invite you to pause, get off the safety net of the highways you travel, and journey the dirt paths described in *Cousins*. From the first hand accounts to the professional perspectives offered by child advocates, this book offers an education for our spirituality and culture as it enhances our understanding of residential care and relationships that are formed and nurtured between children and between children and staff throughout their lives.

J. Andrews Smith

1

Conversations with Child Advocates

The Spiritual Care of Children in Care: A Chaplain's View

Dr. Keith A. Bailey, Ph.D.

History of Child Care by Faith Communities

The Judeo-Christian tradition has evolved in its role of the care of children, especially those considered orphans (literally, the "fatherless"). The early Old Testament scriptures urged the people of God to not take advantage of or oppress the fatherless (Exodus 22:22; Jeremiah, 7:6). Later in the Psalms, God was identified as one who helped, defended, or was the Father to the fatherless. (Psalms 10:14, 68:5, 82:3). Later in the New Testament, the book of James holds that God sees the religious community, as a whole, as one that is "pure and faultless" and one that looks after the fatherless and keeps them from being "polluted by the world" (James 1:27). Finally, in the Gospels, Jesus equated all children with those who possess the kingdom of God (Matthew 19:14 and Luke 18:16).

Similarly, the physical and spiritual care of children who are orphans and those who are in out-of-home care due to abuse, neglect, and mental health issues has evolved over time. From a secular standpoint, the ancient Greeks saw it as the duty of the State to educate the children of citizens and soldiers killed in war, and Plato believe that orphans should be placed under the care of guardians, so that they could show sympathy for the "loneliness" of the orphan, respect the souls of their departed parents, and care for the property of the orphans. (Catholic Encyclopedia. "Orphans and Orphanages.")

One of the early Roman Emperors, Antonius Pius (138-161 C.E.), who was influenced by the early church, stated that orphaned boys and girls should be cared for at the expense of the Church; the girls should be married off when they reached an acceptable age to Christian husbands, and the boys should be taught a handicraft, so neither would be an ongoing burden to the church. (Catholic Encyclopedia. "Orphans and Orphanages.") [

The rise of the Christian orphanage came about in the Middle Ages as religious orders developed and orphaned children were cared for in monasteries or convents. Most prominent in the development of these orphanages in Europe were St. Vincent de Paul (1576–1660) and the Sisters of Charity. (Catholic Encyclopedia. "Orphans and Orphanages.") However, in the Americas, a Spanish order was caring for orphaned girls in Mexico as early as 1548, and the first orphanage in what is now the United States was founded in New Orleans in 1727. The first orphanage, in what was considered U.S. Territory at the time, was opened by Roman Catholic nuns in 1729 after Indians allegedly killed all the adult settlers in Natchez, MS.

Even though orphanages in the Americas were established by the faithful as a way to fulfill their duty to God and God's children by caring for both the bodies and the souls of the orphans, some of the practices, especially while caring for indigenous children, are looked back upon as being culturally insensitive, at best, and abusive, at worst. The role of the Church, then as now, was to spread the gospel and make disciples of all nations (Matthew 28:19). However, at the time, there was no regard given to a person's culture or belief system as the church sought to convert them. Children were the most vulnerable to such crusades, especially if they were deemed to come from pagan belief systems.

Indigenous children were sometimes taken from their cultural lands and heritage and "Europeanized" and "Christianized" by those caring for them in the orphanages. Their hair was cut, they were dressed as Europeans, and they were not allowed to speak their language nor engage in their cultural practices as a part of the conversion process. The country of Canada is now in a settlement process with its indigenous, First Nations population due to the sanctioned use of boarding schools and orphanages used in this way, which has now been deemed "cultural genocide" perpetrated by the Catholic, Anglican, and Methodist churches that sponsored some of the early orphanages.

In what is now St. Ignatious, MT (called Mission, by the locals), the tribal elders of the Salish Tribe got word of the Black Robes (Catholic Priests) who had a strong magic and a connection to The Great Spirit that they wanted for their people. They sent a delegation of elders to invite the Black Robes to their lands to share with them their magic and their understanding of The Great Spirit. A part of the process was to take the tribe's children and strip them of their clothes, language, and practices and turn them into Europeanized Christians. In the midst of bringing this great magic, the Priests also brought small pox to the tribe, which killed an estimated one half to three quarters of the Salish and Pend d' Oreille Tribes. [To this day, there is still tension between the Church and the Tribes due to this history, even though many of the Tribal members consider themselves Christians. (Indian Education, 2010. "Flathead Reservation Timeline Confederated Salish and Kootenai Tribes.")

As we reflect upon the history of orphanages that offered bodily and spiritual care to children to bring about the ultimate goal of Christian discipleship, we must also acknowledge the practices, which were acceptable then, but are now viewed through a different cultural and therapeutic lens.

Orphanages that were sponsored by the churches had priests, nuns, or ministers who lived and worked with the children daily and who were responsible for the religious upbringing of the children. With the rise of the Government run orphanages in the mid 1900's, the spiritual care of children was attended to by the staff or local ministers who visited on a weekly or monthly basis to do religious education and hold worship services. The day-to-day spiritual care of the children was left to the interactions of staff who cared for the children and who would usually convey their own belief systems to the children in whatever way they say fit, without any formal structure or oversight.

With modern Government funded child care institutions in place, and even with private agencies that operate under Government funded contracts, there is a greater sensitivity to spiritual care of children based upon their rights and beliefs, and those of their families, due to the separation of Church and State. Government funded agencies can no longer require children to participate in religious services or activities and cannot, without the children's and families consent, approach them to educate or indoctrinate them within any specific belief system. In fact, as a part of the modern therapeutic approach, it becomes beneficial to help children explore their own unique spiritual interests and support systems as a part of the holistic approach to care.

Vignette

When I came to a United Methodist Home for Children as the Chaplain in 1992, there had been a long history of Methodist and United Methodist ministers being appointed as the Executive Director or Chief Executive Officer of the Home. Since the 1980's, a full-time Chaplain had been appointed to serve the home; the Chaplain was both the minister to the children and the Chaplain to the staff. Since, the home received the majority of its funding from the State, we had to balance our Christian focused heritage and ministry in the United Methodist tradition with respect for children and families who came from different traditions or who wanted nothing to do with Christianity at all. Living in the Southern United States, where there are not clear divisions between Church and State, it was assumed that families, and the children, themselves, would want to be a part of the Christian activities of the agency. In the late 1990's, as we update our intake process and treatment models, we had a question on the intake form about what faith background the child and family came from. Although it was on the form, rarely did anyone, including myself, at the time, give much attention to it. Although we were respectful of other's backgrounds and wishes and were willing to accommodate them, we rarely had anyone push the issue.

We gave the children the option of attending weekly religious education classes (Sunday School) and Worship on Sunday mornings, a Youth Group Meeting on Sunday nights, and various religious observances and activities that the agency held or allowed visiting groups to do as a part of their ministry to the children and support of the agency. However, knowing that given the choice to sleep in on a Sunday morning or to get up and get ready to attend Sunday School and Worship would get very little participation, especially from teenagers, we developed a choice for the children. They could attend the Sunday Schools and Worship service or they could come down with their group to the Chapel and go to a separate room to do life skills work, which usually consisted of several worksheets for them to finish under the supervision of staff. Given these two options, the majority of children would opt to attend Sunday School and Worship. Many did not like to do the "school-like" worksheets, and I would be less than honest if I said that we didn't use this to our advantage to get children to attend Church; however, they were given a choice and that choice was always honored.

There were several teenagers who lived at the home during my years as the Chaplain there who truly wanted to explore other forms of spirituality other than the dominant, conservative Christian tradition that many of them had seen in their families and communities. Some wanted to break away from and rebel against some of the belief systems that they felt constricted them; some wanted to exert what little control they were given while being in State custody and in a treatment program so that they could exercise a chance to make a rare choice; and, some truly wanted to explore belief systems that might be meaningful to them.

One child wanted to explore Native American spirituality loosely based upon the Medicine Wheel and the Four Elements. I would meet with him once a week to place symbols in four directions, relating to the four elements, so he could meditate on their meaning for him and the world. He wanted to light candles for each of the four directions, however, we were prohibited from using fire in his residence area, so a rock (earth), a leaf (wind), an unlit candle (fire), and a glass of water (rain) would stand in to represent the four elements.

One afternoon when I was visiting the children's residences, a staff shared something she had confiscated from a child's room and that she was very concerned about it. It was a small statue of a Buddha, with Rosary Beads draped around its neck, sitting on a Pentagram. She had confiscated it because she was worried that it had a Satanic message and was inappropriate for the child's room. I suggested that we talk to the child about its meaning, return it to the child out of respect for his religious rights, and allow the child this symbol of exploring spiritual meaning. I talk with the child, and he had a very insightful explanation about the goodness that could be found in different faiths and how we should respect the beliefs of all people. It was a positive expression of his spiritual journey, and he was allowed to keep his conglomerated symbol of acceptance of others and his spiritual journey.

Very few of the children who wanted to rebel against the Christian norm of Southern culture professed atheism; that was just too taboo in the South, even for rebellious teens. It seemed that most children who wanted an alternative to a Christian belief system wanted to follow the Wiccan religion. When I talked with them about what the Wiccan belief system stood for, very few knew the details. They would often explain it as the ability to use the power of the earth and nature to help them; they knew that such power was used for good and not for evil and that is was not associated Satanism. I would explain some of the very few things about the Wiccan religion that I knew, which was, most often, more than they knew, and I would talk about the references to the earth and symbols of the earth and elements that were in the Bible. I would tell them that I looked forward to talking with them more about it, learning from them, and sharing more about the similarities and differences between Wiccan and Christian beliefs. Usually, that was the only time the child would bring it up, and they didn't want to pursue it in any regular way beyond that. I think that some wanted to explore and some wanted to push against the norm in Southern culture. Once their exploration or exertion of control was acknowledge, accepted, and most importantly, not punished, they either decided to move on or, I hope, see that there was room for acceptance and dialogue between people from different belief systems. I wanted them to understand that, usually, different religions have much more in common than difference to fight about. I can't help but believe that once no energy was given to opposing their beliefs, there wasn't much of a need for them to fight about it—for whatever reason that fight was important to them.

There were rare occasions when families wanted to have their children attend specific denominational Worship services, and we would work to accommodate that by allowing the families to take the children off campus to the specific churches or have approved volunteers or staff to take them to worship services on a Sunday or Saturday morning. As someone who came into the Chaplaincy role as moderate and who became more liberal over time, I really wanted to protect vulnerable children from what I felt was the emotional manipulation that some denominations used—the turn or burn approach—especially with teens. I wanted them to spend as much time hearing the more grace-filled messages of the Christian faith than the condemning message. So, early on, I didn't promote this. However, as I matured in my understanding of the role of the family and community in the ongoing healing and social development of these children, I came to see that the support systems of their families and communities, including their unique churches and faith messages, were ultimately important and that they needed to connect with those traditions in order to have a more comfortable transition back to their homes, communities, and faith messages that were inherent in them.

Child Development and Spiritual Development

Many Chaplains and Ministers who work with children in care have the customary training for ministry, including Bachelor's Degrees in Religion, Biblical Studies, Youth Ministry, or a Master's level degree from a seminary. However, those working with children and youth in any ministry setting should have additional training to help them understand child and adolescent development based upon the latest social science research. James W. Fowler, former Professor of Theology and Human Development at Emory University and Director of the University Center for Ethics, wrote *Stages of Faith* (Fowler,), to show the stages of spiritual development that parallels the process of human development. He used the theories of psychosocial development (Erikson), cognitive development (Piaget), and moral development (Kohlberg) as the basis for understanding the dynamic process of spiritual development from infancy through mature adulthood. This book is a good resource for anyone who works with children and youth and can serve as a guide for understanding their unique stages of spiritual development. Other theorists who combine the theories of psychology and spirituality include Alfred Adler, Gordon Allport, and William James. The *Handbook of The Psychology of Religion and Spirituality* is a good guide to the ideas of these theorists and more. [See the Resources section at the end of this chapter.]

Children in care, however, often have an altered developmental pathway and have developed survival thinking and behaviors [some use the term psychopathology or anti-social behavior] due to the abuse, neglect, trauma, and resulting mental and emotional health manifestations. All children who come into care and who are moved to different caregiving settings while in the system of care suffer trauma due to physical, sexual, or psychological abuse, neglect, and the trauma of being removed from familiar caregivers. It should be noted that even removing a child from a traumatic situation is traumatic, in and of itself. Children do not assess their situation as good or bad, abusive or non-abusive, however, they often assess it as familiar or unfamiliar. Removing children from even abusive situations that they have learned how to survive in and that is familiar to them creates a separate from the familiar that is traumatic to them. The more often they are moved while in care, the more they are traumatized. Those who work in with children in care, in whatever capacity, must have an understanding of trauma-informed care. The work of Dr. Bruce Perry and Dr. Sandra Bloom can offer good starting points for understanding the impact of trauma on child development. There are even some writings and ideas on how to create trauma informed congregations that helps religious leaders and parishioners to understand the traumas that people experience due to, for example, violent are in which they live, and some of the usual trauma's that people face throughout their lives, which can range from death of loved ones, and intrusive, painful medical procedures, to accidents, and natural disasters. Trauma informed congregations take intentional action to support recovery after traumatic events by providing resources for traumatized individuals and communities

Dr. Perry's work argues that most of the psychological diagnosis given to children can really be summed up under the umbrella of trauma related symptoms. However, other theorists and research in the field of psychology and religion focus on how people with certain diagnoses develop a spiritual understanding of their relationship with God that parallels some of their skewed views of relationships with others. To give some simplistic examples of this, those who have anxiety and positive self-identity issues can see themselves as someone who can never do or be enough to please God. Those who are depressed may see God as distant and uninvolved. Those who suffer from paranoia may believe that God, like everyone else in the world, is out to "get them," and those who are traumatized may feel that an angry or vengeful God will bring more harm to them. Some psychiatrists point out that it is hard to distinguish, though, whether one's unique viewpoint of God add to their mental and emotional struggles or whether these struggles cause this unique view of God. Dr. Harold Koenig, a Duke University psychiatry professor stated, "My suspicion, though, is that…people with emotional problems see their entire world in a negative light and often feel a need to blame someone -- and God is often the target." (The Huffington Post. "Religion & mental health: New study links belief in "punitive God" to emotional problems".)

Vignette

One older teen I worked with came from what I would describe as an ultraconservative church background. However, when he came into our care, he refused to attend any church services or events; he was polite about it, but adamant. As I was exploring his choice not to attend services, a staff member who knew his background told me that the boy had been caught in a sexual act by his parents and was made to stand up in from of the entire church congregation one Sunday morning and give a detailed confession of his acts, so that he could seek forgiveness from God and the congregation. Due to this, he no longer saw God or the church as a positive means of support, but as something that brought about hurt and humiliation. Whatever personal or family issues the boy was struggling with became exacerbated by this approach to spiritual cleansing by confession. All we could do was to provide an alternative view of what a community of faith could be by, first of all, respecting his choice not to attend religious services and offering an example of love and acceptance that was affirming of who he was, as he was.

Many institutional child care settings and many local schools use a behavior modification approach to change children's behavior, based upon the giving and taking of prizes, privileges, points, tokens, and or levels that are related to the children's behaviors. [Many researchers and progressive practitioners believe that such behavior modification approaches, or token economies, have little if any lasting impact on children when they are outside of the settings that reward and punish behavior in such a manner. In addition, the growing field of trauma informed care shows that the constant taking of points and privileges adds to the sense of loss and the poor sense of identity that these children have due to their traumatic experiences. Webb-Mitchell (1993) shows that the concept of behavior modification can actually hinder the healthy development of spirituality in a chapter entitle, The Behavior Mod God, in which he argues that such an approach to child care and treatment, when tied to a program of spiritual development, brings about a works-righteousness approach to spiritual development. The children may believe that, as long as they are doing the right things (earning their points) that God will love and reward them, but when they fail to do the right things (losing their points), that God will not love them and will punish them or take from them.

This goes against the unconditional grace, acceptance, and love that children in care need to feel in their relationship with God and all other healing relationships in their lives. Those who are ministering to children in care should be aware of the complexities of this contradiction if they are trying to offer a positive and healing message about God's unconditional acceptance in a setting where the children are constantly being judged on their conditional behaviors.

The goal of spiritual development of all people, no matter what age, is to bring about a more mature and healthy understanding of and relationship with one's God, one's community, and oneself. Those who work with children who have not had positive, supportive relationships from caregivers or who have mental health issues that have drained a families resources know that those children are coming to term with a deficit of positive interactions with others and a negative self-image. As Fowler points out, the positive images of God often comes about from positive images of a caregiver that children experience in infancy. When children come into care, a church or minister must start building positive images of caregivers who meet children's needs and, thus, who can be trusted. It is only when children see the physical manifestations of needs met that they can start to build an image of a Spiritual Caregiver who will be present and meet needs. When children see that there is a community—a congregation or a church—who meets needs and who is supportive, then they can trust that congregation and become a part of it, finding community, purpose, and being part of something that is bigger and beyond themselves. Research has shown that those who are a part of communities where there is a sense of belonging, support, and purpose have greater emotional and physical health benefits. So, it must be a goal of those who are working with children in care to not only ensure that they have a positive sense of a God but also a positive sense of a faith community; all of these relationships bring about restoration of physical and psycho-emotional health and gives them a place where health and wholeness can be nurtured in community.

My Experiences

In my experiences as the Chaplain at a facility that cared for and treated children who had been neglected, abused, and traumatized and who, as a result, had developed mental and emotional health challenges and survival behavior that were deemed as unacceptable and anti-social, I found that most individuals who did not have a background in working with these children did not have an understanding of their deficits of relationships nor of how to bring about healing. Many churches, youth groups, and individuals wanted to help the children out of a genuine calling to care for the "orphans" and the "least of these" and to bring these children into a relationship with God. Many would raise money or send resources for their care. Some would come and spend time with the children for a day or during a youth group meeting. Few developed long-term relationships with the children.

Some thought that brining these children to salvation was the main and end goal; they merely wanted to come and preach and pray with these children, give an alter call, and leave the rest up to God. They thought that this one-time act would simply be enough without understanding how long the road to restorative relationships takes for these children. The prayer of salvation is quick, but realization of the fullness of salvation is a lifetime journey that requires ongoing compassion and support.

There were times when the mentality of bringing children to Jesus without being an embodiment of Jesus alongside them was not just true of those who visited and didn't understand the needs of these children, it was sometimes true of those who knew and who should have known better. I was told of an incident that occurred just before I arrived as Chaplain, in which an eager staff member at the home baptized a child in the bathtub in one of our cottages. Similarly, a minister who had gone through the volunteer process at the children's home and was educated as to the children's backgrounds was out on a visit with the child, which, to his credit, he did quite often, and, after having the child pray the prayer of confession, baptized the child in the creek where they were fishing.

What both of these individuals did was to take away the church community's preparation for and celebration of the baptism. Also, neither felt that it was important to pass the information on to the chaplain or the leader of the church community, who could offer support for the spiritual growth of the these children. Baptism was seen by them as an individual act that affirmed one's belief. However, baptism is a communal act, whereby the community of faith acknowledges, celebrates, and supports the baptized person. The mentality that just an instantaneous acknowledgement of Jesus and that symbolic affirmation—baptism—would suffice theses children's spiritual needs negates the supportive role of the church community in this process of ongoing spiritual development. A relationship with God is therapeutic, in that it can bring healing on many levels. However, children who have such relational deficits need more than just one visit with a doctor or a therapist. There journey of holistic healing will often take a lifetime and a community of support. The prayer of confession and baptism is only the start of this journey, and there must be community of support in place for growth.

The approach that I chose to take was one of invitation to participate in the community of belief, to become a personal faith, and to experience growth over time. I had found that some of the most significantly influential Christian people I had met or heard about were ones who were mature in their faith and who lived an authentic Christian life, embodying the grace, forgiveness, and love of Christ in an everyday, real way, even when it was hard; it was not a one-time act. This level of maturity is where I wanted these children to end up. I didn't want to leave them at the dramatic place of a conversion experience. I wanted them to grow.

There were some individuals on staff and some churches who came in to "minister" to the children and whose goal was, simply, for the children to have a conversion experience. Some would use the emotionally manipulative technique of asking them where their souls would end up if they died tonight or on the way home from the revival to scare the hell out of them, or rather to try to scare them out of hell. As I became more aware of these children's live and the trauma they had experienced, I found that this approach fed into their fears of pain, death, and suffering, based upon their real life trauma experiences and was, actually, re-traumatizing to them. I became very selective of what individuals I would allow to speak to the children about their spiritual journeys and what churches I would allow to come in to "minister" to them and what churches we would take children to for special youth events.

However, educating churches who wanted to minister to these children became an act of helping them to understand their struggles from the past and the present and to be sensitive to them. One youth group came in to put on a play for our children on a Sunday afternoon that they had written. In the play, one of the characters was acting strange, which prompted another character to jokingly ask if he had taken his medication that morning. I wrote a letter to the youth group leader explaining the over 60% of your children, at that time, was on psychotropic medication, and explained how such a commonly used joke in our society was insensitive, especially in that setting. The leader didn't respond to me, and the group never asked to come back. Although we may have lost what our fundraisers called "Fiends of Children," I wanted these "friends" to have a thorough understanding of the children's lives and needs and how best to "befriend" them.

16

Normalizing the Faith Community Experience

A treatment setting for children is such an artificial and highly regulated community, but one that is justifiably so under the circumstances. However, the goal of treatment is to prepare the children to live, cope, and thrive in real communities—ones without all the protections and supports. The goal of a community of faith that is established in such an artificial community is to meet the children where they are, based on their needs and experiences, but to also help them to connect to communities of faith once they leave. To do so, they need to have some normalization of the faith community while in care and the ability to transfer experiences there to a familiar faith community at home. I would always tell the children that, if they want to find a place to belong when they get home, find a church. In the South, there is not a community health center or provider on every corner, but there is a church on every corner, and, if a church is being the Church, they will be welcomed and supported.

Vignette

We wanted to give the children who left the home something to take with them as a symbol of the care they received there. We decided to give each child a Bible that was personalized with his or her name on it. [Even if children went to a youth detention center or a psychiatric hospital, we would have someone to deliver the Bible to them or ship it to them, if it were not possible to visit them.] One of the first Bibles I gave to a child who was leaving was to a girl who was leaving the Girls Group Home. She was in her late teens and was an understandably cynical child. It was the early 1990's and she had big hair and identified herself, by her clothes and style, as a heavy metal rocker. I said goodbye to her and handed her the Bible and told her it was from everyone at the Home so that she could remember that we loved her and God loved her. She took glance at it and had the look on her face of a child who receives socks or underwear for Christmas, but gave a polite yet insincere, "Thank you." Then she took a second, closer look at it and saw that her names was stamped on it in gold lettering. A big smile came across her face, and she ran to show her staff yelling out, "My name is on it! May name is on it!"

Her name was on it. Her name was in it. She was the child of God it spoke of. All of its promises were hers. We wanted her to take that with her.

If you came to the Chapel on any given Sunday, it would look like Church most anywhere else—except that the congregation was made of children who happened to be in treatment. There was Sunday School in the morning before the Worship Service for the older Youth. Due to the amount of children at the home, and some who were in specialized setting, Sunday School was held at their cottages at various days throughout the week and in ways that met the needs of the children in those particular cottages, whether it was due to age or developmental levels. There was a full worship service on Sunday mornings that looked like most services in the United Methodist tradition, except for the fact that the children were not just the acolytes, but they read the scriptures, took the offering, served communion, comprised the choir, and sometimes played the instruments

One boy came to the campus because he was having behavior problems in his school and community. He also happened to play drums in an alternative band, and he desperately wanted to have his drum set with him on campus. Since he couldn't have the set in the cottage, we worked it out that he could keep them in the chapel, if he would be willing to play drums during the worship services, which often had contemporary Christian songs and choruses. He benefitted by being able to play his drums; he could play whatever he wanted and however he wanted after the service and occasionally throughout the week. He was a talented drummer who could lay down a soft beat with brushes for Amazing Grace and other toned down songs during the service and then play a driving double bass on alternative rock songs after it was over. He taught me to play Inner Sandman on my guitar so that he could accompany me, or rather I could accompany him.

Another child who came to us when he was about nine or ten years old, was from a very active black church. While few of the children who live on campus had "church clothes" and came to services in their everyday clothes (we were ahead of our time in the elements of contemporary worship), this child wanted to wear a three-piece suit and tie to Church because that's the way it was supposed to be, according to his tradition. He asked if he could play a tambourine during the hymns and songs, just as he did at his church. So, he was one of the regular musicians during our services.

On Sunday nights, there was a youth group meeting that, like many at other churches, was composed of a devotional, a meal, and free time/fun time. It was the only time during the week that all of the youth on campus were together, at the same place at the same time. When this idea was first proposed, to have such a "normal" youth group meetings and let the kids hang out with each other—with no program, structure, or overt therapeutic tasks – the staff and leader ship thought it would be a disaster and that having that many of our children in one place would lead to chaos and anarchy. There were rarely problems, and when there were, they were normal, everyday teenage problems that we could help the kids work through, just like parents or youth counselors at a church would do.

We would also take the children to special services at other churches in the community. Some would go to church camp and youth assemblies in the summer (as long as staff went with them and stayed the week, which is something some of our staff enjoyed and would volunteer to do). We also tried to take as many children as possible to some of the community wide and conference wide youth events, as possible. There is a weekend-long United Methodist youth event held in Gatlinburg each year, called Resurrection, that has become the largest collective gathering of Methodists in the world; a total of 5,000 to 6,000 youth would gather each weekend over two weekends (for a total of 10,000–12,000 youth) for worship and fellowship. We would usually take 20–25 youth to the event with several staff chaperones. One year, a boy asked to go back to the campus, because he could not handle being around so many people, and realized it was making him anxious and angry, and he said he was not sure how he might behave. That was the only issue we ever had in all the years we took children to this event. Inevitably , every year I would hear stories from other youth leaders and pastors about some youth they took on the trip who trashed their hotel rooms, got drunk, or were found having sex.

Even though there was an attempt to "normalize" things as much as possible, at times it was evident what traumatic lives the children had lead and that emotional and behavior issues were still a struggle. There were kids who cursed and dropped the "F-bomb" when they were mad or frustrated at church and at youth meetings. One Sunday morning, as I was counting the offering money, I found a picture from a porn magazine that was put in the plate. Then there was the time when we took a group of kids to visit another church in town for special Christmas Service. We usually sat in the balcony. One boy was not happy to be there, and to show his displeasure, during the middle of the service, he fliped his hooding over his head and yelled out a line from Beavis and Butt-head, "I am Cornholio! I need TP for my bunghole." Those who work with these children must have a grace and tolerance about their behavior, as well as a good sense of humor.

I would be at ministers' meetings and conferences and hear ministers share their frustrations with one another about the attitudes and actions of some of their parishioners. After hearing their stories of how some of the adults were acting in their churches, I found that I had less problems in a congregation of children and youth who were struggling with emotional and mental health issues, some of whom were adjudicated as juvenile delinquents and came to us out of detention centers.

Vignette

Steve, a 15 year old boy, came to our Boys Group Home through the child welfare system, like most children, but he came in a wheelchair. He had cerebral palsy. His speech was labored and his hand and arm movements were hard to control, especially when he got excited, and he had virtually no control of his legs ….. but he had a fully developed sense of humor. I called him "Wheels," and he would laugh every time. If I didn't start the joking around, he would.

Steve joined the group that attended Resurrection, a weekend gathering of over 5,000 United Methodist teens in Gatlinburg for worship, preaching, and fellowship. It was a big production with loud music and a celebratory atmosphere. During most of the songs and musical presentations, the youth were on their feet, clapping, swaying, or dancing. Steve was bouncing along with his body rocking back and forth in his wheelchair.

I danced in the morning when the world was begun, and
I danced in the moon and the stars and the sun, and
I came down from heaven, and I danced on the earth,
At Bethlehem, I had my birth.
Dance, then, wherever you may be,
I am the Lord of the Dance, said he,
and I'll lead you all, wherever you may be,
and I'll lead you all in the Dance, said he.

In addition to struggling with cerebral palsy, Steve had lived with an alcoholic father. He said that when his dad would be out drinking, he would come home and demand that Steve sleep on the couch so he could have the good bed—Steve's bed—so he could sleep it off. One night, his father came home so drunk that he didn't even recognize that Steve, as usual, was lying on his stomach, already asleep on the couch. His father just plopped down on top of him, sitting down right in the middle of his back. Steve cried out in pain and continued crying, he was hurt so badly that he had to be taken to the emergency room. He was taken into State's Custody straight from the hospital.

I danced on a Friday when the sky turned black;
it's hard to dance with the world on your back.
They buried my body and they thought I'd gone,
But I am the Dance, and I still go on.
Dance, then, wherever you may be,
I am the Lord of the Dance, said he,
and I'll lead you all, wherever you may be,
and I'll lead you all in the Dance, said he.

Steve thrived in every way at the Home. He received counseling, he received medical care, he went to the local high school, and he had a bed of his own and never had to worry about having to sleep on the couch. He thrived socially, as well; he went the group of boys everywhere they went and engaged in as many activities as he could. He even participated with the group when they would go to the high ropes course. The staff would hoist him up to participate on the high elements just like the other boys were doing.

That night at the Resurrection worship service, he was with the group, enjoying the songs and energy, just like the other kids. He was rocking so hard in his wheelchair, we were afraid it would turn over. Two of our staff, Jim and Kevin, saw that Steve couldn't see the stage because the other youth were standing up and dancing, so, they got on each side of Steve, yoked their arms under his arms and picked him up. He was at the same level of the other youth, and what's more, he started swinging his torso and spastically moving his legs, and he danced, just like everyone else, with a smile on his face.

They cut me down and I leapt up high;
I am the life that'll never, never die;
I'll live in you if you'll live in me -
I am the Lord of the Dance, said he.
Dance then, wherever you may be ...... (Carter, 1963)

21

Preacher, Teacher, Pastor, and Priest-Chaplain

Although the population that makes up the church/congregation at a children's treatment facility has a unique demographic and set of needs, the role of the Chaplain or Pastor is the same as with other congregations. If I had to break it down into three points, it would be to preach, teach, and be present, with the last of these being the most important.

The preaching and leading of worship calls for the chaplain to adjust the service or liturgy to the needs and developmental level of the children. As stated above, the children were a regular part of leading worship, and the language, songs, and content of the messages were geared to meet them where they were in their cognitive and developmental levels. Having said that, the congregation I serve ranged from developmentally delayed youth to very bright adolescents in their late teens and early 20's. So the challenge, like that for any congregation, is to present the worship service and message so that there is something for everyone at every level.

The ritual of the service is very important. Children in care, who come from chaotic, unpredictable environments benefits from what is routine and predictable. Anything I introduced that was out of the ordinary, like drumming or role plays in the service, was always lead into by something that was predictable, so that the transition into something new was attached to something familiar.

The main goal of worship was to have an experience with the Divine. With so many children coming from so many different denominational backgrounds, or without a church background, the goal was to offer something to them that they would recognize or find familiar in any congregation they came from or that they might go to in the future. I was not always successful. One child, who came from a very conservative denomination and who was used to very loud, boisterous sermons told me that I didn't yell at them enough. Just like every other congregation, a minister not going to meet everyone's needs all the time.

Similarly, the teaching role of the chaplain is to meet the children where they are with their level of cognitive understanding and spiritual development, which, like in any congregation, can be a challenge. Our Christian Education (Sunday School) occurred throughout the week, due to scheduling challenges and since I was the only one doing them. The classes would sometimes meet in the Chapel or school, which the chapel was attached to, or in the children's cottages. Since the children were often grouped by age, I would adapt the lessons to their developmental ages. As was stated above, the developmental and chronological ages are not always sync, so the teaching must fit the children where they are at a cognitive and emotional level, and the teaching should be something that is readily applicable to some of the unique struggles and challenges that they are facing based upon their backgrounds and settings. In addition to the basic Bible Study, the teachings and sermons were often about grief, loss, feeling alone, being accepted, being loved, being forgiven, and the hardest message (even for adults), to forgive. I always tried to teach and preach on the side of God's grace and love rather than on sinfulness and judgment, because the children had experienced too many harsh messages about the latter. The main message was, "You are God's beloved child, and you have a place in the Church and the Kingdom."

The most important role was to be present—to be an embodiment of God's love on an everyday basis. I would visit in the cottages or school and check in with the children, because they needed to see that the God-thing was just not a Sunday-thing. Like many successful inner-city ministry programs, there should be a presence in meeting daily needs and participating in daily activities. Those who live with so many deficits need to see that the Church and the earthly representation of God's love is present all day, every day. A Chaplain should be involved in sports, music, service, education, and other programs outside the usual activities and programs of the church, again, as a way to show continuity beyond the Sunday Services and show the depth and breadth of where the love of God is willing to be.

I learned from the first President/CEO I worked under at the home, that one of the most powerful and humbling ways to be with the children was to eat with them, because it put everyone on the same level. Since my family and I lived on the campus for several years, my wife and children would eat in one of the cottages on a Sunday afternoon, just like in the old days when the pastor was invited to a home on Sunday after the services, and we would eat in another cottage at least one other night out of the week. Not only was it the Chaplain (Pastor/Preacher) coming to spend time with them, but it was a rare, and I hope meaningful, interaction with an intact, functioning family that many of them had not had an opportunity to be a part of; my wife and I really wanted to model to them what "family" could look like, and like many pastor's wives, she played a significant ministerial role in the lives of the children.

Visiting during crises was another aspect of the role that paralleled with the role of the pastor in a congregation. In addition to visiting in their homes (cottages), there were hospital visits, as well, for illnesses, injuries, and surgeries. However, some of the visits were to psychiatric hospitals and to community hospitals where children were being held for stabilization or recovering from suicide attempts. One of the youngest children I ever visited while he was recovering from a suicide attempt was eight years old. Again, it is imperative that the Chaplain have unique training in understanding the mental health issues of children and teens and have some supervision in counseling techniques for situations like this. The overly simplistic messages of the pastors and trite theological platitudes, such as, "God has His reasons of this, even if we don't understand it," or, "If you will just pray about it, it will be OK" or, "Just give it over to God and let Him fix it", falls short and is often damaging during and after the crises that these children continually live through. Just a little dose of Jesus will not fix it. The love of God embodied in the community that surrounds the child in time of crisis is what will bring healing in the short and long term.

There were also visits to prisons, both to youth detention centers and county jails, when some of the congregation aged out of youth services and found their way into adult processes. Again, understanding the dynamics of the psychological and emotional processes that goes with crime and punishment is necessary for anyone working with this population. Understanding the guilt and shame that can go with this process, or why there is a lack, thereof, is essential. Also, as a pastor, one must be prepared to help these youth deal with issues of fear, isolation, and self-image from a constructive and redemptive perspective. Developing a good relationship with the Chaplains at the various prisons can help to gain access to those of your congregation who end up there and to understand the parameters of your visits.

One of the roles that I was never prepared for was serving as the Priest at a child's funeral. I had conducted many funerals and burial services for adults, but presiding over the funeral of a child is something that is deeply saddening and challenges even the most positive of theological constructs about the "Why's" of the world and the role of God before, during, and after such a tragedy. Words do not suffice, even Biblical words, to comfort and heal the family, peers, and staff of a child who has died, or even more tragically, taken his or her own life. In fact, some of the trite, poorly thought out explanations bring more pain and questions. The best we can often say, when faced with the questions is, "I don't know why, but God is present and others are present as you go through this." This is not the time to be Philosopher, Precher, or Teacher, but to be Pastor.

One can only be present, even as inadequate as that may seem, as a representation of the community of faith and the presence of Love in a physical form during the process. During any major loss, people rarely remember the words we say, but they do remember that we were present and that they were not alone; it is truly an act of compassion – suffering alongside someone. Again, the Chaplain must have training about and knowledge of the grief process and how children and teens process grief in their various developmental stages. The Chaplain must also be acutely aware of how the loss of a peer or family members often exacerbates the innumerable losses that many children in care and their families experience and be prepared to offer long term care throughout the process. Finally, the Chaplain must be aware of his or her own suffering and to seek support during and after the process. The grief process is often put on hold for the Chaplain, as he or she takes on the professional role of Priest and Pastor. Even though there is often a sense of support from God, it is often necessary to seek support from a peer or a professional to help deal with the unnatural loss of the death of a child and strains of being a helper and caregiver for others who are also suffering through this trauma.

In addition to being a pastor to the congregation of the children, the Chaplain may also act as a pastor to the staff. Some staff may already have connections to a community of faith and have someone who is a pastor or spiritual leader. However, some do not and may seek out the Chaplain as a source for comfort and spiritual guidance during difficult times. It is a common theme that the social work field attracts people who are seeking not only to support those in need, but also to "right" some "wrongs" in the world, some of which were "wrongs" that occurred or are occurring in their personal lives. The Chaplain should be aware of this unique dynamic and have the same sensitivity to staff as s/he does with the children. Additionally, the Chaplain serves in the role as the Spiritual Leader of the agency and may need to take on the role as Prophet in a variety of situations, ranging from advocating for the holistic care of the children and staff (as opposed to a traditional medical model or behavior modification focused approach to care), to human rights, and cultural competence.

Sadly, I have heard the term Chaplain used in a pejorative manner by clergy who serve traditional parishes, as if the role of the Chaplain at an institution, college, or agency is a shallow representation of professional clergy with less responsibility and stress than that of someone serving a traditional congregation. I hope that the description I've offered of the multi-dimensional role of a Chaplain for children in care and the depth of knowledge and range of skillsets required to serve that congregation effectively will contradict such a shallow understanding and false criticism.

The Power of Service

Sponsoring Children through Children International

As a part of the worship service, the children had the opportunity to give an offering. (The each got an allowance of $5 a week, since they were in State Custody.) I tried to come up with ways that they could use the offering to serve others, since, unlike a traditional congregation's offering, the money did not go to the minister's salary or the expenses of up-keeping the church building.

I thought it would be interesting if they sponsored a child from another country through an international ministry organization; I put it to the congregation of children, and they agreed to take this on as an act of service. After researching several, I thought that Children International would be a good fit. So, I wrote to Children International and told them that my congregation wanted to sponsor a child. As was there practice, they sent three profiles and accompanying pictures of children for the sponsors to decide between; we were sent information for two boys from the Philippines and one girl from Chile. I explained to the children that we would need to choose one of these children to support with our offering.

I read all three profiles and showed all three pictures to the children, and then I asked for them to vote. I asked who wanted to support Boy #1, and all their hands went up. I asked who wanted to support Boy #2, and all their hands went up. Then, I asked who wanted to support the Girl, and all their hands went up. I asked them if they were sure that they could support all three and told them how much offering we would have to have each week to do so. I got a collective affirmative nod from them.

These children, many of whom had experienced poverty and neglect, were not going to let any one of these children from half-way around the world go without support. They could not pick one and let the other two go uncared for. They could not do to others what had been done to so many of them. From that point on, the pictures of these three children set on top of piano in the chapel, much like in homes where the family pictures set atop the piano in the living room; they were a part of our congregation; they were a part of our family; they were children in need, receiving a loving and helping hand from others in need; the children saw themselves in the family pictures that sat on the piano.

For many years, even when a new Chaplain took my place, the children of the home sponsored three children in developing countries, so that they could have food, medicine, clothes, school supplies, and care. It was a true act of compassion, service, and healing; in this act, they were in control; they brought care and healing to other children, and in turn brought it to themselves.

Painting Houses

There was an elderly woman who was a Volunteer Grandparent at one of our Child Day Care centers operated by the children's home. She was a faithful volunteer, working several days a week with the children. She also was a poet, which led me to her home to see a book of poetry that she had self-published. When I arrived at her modest, white clapboard house, I found it was in sad shape and needed a paint job; it hadn't been painted in over 10 years. The irony of this was that her recently deceased husband was a house painter, and an alcoholic, who didn't attend to the needs of his own home. Painting old houses was something I knew how to do, and I thought it might be a good idea to help the children to participate in service in a hands-on way with someone in their community rather than just donating money to a passed plate to children who were only real through pictures and quarterly letters. There was money left over from the offering each week, enough to buy a few gallons of paint and paintbrushes.

I put it to the congregation one Sunday morning about using the additional offering monies to take on this service project, and they voted yes, without really knowing the details of the work ahead. I asked the Grandmother if we could paint her house, and she was thrilled. We set a start date.

Once I had done this and headed back to the campus to start working out the details of buying the supplies and organizing the children, mainly teenage boys and a few teenage girls, to work on the house, the reality of it set in. It dawned on me that I might be painting this house all by myself if none of the children wanted to spend hot summer afternoons scraping and putting two coats of paint on that house.

When I went from cottage to cottage to get volunteers and set a schedule, I expected maybe eight or ten of them would want to go out and do the work. By the time the volunteer list was done, there were somewhere between 25-30 volunteers, and we would have to take them out in shifts. Staff who were there to supervise the youth felt compelled to work alongside them. We spent summer afternoons, for several weeks, working on the house, and when we were finished, we put before and after pictures, and pictures of the work in progress—pictures of the children working to help another – on the Chapel bulletin board. They would go by and look at the pictures and find great joy in finding themselves in the pictures ….. finding themselves as being the helpers and not the helped.

This tradition of service went on for another seven years, as we would find houses that were just a few blocks from the children's home campus to paint. I felt that it was important for them to see that they could have an impact on their immediate community to change the lives of others. During one of the summer painting projects, we were painting the house of another grandmother in the community. However, this one was one who had once had a grandchild whom she was raising in her home to receive our services. Sadly, like many kids in that time who did not receive adequate aftercare or wraparound services, he went from being successful at the children's home program to struggling in the outside world. He started selling drugs and ended up in and out of jail. She didn't see much of him anymore.

There was one teenaged boy who had volunteered for the project who was working hard – surprisingly hard. This was a boy who didn't really engage in the treatment program, who had to be prodded and consequenced to get his chores done, and who we often wondered about whether he would make it through our program, much less in the world he would return to. He worked diligently on his shifts. When the other boys would take breaks, he wouldn't, and we would have to prompt him to stop long enough to get a drink and stay hydrated. When the other boys would linger too long under the shade tree

28

or at the water cooler, he would scold them to get back to work. We were all befuddled by his work ethic on this project; it was like nothing we had ever seen from him.

It so happened that, later in one afternoon shift, I ended up on a ladder next to his ladder, talking, sporadically, about everything and nothing, like you do when you are painting for hours. After a long bout of silence, out of the blue, he said, "When I was a kid, a church came and painted me and my Mom's house."

It started to make sense then. The kid who was always on the receiving end of help and services had the opportunity to be the one who offered help to someone else. He was the Church now, and he wanted to ensure that he and the rest of his Church served well. It was a transformative moment.

UNICEF

Another project that our congregation did on a yearly basis was to Trick or Treat for UNICEF. Rather them going from house to house, we would have two to four youth at a time stand out in front of local grocery stores and department stores and ask for donations. We educated them on what UNICEF did with the funds to help provide medical care for children in developing countries so that they could answer questions when people asked what the money would go for. Most of the children were very successful at asking for things, because they were used to it, and many did not have good boundaries. So, asking strangers for money is something that was not a problem for most.

We would end up with buckets full of change, a few one dollar bills, and occasional, rare five dollar bill. It was a chore to sort, roll, and count all the change and paper money. Since about half of the children on the campus went to a day treatment school on campus, we would often take advantage of their down time between lessons to ask them to volunteer to sort and count money after an evening to collecting donations. One year, one unlikely volunteer was a teenaged boy who said he was bored and would help out. I left him under the supervision of a teacher's aide with buckets of change and dollar bills. I came back about an hour later to check on his progress and saw an elaborate and concise organization of pennies, nickels, and dimes stacked in groups of tens, quarters stacked in groups of fours, and dollar bills stacked crosswise on top of each other in groups of tens. I was amazed at his organization and the precision of his counting. I complimented him on his abilities. He told me it was something he had learned when he was dealing drugs, because his supplier would get very upset if "the money was not right" when he turned it in. A skillset, developed under nefarious circumstances, was redeemed, and maybe a boy found that, as we say about comic book villains, his powers could be used for good instead of evil.

Many years ago, Boys and Girls Town, a Catholic organization, conducted research on the spiritual development of children in out-of-home care, and as one can image, the children in their study showed deficits in every category of spiritual development compared to their peers who had not experience out-of-home care, except in one, single category – the desire to serve others. These research findings played out over and over again in my experiences with children in care. They wanted to be of service. They wanted to experience the positive feelings of reaching out to others in a self-less way. They wanted to be the ones "doing for" rather than being "done to." It is uniquely empowering for them to be the ones in control, and it is transformative on every level.

An Evolution of Theology

I came into the role of the Chaplain at the children's homes as theological moderate, with a traditional bachelor's training in psychology and religion and a seminary education. I was educated to provide exegetical biblical justifications and tight theological explanations for everything ranging from sin and salvation to suffering and death. Many of those explanations sound good from the pulpit and can be left in the abstract there. However, as any pastor knowns, the real challenge of living out faith is how those arguments—and resulting justifying actions—are lived out in the midst of crises. Even the best theological arguments have imperfections and appear lacking in the face of tragedy when it appears that no words, not even God's, give a good explanation for why something so bad had happened to a real person.

Take that sense of speechlessness and multiply it by every child and family served in the child welfare system, and you can begin to get a sense of how trite some of the theological explanations are for why people, and especially children, suffer. The absolute worst of these explanations we use when we don't know what else to say is, "We don't understand it, but God has a purpose for this." That argument that we use to give God the easy way out by blaming our own intellectual or spiritual shortcomings, actually makes God complicit to the abuse and neglect from which the children seek refuge from and a lifetime of healing for.

As I spent years wrestling with the biblical justifications and theological explanations for the trauma that the children in our care have lived through, I found little solace in the apologetics. I found myself re-thinking and un-believing many things that worked for me in my upbringing and spiritual development and for the majority of those I served in traditional middle-classed congregational settings. Even as someone steeped in liturgy and orthodoxy, I had a harder and harder time instructing the children to ask for "forgiveness of their trespasses" when they would struggle their whole lives because of those who had "trespassed against them." I didn't need to talk about Hell; they had lived it and were struggling to get out and stop having intrusive thoughts of it. I even had a hard time putting "Amazing Grace" on the bulletin and have them sing that they were "wretches;" even though it is a favorite, emotion-laden song, that talks about being found and saved; the message of the song inadvertently puts the blame on the children for being "wretches" instead of being victims of "wretched situations." Such theology insidiously blames the victims, even though the goal is to attain God's love and salvation. If you think about it more deeply, it destroys conventional theology, and if you don't think about it at all, the theology perpetuates blaming the victim. In the end, I could only, in good conscience and in good faith, present the presence of Love, God's and humanity's, as a path to transforming hearts, minds, and bodies wrecked by abuse, neglect, and trauma. The starting point had to be Love, and the ending point had to be Love, without any transgressions of the children coming into the theological or liturgical equation. We must constantly re-construct the narrative of faith as we learn more about how it impacts all the conditions of humanity—especially the powerless and traumatized.

A Chaplain serving the most vulnerable and victimized part of humanity must be ready for his/her theology to be challenged and to evolve. The Chaplain will need a strong faith and community for support. It is simultaneously a heartbreaking and fulfilling service. In the end, the best you can hope to do is to offer Hope by being the embodiment of Love… and the Word became flesh and dwelt among us.

About Keith A. Bailey, Ph.D.

Keith has over 25 years of experience working with children and families. He served for 15 years at Holston Home for Children, Greeneville, Tennessee (1992–2007) in multiple positions; he was the Chaplain/Director of Spiritual Life for nine years and later served as the Administrator of Best Practices. He was a Consultant for UT's Social Work Office of Research and Public Service (2007–2012), where he trained Tennessee Department of Children's Services Staff and foster parents, developed curricula, and offered technical support. He went on to work as a Curriculum Coordinator for UT's CAFSP, developing curricula for the Food and Drug Administration and Department of Homeland Security (2012–2016). Keith also has operated his own training and consulting business since 2007, serving schools and child welfare and social service agencies. He has trained and consulted across the U.S. and in Canada as an independent consultant and on behalf of the Child Welfare League of America, the National Technical Assistance Center, and SafeGuards. He has taught at Tusculum College as an Adjunct Faculty in the Psychology Department at since 2009.

In 2016, Keith joined Harmony Family Center as the Director of Training and serves as a member of the Executive Team. While at Harmony, was certified in Dr. Bruce Perry's Neurosequential Model of Therapeutics.

Keith earned a B.A. in Psychology from Tennessee Wesleyan College, an M.Div. from Duke University, and an M.S. in Child Development and Ph.D. in Human Ecology, with a concentration in Child and Family Studies from the University of Tennessee.

He is a Professionally Certified Trainer for Therapeutic Crisis Intervention through Cornell University and a certified Therapy Dog Handler through Therapy Dogs International.

Keith is married to Angela, and they have two adult children, Kaitlyn and Taylor.

References

Carter, S. (1963). Lord of the dance.

Catholic Encyclopedia. Orphans and orphanages. Retrieved from http://www.newadvent.org/cathen/11322b.htm

Fowler, J. W. (1981). Stages of faith: The psychology of human development and the quest for meaning. San Francisco: Harper & Row.

The Huffington Post. Macrina Cooper-White. Religion & mental health: New study links belief in "punitive God" to emotional problems. Retrieved from http://www.huffingtonpost.com/2013/04/24/religion-mental-health-angry-god-brain_n_3097025.html

Indian Education. (2010). Montana Office of Public Instruction—Flathead Reservation Timeline Confederated Salish and Kootenai Tribes. Retrieved from http://opi.mt.gov/pdf/IndianEd/iefa/FlatheadTimeline.pdf

Webb-Mitchell, B. (1993). God plays piano, too: The spiritual lives of disabled children. Crossroads Publishing Company.

Resources

Adler, A. (1951). The practice and theory of individual psychology. London: Routledge & K. Paul.

Allport, G. (1950). The individual and his religion: A psychological interpretation. Oxford, England: Macmillan.

Bloom, S. (2013). Creating Sanctuary. Abingdon, Oxon: Routledge.

Creating Trauma Informed Congregations. http://www.mentalhealth.gov/blog/2014/04/creating-trauma-informed-congregations.html

Fowler, J. W. (1981). Stages of faith: The psychology of human development and the quest for meaning. San Francisco: Harper & Row.

James, W. (1985). The varieties of religious experience. Harvard University Press.

Pargament, K. et al. (2013) APA handbook of psychology, religion, and spirituality. Washington, D.C.: American Psychological Association.

Perry. B. (2008). The boy who was raised as a dog and other stories from a child psychiatrist's notebook: What traumatized children can teach us about life, loss, love, and healing. New York: Basic Books.

Behavioral Issues Common in Residential Care

Kevin Orpurt, MSW, LCSW

Before we look at common therapeutic issues that people who have experienced residential care may experience, it seems fair that you know a little about me. To be honest, I've found writing this chapter to be quite intimidating as I was very fortunate to grow up in an intact family who clearly loved me and had the means to provide for me. My parents both had good factory jobs in Indiana and although my father died when I was a teenager there was never a concern about my mother's ability to finish raising my brother and me on her own. Additionally, while I tested a few limits, I was a compliant kid who was at little risk of getting into significant trouble. However, I was drawn to Social Work as my brother and I were first-generation high school graduates and I always understood how fortunate I was to have the resources and education I had.

Professionally, while I have spent most my career providing outpatient psychotherapy, I am very grateful that two of my earliest jobs were working in residential care. My first job after graduating college was working in an adult alcohol and drug treatment facility in Portland Oregon. It was a truly amazing program in which most residents stayed 6 to 9 months with the option to stay up to 18 months. The other unique feature was we only served people who could not afford insurance and if we found out someone had insurance, we arranged a transfer to a different facility. From a clinical perspective, I have always appreciated this experience as we had a very structured program that allowed me to learn a specific treatment approach. I believe it is good for young therapists to have the foundation of a specific treatment approach from which to adapt as they gain experience.

My second formative experience was providing psychotherapy for a Methodist Children's home in East Tennessee. My role was to provide therapy to the children and adolescents as they were transitioning out of the home and into either foster care or returning to their birth families. This experience allowed me to see how the kids would take what they had learned in residential care and use it back in a more traditional environment. While a don't claim to be an authority on residential care per say, I have had enough experience to see significant patterns and both experiences have greatly influenced my approach to therapy throughout my career.

In working with children and youth in residential care, as well as adults who have experienced residential care, some of the common behavioral issues that arise include issues with bonding, trauma, and conflict management. At some level, this is a brief list of core issues all people have to manage at times. However, it can be greatly influenced by life events as well as general coping predispositions. Certainly, residential care and the issues that lead to it are significant life events.

Before we take a more specific look at these issues, let's look at general coping, the common ways that the average person copes. The key to understanding coping is knowing that we usually do what we think is best for ourselves in the moment. Often, we respond to events in ways that lead to positive outcomes. However, there are other times our solutions actually create bigger problems. When this occurs, we either recognize that we've created a bigger problem or we continue to cope in ways that perpetuate or increase our problems unwittingly. When we recognize we are perpetuating or increasing our problems, we can look for other solutions, or knowingly increase our troubles. When we knowingly increase our problems, it is usually because we can't imagine a better solution. So, when people are seen by a therapist, either by their own choice or at the demand of someone else like a judge, parent or spouse, they usually have already tried in some way to solve a problem.

The classic example of the solution causing a bigger problem is panic disorder. At some point in our lives, most people experience the level of physical reaction to stress that could be classified as a panic attack. This reaction may include shortness of breath, tingling in the arms, sweating, chest pain and several other symptoms. However less than five percent of the population will have panic disorder, which is recurrent panic attacks that interfere with their daily lives. Anyone who has ever had a panic attack knows they are miserable. But, given that anxiety is a normal part of life, our bodies are naturally designed to allow the panic to subside, which most people can do. The problem with panic disorder is that some people are so overwhelmed with the experience of panic symptoms that they establish a goal of not feeling panic again. In order to achieve this goal, they avoid activities that can cause panic and become vigilant about the symptoms themselves. This combination of avoidance and vigilance leads them into a pattern of missing out on many of life's activities and inadvertently increasing their anxious reactions to life's inevitable stress. Thus, the desire to avoid anxiety has created more anxiety. The good news is that once someone recognizes how they are accidently making their panic worse, the alternative becomes clear. If anxiety is a nature part of all life (even plants experience stress) and our goal of not experiencing anxiety is unrealistic and counterproductive, then a new goal of being ok even when we are anxious allows us to stop adding stress to our stress and thus allows our body's natural calming powers to kick in.

Now, with this general understanding of coping, let's take a closer look at some common therapy issues that are seen in residential care or that people who have experienced residential care may struggle with throughout their lives. Please keep in mind that this is a discussion of common or general themes and that everyone's circumstances, influences and inclinations are uniquely their own.

Issues of bonding and attachment are central to the human situation and often pronounced in people who have experienced residential care. Put simply, as infants, humans are completely dependent on someone else for all issues of safety and nurturance thus we develop a bond or attachment to our primary care giver. The more stable, safe and nurturing the care giver, the more secure the attachment is likely to be. As we develop, the older we get, the more independent we become.

It's a bit like a big game of tag. If home base is always present and in the same place, we can gage our risks appropriately. The bigger and faster we become, the further we are likely to stray. The more we stray, the more confident we become in our own abilities. If a new base is added to the game, we are likely to trust the base, given that our experience tells us bases are safe and dependable.

However, if our early experience of base is that it is not dependable, we will play the game much differently. Some of us are likely to become vigilant about the base, focusing our attention on where the base will be rather than where the opportunities or threats are elsewhere in the game. If we choose, or are inclined toward this path, our sense of self confidence is likely to be stunted, given that we spend more time worrying about the base than learning our own strengths and limitations. Others may just leave the base altogether, concluding they are safer on their own than on bases.

Once additional bases are introduced, our approach to them will be informed by our original experience of bases. Some of us will be so relieved that we move quickly to the next base. But, if experience teaches us that bases move, we may become skeptical of the base in a short period of time. Once it does show signs of movement we can either cling to it (and possibly tolerate tremendous instability) or dismiss it (maybe prematurely) and move on in search of the next base. Those of us who struck out on our own at the beginning of the game may become indifferent to bases altogether. Others may actually develop disdain for bases, choosing to attack them as the worthless objects we know them to be.

So it's not hard to imagine that people who have experienced residential care often have difficulty knowing who they can trust and how to relate to other people. Even in the case of someone who has had an excellent biological mother (the most obvious potential example) as their primary attachment, the mere fact that they are or have been in residential care indicates there has been a break in their ability to depend on "home base" before they are ready to be independent. If it is the case of the death of the mother, the child has learned at too early an age that no relationship can be counted on to be permanent (and the secondary attachments are not able or willing to fill the void). Of course a child who is in residential care because they never had a safe, stable primary nurturer is likely to have even more significant issues with bonding.

There are a variety of behaviors that can result from issues with attachment and bonding. One of the most extreme examples is the young charmer who is great at attracting others (including care givers) only to turn disinterested or aggressive when they get the attention they sought. Remember, they have already learned at a very early age that no one can really be trusted and if they actually start trusting, they endanger themselves. In the milder forms they may simply start to emotionally disconnect from others when they begin to feel close or safe. On the other end of the spectrum we see people that are willing to latch on to people who show them interest even though the other person is really not safe to be with. If someone's childhood experience is that primary relationships are filled with emotional or physical abuse, why would they leave the relationship? Experience has taught them they are lucky to have anyone that cares about them and that the next person will be just as abusive anyway.

I used to have a pastor that I would have coffee with occasionally. When he found out that I was a psychotherapist who had experience working in foster care, he used to pester me about doing a lecture in his Sunday school class about attachment. He explained to me that he had an attachment disorder that he attributed to his childhood experience of growing up in an orphanage. He went on to explain that he had the ability to detach from anyone except his wife and children. He would say, "if you violate my trust, I can cut you off and never care about you again." After several similar conversations, I finally told him that I would be willing to prepare the lecture but I did not believe he had a disorder. I went on to explain that what he described were very legitimate survival skills he had learned from his childhood experience in an institution. The next time we had coffee, I asked him when he wanted to schedule the lecture. He told me not to worry about it, he realized he doesn't have an attachment disorder.

Now the reality is he does not have a disorder but he does have to be aware of his issues with attachment. He sometimes has to make conscious decisions to stay engaged in relationships when his inclination may be to just walk away. Whether you are someone working through your own attachment issues or someone working in residential care or even the loved one of someone that has had issues with bonding, the key really is awareness. If I am aware of my behavior and motivations, I can learn to manage them. However, if I am not aware, I cannot manage them and they really may develop into a disorder.

Specifically for caregivers, it is important to understand that the child who is acting out really is doing what he or she believes is in their best interest. We tend to find it easier to disengage from power struggles when we understand that the child is behaving in a reasonable way even if it is dangerous or misguided.

Our second category is issues related to trauma. Trauma can be described as our response to very difficult or damaging situations. Many children in residential care have experienced significant danger in their lives, both physical and emotional. The coping strategies we use for survival in acute stress situations are not the same as those we use to thrive in everyday life. Sometimes we become aggressive to fight our way through situations and other times we become withdrawn and emotionally shut down. This is especially true for children and those in situations in which they are or feel powerless. However, coping strategies are like all skills, the more we use them, the better we get and the less we must think about them. Therefore, it is not uncommon to continue to use the survival skills on auto pilot even when the threat is removed.

This brings us to a critical point. It is asking a lot of a child and sometimes even dangerous to ask a child to switch out of survival mode or learn alternative coping skills when they are returning to the same environment. I'll give two examples of children I worked with in school settings recently. The first example was a ten-year-old girl who lived in a dangerous home. The mother appeared to be well intentioned but had struggles with addiction and her live in boyfriend had a significant record of violent behavior. The school had made multiple reports to both the local Children's Services and Sherriff's departments. The girl was very withdrawn and failing in school. She had stolen from her favorite teacher and could be aggressive, although that was not her tendency. The principal and teachers encouraged me to work with her on emotional identification/regulation and social skills. I had to explain to them that if their suspicion of her home was accurate, then they were really asking her to learn skills that could make her more emotionally vulnerable at home. We focused instead on providing a safe, consistent, accepting environment for her during the day. She continued to be emotionally withdrawn and displayed a limited range of affect. One random day, however, I was standing in the office and looked out into the hall. I saw her giggle with a peer as her class transitioned to their next activity. When I pointed this out to the school principal, she informed me that she had been removed from her family earlier in the week and placed in temporary foster care with one of the substitute teachers. She went on to have a very successful rest of the school year. She was highly engaged with both peers and teachers and her grades made dramatic improvements.

How does this relate to residential care? We have long recognized that while it is often easier to help children make positive changes, it is critical that if we are preparing them to return to their previous environment, we often must help those they are returning to make positive changes as well. While the beginning of this example is nice, the best part is the reunification. It turns out her mother was just as scared of her boyfriend and was living in an acute survival state as well. Once he was facing legal charges, he burned the family home and left the state. The mom was very compliant with all the recommendations from the court and agencies involved and was able to provide a safe place for her daughter's return.

The second example is a little more difficult. Around the same time, I was working with a fifteen-year-old high school student. He previously had been in residential care but at the time I saw him, he was back with his biological family who was still struggling with the initial issues that caused him to be removed from the home in the first place. This young man's mother had a significant mental illness which was exacerbated by her drug use. She was often psychotic and paranoid, frequently verbally aggressive with him. His father coped largely by staying out of the mother's way, working long hours. When he did discuss leaving her, he talked about getting a one-bedroom apartment, essentially leaving his child and my student to fend for himself. The student was a very large young man and would often intimidate his mother then stay in his room playing video games.

The school referred him to me because he was failing all his classes and spent a lot of his time in in-school suspension for refusing to comply with teachers and disrupting the class. In our sessions, he was very pleasant and often funny. He was able to verbalize tremendous rage toward his mother and indifference toward school. Given that he was five years older than the child in the previous example, his increased development allowed him somewhat better insight into his behavior. Over time, as he began to trust me, we were able to identify that his primary coping strategy was to tell himself that he didn't care. This strategy was very effective in helping him survive his home life. If he had given into the rage that did come along with allowing himself to care, he may well have killed his mother. Knowing that I could not ask him to establish a goal that would interfere with his survival instincts at home, we began having open conversations about the difference between survival strategies and thriving strategies. I completely validated his strategy of emotionally cutting off at home but did ask him to work on being aware of when he was using the same strategies of not caring in school. This made sense to him and he was able to begin making the distinction between not caring and feeling overwhelmed at school. Sadly, one day when discussing school, he looked at me and said it had been so long since he had tried in school that when he does try, he is often completely lost.

Unfortunately, I transitioned out of that school and do not know how he is currently doing. As we anticipated this transition, I tried to share some insights with a couple key staff, because if he does graduate it will not only take effort on his part but the understanding of at least one or two empowered adults in the school as he has one other coping mechanism that is worth mentioning. When he is anxious, he often smiles and in extreme cases can start to get the giggles. While this has the appearance of disrespect, it really is merely a stress response. However, when this is not recognized by the adults they tend to unwittingly perpetuate the cycle by demanding that he not smile and be respectful, thus causing even greater internal stress. It is good for all of us in the helping professions to be mindful that what appears to be indifference or intentional disrespect, is often merely a desperate response by the most anxious of the people we are trying to help.

Having looked at coping in acute stress situations, it goes without saying that many who are in or have been in residential care, often are struggling with past trauma as well. It is important to understand that trauma is not caused by the event itself. Two people can experience the same event and only one of them be traumatized. How the event is experienced and/or processed and the response to it determines the trauma. Post-Traumatic Stress Disorder (PTSD) is the severe struggle to cope with a past event. People with PTSD can re-experience events through intrusive thoughts, flashbacks as if they are reliving, nightmares, etc. They also avoid places and situations that remind them of the event.

A simplified way to understand PTSD is that the person is afraid of the memory of an event. The experience of the event was so uncomfortable that they are afraid of re-experiencing it. Much like with panic disorder, they are so afraid of the memory that they become vigilant about having it. Of course vigilance requires people to look for that which they are afraid of, thus causing the cycle to start.

There are several effective methods to treat post-traumatic stress issues, but they tend to follow a common formula of teaching people coping strategies to employ once the response starts and then guiding them through the memory. The critical piece is in allowing themselves to experience the memory. Once they break the avoidance cycle, they begin to gain confidence that they can get through the experience, thus taking some of the anxious energy out of their avoidance or reaction. This doesn't mean they will no longer have PTSD symptoms but that as they gain confidence, the symptoms tend to become less severe and happen less often. Yet, when they do happen, they have the knowledge of how to get through them.

In the beginning of this chapter, I mentioned that people tend to do what they think is best for themselves in the moment. Another theme that is coming into focus is that we often get into unconscious coping patterns that accidently make a situation worse and once we become aware of the patterns, we can start to unlock them. Often times, merely recognizing this cycle while it is occurring is enough as long as we choose to treat ourselves with a bit of compassion and not berate ourselves "for making it worse." Given that there is so much information available on PTSD, I will not linger on the topic itself but will share an experience that illustrates this point.

I used to see a lady in her mid-sixties whose husband had had an affair twenty years earlier. This event had consumed her life, causing significant episodes of depression and self-doubt. She could identify how she had been emotionally distant before the infidelity thus she blamed herself although her husband did not appear to blame her, as he had been remorseful of his own behavior, and had been quite attentive and loyal to her in the subsequent years.

In one of our sessions, she was explaining to me that she can be having perfectly good days and be overcome with the memory of the event, as if is she were there. She also reported that there was very little else in her life she was unhappy with. As we discussed this issue, she also told me that a couple mornings prior, she woke up and the experience was just present with her. It colored her entire day. As I asked her about the events of the previous day and evening, she explained to me that it had been very nice. It was the first warm day of spring and she and her husband sat out on their deck, having a very nice evening. She went on to tell me that the weather was so nice they let the dog stay outside and they opened the windows to sleep in the nice breeze. Unfortunately, the dog barked all night and she slept very little. I quickly realized, this was where her unconscious coping pattern started. By the time morning arrived, she was very frustrated and tired. However, she had become accustomed to blaming all her depressive thoughts on her perceived inadequacy as a wife. With a respectful grin, I looked at her and explained that she in fact should have been tired and grumpy and that the real culprit was their dog. She gave an embarrassed but relieved laugh, recognizing the error she had made.

It is very common for people who have experienced trauma or who have had issues with depression to have those "go-to thoughts or ruminations". Any time she experienced distress, her brain's go-to thought was of the infidelity and her perceived inadequacy. I asked her to start playing a little game with herself. I suggested that she try and catch herself having the automatic thoughts of his infidelity and think about what was really causing the stress in the moment. Not surprisingly, she got quite good at this and as she increased her ability to be mindful of her present situation, intrusive memories of her husband's infidelity diminished significantly. Note, the real liberation occurred when she was willing to start noticing the unpleasant thoughts rather than avoiding them.

The final therapeutic issue I want to look at is coping with conflict. It's not hard to see how this ties in with all that we've already discussed. Childhood, by its very nature, is filled with power differentials. Certainly, this is magnified with institutional care. The reality of all healthy relationships is they all involve conflict and the more constructive conflict we've experienced the better we will be at managing future conflict. Conversely, the more we have to struggle to get our needs met, the more we are tempted to become aggressive or just give up. If our childhood has taught us that we have very little power, our automatic tendency toward either will kick in. As in our previous discussion of trauma coping, when we learn to recognize these unconscious patterns as they are happening, we can begin to work through them.

As care givers, it is imperative that we be aware of our own issues with power if we are going to try to help people manage conflict. The following may be my favorite therapeutic story. When I was working in the high school, a 16-year-old junior boy was referred to me. He apparently had been having issues with authority, talking back to teachers and administrators. Given that he was 16 I could only see him if he were willing. I spoke with his mother who explained there had been significant issues in the past but gave very little detail. She said that she would love for him to see me but didn't believe he would agree to see me in sessions. We made an agreement that I would call him into my office and explain my services and how I conduct therapy then let him decide whether or not to continue.

A few days passed before I was at the school again so on the morning I called him into my office, I asked his guidance counselor to remind me why she made the referral. In a rather loud voice, she said, "Because he's a punk".

When he came into my office, I explained that he was referred to me because of issues with anger and I told him my two rules for therapy. My first rule is that I don't fuss at my patients. They are always welcome to continue what they are doing and question me about what I am doing. The second rule is a general statement about confidentiality and not asking me about other people I also see. Then with a smile I usually tell them if they break rule number two I may break rule number one.

He was very calm and respectful then started to recap his understanding of what I said. He started with, "You said I have a problem with anger..." At which I point I quickly interrupted him saying "Whoa…" and threw in some arm gestures. Rather than get angry with me, he was clearly thrown off and started stammering about rules number one and two. After we clarified that he thought I was breaking rule number one, I looked directly at him, then pointing to the rest of the school, said with a genuinely disgusted voice "**they** said you have an anger problem. I don't care what they think!" To which he regained his composure and said, "well okay, I think I can work with you."

As it turned out he was a real joy to work with. He had suffered sexual abuse from an older brother and the family had significant interventions from the Department of Children's Services. At the time I started seeing him the perpetrating brother had been reunified with the family. He was aware that he had significant anger but also possessed a level of charm and genuine self-motivation that allowed him to be very successful in one of the school's clubs He was actually very talented and a leader, but if he perceived he wasn't being treated with respect, he could be very challenging with teachers and administrators. Given that he knew I respected him, he not only allowed me to challenge him but appreciated and enjoyed it. Recognizing that his aggressive nature could be both helpful and undermining, we were able to work on recognizing what triggered him and appropriate alternatives once he was triggered.

The reason I like this example so much is that it encapsulates or summarizes all the behavioral issues and treatment themes we have been discussing. Even though he has not experienced residential care, he did have a very similar family experience as many that have, and in his case, some of the school officials treated him with the rigidity of the worst institutions. As is usually the case, there were others who treated him with great respect.

In the case of bonding, our young man does not have a stable sense of who he can trust emotionally. Superficially, he is good at recognizing who will at least take him seriously and treat him with respect, but on a more intimate level he has struggled to know who he is willing to truly depend on emotionally versus who is merely an object for his goals or challenge for his ego. As for trauma, in addition to his own abuse, is his knowledge that his younger sister was also abused. In many ways this is a greater issue for him to get in touch with as he perceives it is largely his fault for not telling what his brother was doing to him, thus unwittingly allowing his brother to move on to another victim. He has a strong desire to care for others even to the point of putting his own self at risk. It is probable that the source of this is his guilt around not protecting her. And as we just noted he is working to increase both insight into and the ability to manage his anger as he is navigating inevitable interpersonal conflicts.

As we look toward the conclusion of this chapter, we can begin to see common issues that children who have experienced residential care are likely to take into their adult lives, especially if the residential program did not have adequate treatment services or if the child was unable to take advantage of those services at that time in their life. The key issues we've looked at are bonding, trauma, and conflict management. What do these issues look like for adults? A recent sampling of my new patients gives us a good idea: The young college age lady who suspects she is too picky in her friend selection and that she is superficial with the friends she does have and the 50-year-old man who has had a series of intense yet failed romantic relationships and is currently estranged from his adult son are both struggling with issues of bonding; The mother who has limited memory of her childhood before the age of 14 and has struggled with sexual intimacy only to start having flashbacks of sexual abuse when her own daughter reaches puberty and the 30 year old man who grew up in a violent home who continued to fight throughout residential care and now dismisses his tendency to lose jobs for fighting on the worksite (and being in a blackout during the fights) as normal are both working on trauma issues. The man who struggles to share an opinion with his wife then resents her for not being in tune with his needs and the woman who shuts down disagreements by becoming enraged are examples of adults continuing to learn how to manage conflict.

We can see in the above examples that there is an overlap between issues and this is not a complete list of treatment issues, just some of the more fundamental ones. It is also important to note that even for adults whose residential experience was in a facility with good treatment programming, these issues may arise and there may be a need to return to therapy for a time. This should not be seen as any kind of weakness or failure. We are all in a constant state of learning and maturing. What we gain from therapy at 15, 35, and 55 should not be the same. As we progress through life, we bring more experience and wisdom into our therapy sessions. Even so, sometimes the coping strategies that help us through our younger years, are no longer helpful in mid or later life. It can be very liberating to revisit some of our therapeutic issues and coping mechanisms as we progress through life.

In conclusion, the overriding theme in effective therapy is that people's behavior is the solution they perceive to be the best for the situation they are in, even when it is perpetuating the problem. So if I am the one that has the problem, it is important to treat myself with compassion. If I can learn to recognize how I am accidently perpetuating or exacerbating a problem and cut myself some slack, I can begin to look at different ways to address my problem. And if I am the professional helping an identified patient or client, it is imperative I treat them with genuine respect. I cannot truly help them otherwise and besides, no one spots an inauthentic or uncaring therapist faster than someone who has experienced residential care.

About Kevin Orpurt, MSW, LCSW

Kevin Orpurt is a Licensed Clinical Social Worker with over 25 years experience in the mental health field, in a variety of settings, including Residential Alcohol and Drug, Child and Adolescent Residential and Foster Care, School Based Therapy, Community Mental Health and Integrated Care. He has a degree from the University of Notre Dame and a Masters in Social Work from Tulane University. In each of his work settings he has balanced a leadership role with maintaining an active psychotherapy caseload. Currently he is the Chief Clinical Officer of Basis Health Group, a tele psychiatry company in Knoxville, Tennessee and maintains a psychotherapy practice at Haven Family Psychiatry. He and his wife, Kim, have five children and have recently welcomed their first grandchild into the family.

Houseparents Crucial
for Residential Children

Jerry Smith, MSW

In 1949, my twin sister and I were admitted into residential care at the Free Will Baptist Orphanage in Middlesex, North Carolina. We were seven years old, and our arrival on campus was recorded in the 'Register of Inmates' book. For the next eleven years, our primary daily care was from our matrons. My sister lived in an all-girls building and I lived with the boys in another building across campus. There were always 90–100 children living in the orphanage at any given time, evenly divided between males and females. My sister and I both left residential care upon graduating from high school in 1960.

For nine of my eleven years in residential care, Mary and Clarence Mitchell were my houseparents — but we boys referred to them as our matrons. In other orphanages in this country, some houseparents were called matrons, too. Other terms used for those in this role include uncle, aunt, mother, mom, father, dad, sister, teacher, and child care worker. Today, working titles for houseparents in residential care include practitioners, children's service worker, cottage parent, and teacher counselor. Regardless of their titles, the responsibilities of houseparents are 24/7 and their care remains the same and principal for each child in care. Whatever the administrative title, those that give 24/7 care for children in residential care, in my mind's eyes, are houseparents. Today, fifty plus years after leaving residential care, I continue to refer to my houseparents, Mary and Clarence Mitchell, as matrons.

Presidents, CEOs, social workers, psychologists, psychiatrists, physicians, nurses, resident managers, and other child care staff go in and out of children's lives frequently, but houseparents are always present. The children know this; these people are their safety nets, night and day. They calm the children's fears and anxieties through storms and inclement weather; they are always within touching distance when electricity fails due to threats of hurricanes and tornados. They are always there in the evening hours to comfort a grieving child from the day's activities or when he or she is missing a parent. The houseparent is truly the soul of residential care, but not the face of residential care.

Houseparent Make First Impression

At various times, society has both glorified and vilified the houseparent. Yet, to the child coming into residential care, the houseparent is the first adult the child is left in care with for modeling genuine parenting protection and love. It is the attitude of the houseparent during the initial intake that reaffirms adult care and trust. The houseparent, often with little professional training, meets a child after the "normal" family structure breaks down, and is expected to assist the child with achieving a satisfying standard of future life and health.

The job description for a houseparent calls for someone who is warm, wholesome, tender, loving, kind, and flexible, but able to set limits. This person also needs to be capable of tolerating verbal and physical abuse that would try the patience of a saint.[1]

The majority of children who are placed in residential treatment have exhausted other forms of community service and need total environmental management or a restructuring of their reality to help foster more healthy personality development. In many respects, the residential staff person who is predominantly responsible for helping to effect personality change is the houseparent, and if the total milieu is to be utilized effectively in the treatment process, the role of the houseparent becomes critical and requires sophisticated skills.

In any human services program, affection and warmth in personal relations are necessary components, but "love is not enough." Recognition of interpersonal attitudes and feelings and their significance and management require special training and awareness in order to utilize the interaction between child and adult productively.

The houseparent's task varies from one residential care facility to another so that the houseparent's care role will reflect the differences in the overall treatment philosophies of the particular residential care home he or she is in. Residential practice may range from custodial care to interventionist process where the houseparent might function as an adjunctive or even major therapist. The majority of residential care, however, continues to utilize the houseparent mainly in a caretaking capacity, or as a surrogate parent.[2]

Responsibilities to Residential Culture

In addition to personal obligations of their own family and lives, a houseparent has three primary responsibilities to the child care institution and child:

- to create a home-like atmosphere with the children where the individual child's needs are met and potentials realized.

- to adapt to living with their colleagues and learn to get along with them, even though they may not be the type of people they would have chosen to live and work with.

- to understand and accept the administrative policies and requirements of the residential home, even though they might disagree with them. Often these policies are laid down by a president/CEO with no child care training or experience.[3]

The facility may impose many restrictions, and

…the amount of independence given to houseparents varies. In all cases, they have to be accountable to the administration, keep the rules about fire drills, medical care, bookkeeping, case records, and shopping. They must be ready at all times to receive visitors, committee or board members, child care officials, and parents. And they must be prepared for discussions on the children in their care. They often must maintain contact with the community, and visit the children's schools, churches, etc. Their own leisure interests may have to take a back seat to the needs of the children and the institution. It is only too easy, therefore, for houseparents to become so bound up with their work that they are in danger of losing touch with community life and friends outside. This problem intensifies its stranglehold when there are staff shortages and very long hours have to be worked.[4]

Houseparent, Natural Parent Responsibilities Parallel

There has been little change in the houseparent of today compared to years ago. Real wages, education, marital status, experience with people, and length of service has remained about the same. The average houseparent is still a widow, age 53, a high school graduate but not a college graduate, and has been working on the job less than five years.[5]

In some ways, her responsibilities are like parents outside the institution. The hours are long and she must account for the child at all times; her relationship with the child cannot be too strict and is usually on an informal basis; she must recognize the child as an individual; she needs to be aware and concerned when others criticize the child; and she must recognize the normal growing behavior.

Likewise there are significant differences between houseparents and natural parents. A houseparent receives a salary, has no blood relationship to the child, and can resign when the going gets rough. She must supervise a group of children who are not siblings, and she takes regular time off with the child. She has no financial responsibility for medical bills, clothing, or food,[6] and will not suffer any stigma on her family name due to any misbehavior on the child's part.

Public Perception

The public has many false beliefs about the houseparent. One is that any motherly woman with a kind heart and common sense can be a successful houseparent. This is unrealistic when one considers the emotional and disturbed children under their care. Another is that there is a sufficient number of workers available for orphanages or children's homes. In fact, there is a national shortage which remains consistent through the years. Even the public view that the staff is "always" properly trained is not true.[7]

Government, private, religious and secular organizations supporting residential care need to realize the importance of having qualified houseparents to care for children. The days should be gone when the little "ole" widow found in residential care finds a secure place to live out her last days watching the sunset and without having knowledge of parenting the troubled child for which she is responsible. Houseparents need a more professional image. Their status, training, and conditions of pay must be improved. It is heartbreaking knowing there is high national employment turnover with houseparents.[8]

Training for houseparents is not consistent unless the children's home of employment is nationally accredited by Council on Accreditation (COA), or other accepted accreditations for providing quality child care.

Houseparent Training

My knowledge and experience of residential care, besides spending my childhood in an orphanage (1949–60), has evolved from my graduate studies in social work, my career in social work, and from the work of Dr. Alan Keith Lucas, Ph.D. He is Alumni Distinguished Professor Emeritus of the University of North Carolina, and founder of that University's Group Child Care Consultant Services. He consulted with more than 80 children's homes on three continents before his death in 1995. In my opinion, Dr. Keith-Lucas continues to be the authority and expert for residential care. His writings and teachings are sought-after references for quality child care. In his book, *The Church Children's Home in a Changing World*, Dr. Keith-Lucas illustrates what can be done to train houseparents so that they can become professionals who are properly equipped to give the kind of services needed by children:

- Training starts when the houseparent stops being a "matron" without training and becomes an educated houseparent.
- Training continues whenever you send a houseparent to a conference, and whenever this conference stops being a series of lectures by experts and becomes a forum where houseparents can voice their experiences and have their ideas valued.
- It happens when you begin to see administration not as hierarchy in which the houseparent carries out your commands, but as a help to the worker who lives with the child both day and night, when the houseparent is truly a member of the team with as much in her sphere to contribute to the conversation as the professional in his.
- It happens when the administrator or director schedules regular conferences with the houseparent, thereby treating her as a professional who evaluates her performance objectively and in accordance with standards and entrusts her with information that she needs to carry out her job.

Houseparents now have a guide of sorts, since for the first time in this country, a publisher thought it worthwhile to publish a book of reading for houseparents.

In my professional life, I have known and worked with hundreds of houseparents. Some, it is true, have been narrow-minded and apparently insensitive to children's needs, while others were just plainly inefficient. But many have had much to offer the children and have been truly professional people. I am inclined to say that what characterizes the good ones has been a freedom from fear—internal and external. It is not, of course, the whole story, but it is a big part of it.[9]

There is strong implication for a need to have well-trained, professional, and empathic houseparents. Those who recruit child care workers should constantly be aware that:

- The emotional needs of people who are willing to undertake "residential" and foster care are diverse, and their desire to become "houseparents" and foster parents arises from many sources. It is not always reflective of healthy needs.[10]

- The seed that must be good and properly nurtured, to ensure that all child care institutions provide professional child care, is the houseparent.

It is my experience and professional opinion that the single most important obligation of houseparents should be in helping meet the emotional needs of a child. Houseparents should begin their profession by understanding their psychological task and the importance of their responsibility in adequately understanding each child's history and developmental level.

Housemother

It is very important that residential institutions recognize that there are many qualities needed to be a good housemother, and they should be keenly aware of her tasks. The psychological tasks that confront the housemother are in some ways similar to those experienced in natural parenthood, but they are different in significant ways. They are influenced by the child's previous experience with one or more other mothers; by the child's age and stage of development when he or she enters residential care; by the agency's outlook or expectation regarding the length of his or her stay in care; by his or her ongoing relationship with the natural family; and by the needs, hopes, and expectations of residential care in undertaking the child's care."[11]

Housefather

More emphasis should be placed on the recruitment and employment of housefathers. Most literature on parental care seems to give the father a secondary role in child development, and this is also true with the housefather. In truth, his role is as important and demanding as that of the natural father. The role of the father in modern society has often also been reduced to mere financial support. There has been a "historic failure to appreciate the fact that fathers as well as mothers are important in child development."[12]

A good housefather has to understand something about the natural father and the history of the child in accepting his role as a child care worker. A male image to a child, male or female, is important in his or her development. The housefather role in a child care facility is of utmost importance, and it is critical that residential care recognizes his function and psychological tasks.[13]

The inherent psychological tasks of the housefather are less intense than those of the housemother; nevertheless, the housefather is called upon to share the direct and indirect demands brought by the introduction of the child in residential care. His key role in providing emotional support, empathy, and direct help to the housemother in the child-rearing functions is not unlike his role as natural father. His representation of the expectations, standards, and reality of the outside world often is a new and vital experience for the child, who in many cases has had little opportunity for a relationship with an adult male who is, psychologically, the head of the household, the provider, and the representative of the adult world outside the home. In the home the housefather may be called upon to play a critical role in helping the child relate to the housemother or in helping the child overcome his or her fear of himself as the housefather, if the child from previous experience has learned to trust one parent more than the other.[14]

Postscript

As I reflect back to my childhood, I lived in a building with 40–50 boys everyday of my youth. For the eleven years I was in residential care, my houseparents carried an enormous responsibility parenting so many boys. They will always have my gratitude for being there for me. I truly think it was incredible they did as well as they did. Of course, some boys might have felt they could have done better, but one has to take into account the lack of orphanage administration's training support and resources for houseparents. I believe my matrons (houseparents) did the best they could do, and I am sure that their annual incomes did not aptly compensate them for their professional workloads.

Substitute parenting will continue to play an important role in the progression of residential care. The quality of houseparents will, to a large extent, determine the emotional, psychological, social, mental, and physical development of the child, and will greatly influence his or her responsive integration into society upon leaving residential care. The residential child has a right to receive care that will provide him or her with the environment in which he can experience all the growth stages. All residential children will best realize this developmental growth when church and government supports, and society recognizes the total needs of each child and the houseparent's important role in this process. When this happens, support will come forth to train and pay the houseparent as a professional. Only then will administrators flip their organization chart upside down, moving the houseparent to the top position, supported by the president/CEO and board at the bottom of the chart. Staff will then help support the houseparent occupation as the most important in residential care.

Education will improve, compensation will increase, staff turnover will decline, and houseparents will become teachers and counselors with training and skills for working with children from dysfunction families—as we witness with teachers in public school systems.

About Jerry Smith, MSW

Jerry Smith is the author of *Cousins*. His pen name is J. Andrews Smith. He has 30 years experience working in child welfare services, and 11 years of experience living in residential care. Jerry is a graduate of Mount Olive Jr. College and Barton College, and has a Masters of Social Work from the University of North Carolina at Chapel Hill. He has written numerous articles on residential care and has published three additional books: *The Family* (2010, LuLu Press), *Road to Hutchinson* (2009, PublishAmerica) and *I Have Hope* (1978, Era Press). Jerry was President of the Free Will Baptist Children's Home Alumni Association from 1973 to 77, and a Board Member there from 1990 to 97. Additionally, he was an Adjunct Professor, Barton College from 1980–89, President of the North Carolina Social Services Association from 1990–91, and worked with

Arab and Israeli children at Camp Seeds of Peace from 1995–97. He served as a medic with the U.S. Army in Germany from 1961–64.

Over thirty years, Jerry was Social Services Director for the Tazewell County Department of Social Services, Virginia, and Social Services Director for Washington, Swain, and Wilson Counties in North Carolina. He was director of the Holston United Methodist Home for Children (Knoxville Office) in Greeneville, Tennessee, and since 2000 has been a member of the CORE training staff with the home.

Jerry is married to Susan, and has sons: Jerry, Jr., and Mark; daughter-in-laws: Samantha and Anne; and grandchildren: Martha, Miriam, Sayre, River, Jerry III, and Torin.

Resources

1. Harry Finkelstein, "The New Look in Foster Care," *Public Welfare,* Volume XXVI, No. 3 (July 1968): p. 188.
2. American Association for Children's Residential Centers, *From Chaos to Order,* pp. 99-101.
3. Jessie Parfit, *The Community's Children* (New York: Human Press, 1967); p. 53.
4. Ibid., p. 54.
5. Alan Keith-Lucas, *The Church Children's Home in a Changing World* (Chapel Hill): The University of North Carolina Press, 1962), p. 43.
6. Aklton M. Broten, *Houseparents in Children's Institutions* (Chapel Hill: the University of North Carolina Press, 1962), p. 9.
7. Rosemary Dinnage and M. L. Kellmer Pringle, *Residential Child Care Facts and Fallacies* (New York, Humanities Press, 1968), p. 38.
8. Parfit, *The Community's Children,* p. 6.
9. Keith-Lucas, *The Church Children's Home in a Changing World,* pp. 44-45.
10. Jack V. Waller, "Placement and Separation Trauma," *Public Welfare,* Volume XXIV, Number 4 (October 1966), p. 300.
11. Draza Kline and Helen-Mary Forbush Overstreet, *Foster Care of Children* (New York: Columbia University Press, 1972), p. 277.
12. David B. Lynn, *The Father: His Role in Child Development* (Belmont, California: Wadsworth Publishing Company, 1974), p. VII.
13. Kline and Forbush, *Foster Care of Children,* p. 229.
14. Mary M. Diggles, "The Child Care Counselor: New Therapist in Children's Institutions," *Child Welfare,* Volume XLIX, Number 9 (November 1970), p. 153.

Orphanage Alumni Believe in the American Dream

Dr. Richard B. McKenzie, Ph.D.

O ver the last several years, national media have reported discouraging news on the survival of the American Dream. One study found that a sizable majority—just under 60 percent—of Americans have lost hope that they will achieve the American Dream.[1] They are even more discouraged about their children's futures. A recent study suggests a cause: The percentage of Americans earning more than their parents did at the same age has plunged since the 1970s.[2]

Many Americans believe the economic system is "rigged" against them and their children. They accept as fact that only the wealthiest of Americans have improved their financial condition over the last half-century at the expense of all others—and that upward economic mobility has been and remains hamstrung by entrenched poverty, crime and welfare dependency, and an array of trade, regulatory and tax policies designed to benefit top-income earners.

In contrast, surveys and interviews I conducted from the late1990s to as recently as summer 2016 found a substantial majority of Americans who came of age in orphanages, or "children's homes," from the 1920s to the present—and faced multiple family and foster-care hardships—believe they have lived, and are living, the American Dream.

The critics of modern orphanages—in contrast to 19th-century Dickensian workhouses—range from Sen. Orrin Hatch to novelist J.K. Rowling, and their prescriptions include eliminating such institutions in the United States and discouraging Western support for them in developing countries. There are surely institutions that provide poor care, inadequate education and harmful environments for their charges, but *most of the orphanage alumni I have surveyed avow that the list of hardships they have overcome did not include their orphanage experiences.* Indeed, a substantial majority express deeply felt affection for their stays in their "homes" and claim their orphanage experiences *contributed to* their success.

Success in Life

What is the American dream? People will answer that question differently, depending on their values and life experiences; but most Americans would agree that achieving their dream requires such things as education, steady work and a stable family life. It also requires, or leads to, a positive attitude toward life.[3]

In the mid-1990s, I surveyed more than 2,500 adult alumni of 15 American orphanages on their life outcomes and assessments of their institutional experiences. In the summer of 2016, I surveyed just over 400 alumni from six orphanages clustered in North and South Carolina, ranging in age from 20 to 97 and averaging 66, with their admission to their orphanages stretching back as far as 1925 to as recently as 2012. [See Dream Survey, next page]

Regardless of age or time of survey, the results were remarkably consistent: on measures of education, income and attitude, orphanage alumni scored better than the general American population, even though, in the most recent survey, the average children's home stay was 8.5 years and 70 percent report living in poverty prior to their admission to an orphans' home. (Though I call them orphans, most of the older alumni were in children's homes due to familial economic hardship, rather than the loss of parents, whereas younger alumni came from troubled circumstances.)

Education and the American Dream. Take "Dexter," for instance. As a young boy in the 1990s, he knew firsthand family poverty and homelessness, and emotional abuse from a parent diagnosed with psychosis. In his tweens, he found he could make more money distributing drugs in his middle school than mowing lawns. At age 14 he was caught distributing and was arrested

American Dream Survey, Summary Statistics
(Alumni from Six Orphanages, 2016)

1.	Total respondents	401
2.	Average age	66
	Age range	20–97
	Under 50	13%
3.	Average year of arrival	1959
	Range of arrival years	1925–2012
	Average years in orphanage	8.5
4.	Lived in foster care	20%
5.	Lower and poverty income classes before home admission	71%
6.	Lower and poverty income classes today	2.5%
7.	Middle and above income classes today	88%
	Top income class today	6%
8.	Very favorable and favorable assessments of children's home experience	80%
	Unfavorable	1.8%
	Very unfavorable	0.3%
	(The rest, mixed assessments.)	
9.	Very strongly agree or agree they have lived the American Dream	82%
10.	Have not lived the American Dream	5%
	(The rest, "not sure.")	
11.	Very strongly agree or agree the American dream remains viable for today's generations	88%
12.	Average happiness rating on scale of 1 (not happy at all) to 10 (very happy)	8.86
	Range of ratings	1–10
	Mode	10
	Median	9

in school. His probation officer persuaded a "self-proclaimed modern-day orphanage," which rarely considered children with criminal records, to take a chance on him.

A year behind when he was admitted to the children's home, Dexter graduated from high school on time with a full scholarship to study political science at his state's flagship university. He turned down the prestigious scholarship to take an unpaid job with a presidential campaign, in short order obtaining a paid position. The summer before the election, he was offered another full scholarship to attend one of the nation's elite Northeast universities to study international politics. He graduated with honors.

Dexter's educational experience is not unique: the aging alumni surveyed in the mid-1990s reported a college graduation rate 39 percent higher than the rate for their age cohort in the general white population.

Average students also fared better. For example, "Shellie" was a confident 18-year-old and a recent high school graduate when I interviewed her in 2011, working at a part-time summer job and looking forward to cosmetology school. Before going to her children's home, she lived in poverty with her "pill head" mother, as she described her, three sisters, all by different fathers, and a parade of men in the home. One of her sister's fathers sexually abused her.

"The best thing my mother ever did for me, at age eleven, was to run him out of the house when she caught him in my room," Shellie told me. "But, by my early teens I became almost a full-time truant. I could skip school because my mother was too out of it to know what I was doing, and I didn't like school."

Child welfare eventually took Shellie away, and sent her to several foster homes before placing her in a children's home at age 16, more than two years behind in school. Yet, with a large measure of tutoring, emotional support and focus on her course work, both in-class and online, Shellie graduated on time. By contrast, Dexter's twin sister remained with their psychotic father. She dropped out of high school as soon as she could. She did get her G.E.D.—about the same time Dexter received his university diploma.

Work and Family. In an era of supposedly stagnate income mobility and the prevalence of talk of the tight grip of the "cycle of poverty" on economic advancement, the alumni in my most recent survey report that, on average, they have moved up more than three "rungs" (quintiles) on the national income ladder from where they started before their orphanage admission. Remarkably:

- Some 87 percent of the alumni responding report their household income is in the middle fifth or higher income tiers.
- Nearly half report they are in the top two income tiers ("upper middle" and "upper").
- Only 0.3 percent report they live in poverty today, and only 2 percent are in the "lower income" category (the next level up from poverty).

Most of these individuals started in poverty. Take two examples from the 1990s survey. In the 1920s, "Martin" was taken from a backwoods southern farm to his orphanage because "our father died and our mother was an invalid." He graduated from his orphanage's high school, went into the military, married and spent 43 years as a technician at the Carnation plant in a town near his orphanage.

"Herman" knew "dirt poverty" that came as the child of a single mother with menial work skills in the early 1940s. His mother gave up custody when he was a toddler to the county welfare department, which placed him in a sequence of several failed "welfare sponsored homes" (now called "foster care"). Eventually, he was placed in a rural North Carolina orphanage of over 300 children who worked on-campus farms and shops operated with a handful of supervising adults. He went to college with help from a well-to-do Charlotte couple, then to officer's training school and into the Navy for three years. After military service, Herman married, began his career as a financial adviser and stockbroker, had two children and retired after a successful 50-plus year career.

In the main, these children's homes graduated good, responsible, upstanding American citizens.

Living the American Dream. Over the last several years, national media have repeatedly reported that a substantial majority of Americans have lost hope in their achieving the American Dream. They are even more discouraged about their children's futures.[5]

In the most recent survey, I asked orphanage alumni whether they had lived (or are living) the American Dream. I left "American Dream" totally undefined; thus, the alumni reported according to their concept of the "American Dream."

- In dramatic contrast to findings from a recent poll of the general population, an astounding 82 percent of the alumni respondents report that they have lived (or are living) the American Dream, while only 5 percent have not (or are not). (Most of the rest of the respondents indicated they could not say.)
- An even higher percentage, 88 percent, attest that the American Dream remains achievable for younger generations.
- Only 3 percent had doubts about the American Dream remaining viable today.

When asked how happy they are today on a scale of 1 (not happy at all) to 10 (very happy), the average response was 8.86 (with a range of 3–10). The most frequent response was 10.

Orphanages and their Critics

The alumni in my early surveys were not drawn from "Cadillac orphanages." On the contrary, a substantial majority (at least 87 percent) lived in orphanages in the 1960s and before, when they had to work long hours in their orphanages' farms, dairies, kitchens, and laundries, making their homes largely self-sufficient. They lived in "cottages" that often housed one or two dozen children who slept in group "sleeping porches" and were supervised by a single adult "housemother." The orphanages still operated on tight budgets from private contributions —before the 1970s when homes became ever-more dependent on and controlled by federal and state child-care dollars and a mountain of regulations that have driven up costs.[6]

The Role of Orphanages in Alumni Success. A number of the surveyed alumni offered assessments of their institutional experience—mostly positive, but a few negative, Typical comments include:

- A female alumnus in her late twenties simply said, "I love [orphanage name]."
- Another alumnus in her thirties wrote, "Thank you [orphanage name] for all that you did for us."
- An alumnus in his early seventies, in a common reflection, said, "I cannot imagine where I would be today if I had not been sent to [orphanage

name]. Here I received all the lessons I needed to be successful throughout life. I love this children's home still today."

- A male in his mid-seventies expressed religious sentiments others shared (several of the homes were supported by denominations), saying, "I was blessed that my mother made arrangements for me to enter [orphanage name]. [My orphanage] allowed me to recognize the benefits of self-discipline, hard labor, competition, responsibility and the education that enabled me to accept Jesus Christ as my Lord and Savior."

Some of the assessments were mixed. Although the alumni with foster-care experience often (but hardly always) had favorable views of their foster care, they generally gave more positive assessments of their orphanage care than their foster care. Among the few unfavorable assessments of orphanage life, these two comments are representative:

- A male alumnus in his early sixties, who gave the only "very unfavorable" assessment of his orphanage experience among his cohorts, remains vexed today by his worse memory, saying, "I was raped at [orphanage name] by the boy who slept in the bed beside mine and no one did anything about it even though it was reported."
- A female in her mid-sixties wrote, "Retired and financially secure at this stage of my life but have had a hard time with intimacy and emotional connectivity even though I've been married to the same man for 43 yrs. Also, I feel like I never found my niche in life."

Those with positive assessments attributed their success in life to:

- The education they received (often from on-campus teachers who were more qualified than teachers who taught in surrounding county school);
- The work ethic they developed from extensive work demands;
- The life challenges they had to overcome because of their Spartan orphanage conditions;
- The moral values that were pressed on them because their orphanages were often faith-based and tied to churches and synagogues;
- The comradery they developed from living and working with many other children who understood their past life difficulties; and
- The inspiration to live a "good life" provided by dedicated on-campus adult mentors.

The Evolution of Institutional Care for Children. The precipitous drop in the count of orphanage alumni responding to my surveys in the 1990s and this year can be largely attributed to the closing of many orphanages, to their gradual conversion to treatment centers over the last four decades and to deaths of the remaining aging alumni:

- Three of the six homes have continued to provide long-term care for mainly disadvantage (as distinguished from seriously troubled or traumatized) children, although the children they admit today often have physical and emotional problems beyond poverty not generally faced by children admitted to orphanages in the 1960s and before.

- The other three homes have either morphed into "treatment centers" (which means they often serve today traumatized kids) or have, since the early 1970s, evolved into the equivalent of "state foster-care agencies," administering collections of foster homes and group homes spread over large sections of their home states.

- One home is totally private (and gave up state funding to avoid misguided state controls on children admitted and length of stays); the others rely on state child welfare dollars for upward of 50 percent of their revenues.

Children's homes are no longer self-sufficient due to government regulations. For instance, they can no longer ask children, even in their mid-to-late-teens, to use a mower with more than one and a half horsepower, which effectively means they cannot ask children to do much serious work around campuses with acres of grass. This type of restriction is not imposed on biological and foster parents.

Foster Care or Orphanages? Harry Potter author J. K. Rowling is a recent self-appointed orphanage critic, tweeting that "Orphanages cause irreparable damage [to children in their care], even those that are well run." She paints orphanages as "nightmarish institutions" where young children are "caged" day and night.[7] Many child welfare experts share Rowling's sweeping damnation of orphanages, both in the United States and abroad. Their solution: Shutter them all.

Rowling's tweet is part of her campaign to discourage "voluntourism," under which volunteers from advanced countries spend their "vacation days" working in, say, African and Haitian orphanages by cooking, providing hygiene instruction, and reading to the children.[8] Rowling effectively argues that such warm-hearted charitable efforts unavoidably set back the emotional and physical development of disadvantaged children by reducing the relative costs, elevating the relative quality of care in orphanages, making them comparatively more attractive care options.

Like many other orphanage critics, Rowling claims that children would be far better off with "loving and responsible" biological or foster parents than in "cold and loveless institutions." However, she is dismissing the central child-welfare problem of the ages: the dearth of loving and responsible parents. Many parents, biological and foster, are simply unloving and irresponsible, too often emotionally, sexually and physically brutalizing the kids in their care.

Child-welfare expert Kate Whitten at Duke University has assessed the outcomes of orphaned children on a number of physiological, psychological and behavioral measures in five very low-income countries in Africa and Southeast Asia. Professor Whetten summarizes her findings to date:[9]

"Basically, in our five-country study, following approximately 3,000 orphaned and abused children permanently separated from their parents for over ten years, those children living in group homes (or orphanages or whatever you call them) do as well or better on every physical health, mental health and cognitive measure that we have [than children in biological in-tact families]. In addition, those in group homes experienced less exposure to sexual and physical abuse while in the homes (they experienced more before entering). These findings have been confirmed by a separate National Institute of Child Health and Development-funded study of 3,000 similar children in Kenya, which also found that children's human rights were less likely to be violated in group homes than in individual family settings. A third NICHD funded study found similar results out of China, and I just read another study out of Uganda showing that depression rates and anxiety were lower in group-home-based kids."

The Federal Government Prefers Foster Care. The *Family First Prevention Services Act of 2016,* sponsored by Senator Orrin Hatch (R-UT), was passed by unanimous consent in the U.S. House of Representatives in 2016, but did not come up for a vote in the Senate. The bill would cause federal dollars to flow solely to foster care and "treatment centers," which admit only seriously abused and traumatized children in need of therapeutic medical treatment and penal care, often attributable to the children's poor family *and* foster-care experiences. Federal funds would not go to any child welfare alternative that smacks of an "orphanage," and that admits children who are deemed "normal," or need only a stable and safe place to grow up, rather than those who need medication and "behavioral modification" to coexist with others.

Yet, many foster-care children move among multiple—not infrequently, a dozen or two—foster-care placements before aging out of the system at 18. They make court appearances for each new placement with their few possessions in plastic bags (causing them to be known as the "plastic-bag brigade" among judges and social workers). They are required to adjust to multiple schools and families in which they can be treated as adjunct and dispensable family members, often without being told where their siblings live (few foster parents will take on the burden of multiple siblings).

Worse yet, foster-care children have no say over where and when they will be placed and can be given little notice (at times, only 24 hours' notice) of their reassignments, possibly to another foster placement; but possibly back to one or both of their dysfunctional parents, who may have faked rehabilitation, only to later be pulled from them for another cycle of foster-care placements.

Of course, many foster parents provide exceptional care to their charges, but a problem with efforts to close children's homes (through, say, Hatch-type policies) is that it would increase the already excessive demands on the foster-care system. The resulting greater demand for placements will cause social workers to dig ever deeper into their stable of available foster parents, who are in short supply, and to call on progressively lower income, less adept foster parents who will be subject to less oversight as social workers' caseloads rise.

Those who want to close orphanages and place disadvantaged children in foster care should consider some disturbing statistics:

- More than 60 percent of foster-care youth age out of the system at 18 without a place to live.
- Half of those aging out are incarcerated within two years, and four-fifths of death-row inmates have lived in foster care.[10]
- By contrast, the orphanage alumni I surveyed in the mid-1990s reported an incarceration rate one-third that of the general white population and most arrests were for drunk driving, while long stints in prison were rarely reported.

The first large-scale study offering health comparisons for children in the general population based on a nationally representative sample of more than

900,000 U.S. children, published in *Pediatrics*, included 117,000 children in foster care. The study reports that:[11]

- Foster-care children face double to triple the risks of coming down with asthma, obesity, and hearing and vision problems than their counterparts in the general population (including children in impoverished families).
- They are five to seven times more likely to have behavioral, depression, and anxiety problems than children in general.

The study is careful to avoid attributing the children's problems to their foster care. However, given the many reported problems in the foster-care system, most notably multiple placements, it would not be unreasonable to suspect that foster care is an auxiliary contributor to many foster children's medical and behavioral problems. Thus, it would be prudent to maintain the type of long-term care options orphanages of the past provided.

Conclusion

Michael Morgan, who was one year behind me at my own orphanage, points out the irony of J.K. Rowling's orphanage claims:[12]

> *"Harry is an unhappy, bullied, and abused orphan, fostered by an aunt and uncle for the first eleven years of his life. He wears cast-off clothing, sleeps in a closet, has no friends and is ostracized, marginalized and ignored as a matter of course. He has no sense of self-worth, practically no personal possessions, he has never known affection and his future is as bleak and lonely as his past.*
> *"It is an institution, Hogwarts, that saves our protagonist. He makes friends, becomes a leader, accepts responsibility, and displays a willingness to sacrifice himself for a greater good. He is introduced to sports, a moral code, social skills, and educated for success in life. For the remainder of the series, his foster home is something he has to endure. Hogwarts is his 'Home.'"*

Rowling's fictitious description of Harry Potter's orphanage life reflects more accurately the reality of experiences for the vast majority of the surveyed alumni than does her activist child-care policy claims.

Granted, there have been orphanages in the United States and around the world that have been child-care horror chambers, but the same claim can be made of families, both biological and foster. But no one proposes to model modern child-care programs on the worst examples of orphanages of the past or present.

Two stark facts remain self-evident, given the current state of child welfare:

- First, disadvantage children have different needs. The country needs a menu of care options, just to fit children's undeniable varying needs with their care.

- Second, foster care, adoption, and treatment centers can work well for many children, but hardly all. Children's homes have proven they can be one of a menu of care options—and must be, given the size of the country's child-welfare problems.

What might explain the orphanage alumni's success? Many responding alumni were first taken out of bad environments and often placed in pretty darn good circumstances where many bad influences were held at bay, outside of their homes' campuses, enabling the alumni to find their own paths toward their pursuit of the American Dream.

What can be done to slow and reverse the ongoing "fading of the American Dream," and the several corrosive social and economic effects of the growing pessimism in the country? Child-care pundits and policy makers have a standard list of corrective polices: improve education (especially in the worst school systems in poor neighborhoods), reduce drug and alcohol addition, promote job-creating tax and regulatory policies, and so forth.

My findings suggest two rarely mentioned and unheralded (and, for many, unsettling) policies. First, drawing a lesson from the country's child-care past: Do no harm. Adoptions and out-of-home placements with families should be maintained, but we need foremost to set aside proposed child-care policies that will likely lead to a further acceleration of closures of the few remaining children's homes.

Second, adopt child-care policies that will encourage community groups and churches to return to their important mission of caring for the children in their midst through the development of modern and improved children's homes. The children's homes of the past were hardly perfect, but they had records of care that are worth celebrating, as a substantial majority of their alumni attest today. If you think quality child care cannot be provided in children's homes today, go to the campuses of the Crossnore School in the mountains of North Carolina and/or Connie Maxwell Children's Home in central South Carolina, and expect to be astounded.

About Richard B. McKenzie, Ph.D.

Dr. Richard McKenzie is the Walter B. Gerken Professor emeritus at the University of California, Irvine, and a senior fellow with the National Center for Policy Analysis. He received his B.S. from Pfeiffer College in North Carolina (1964), his M.A. from the University of Maryland (1967), and his Ph.D. from Virginia Tech (1972). He was awarded an honorary doctor of letters degree from his alma mater in 2001. He is a past president of the Southern Economic Association.

Professor McKenzie grew up at Barium Springs Home for Children (near Charlotte, North Carolina), an experience that led him to write *The Home: A Memoir of Growing Up in an Orphanage*, 2ⁿᵈ edition (Dickens Press, 2006). His own orphanage experienced caused him to edit *Rethinking Orphanages for the 21ˢᵗ Century* (Sage, 1998) and *Home Away from Home: The Forgotten History of Orphanages* (Encounter, 2009). He is executive producer of a documentary film on *Homecoming: The Forgotten World of America's Orphanages* (which can be viewed by clicking on the link. The film was screened at several film festivals around the country and received the Best Documentary Award in the Sedona (AZ) International Film Festival in early 2005. The film was aired in 2006-2008 on over 220 PBS stations, including stations in practically all major television markets. Most of his work on his orphanage avocation has been focused on orphanages as they existed before the mid-1960s.

In 2013, Professor McKenzie released his latest book on a self-proclaimed "modern-day orphanage" (The Crossnore School), *Miracle Mountain: A Hidden Sanctuary for Children, Horses, and Birds Off a Road Less Traveled* (Dickens Press). This book conveys the difficulties and triumphs of today's children in distress as seen through their eyes. He also organized the production of a documentary short on The Crossnore School, which can be viewed here. He recently published "Orphanage Alumni Believe in the American Dream" (link to be added).

He is married to Karen Albers McKenzie.

Endnotes

1. Aaron Blake, "The American Dream Is Hurting," Washington Post, September 24, 2014.

2. The study found that babies born into middle-income households in 1940 had, at age thirty, a 92 percent chance of earning more than their parents. In 1992, the percentage was down to 52 percent (as reported by Bod Davis, "Barely Half of 30-Year-Olds Earn More Than Their Parents," Wall Street Journal, December 9, 2016,citing Raj Chetty, David Grusky, Nathaniel Hendren, Maximilian Hell, Robert Manduca, and Jimmy Narang. Working Paper, 2016. *The Fading American Dream: Trends in Absolute Income Mobility Since 1940*, Boston: Department of Economics, Harvard University, working paper, 2016.)

3. New York Times columnist David Leonhardt, reports that James Truslow Adams coined and popularized the expression the "American Dream" during the first years of the Great Depression. Adams defined the expression as "that dream of a land in which life should be better and richer and fuller for everyone." (David Leonhardt, 2016. "The American Dream, Quantified at Last." New York Times, December 8.)

4. Richard B. McKenzie, *Miracle Mountain: a Hidden Sanctuary for Children, Horses, and Birds*, chapter 7 (Irvine, Calif.: Dickens Press, 2013).

5. Aaron Blake, "The American Dream Is Hurting," The Washington Post, September 24, 2014; and David Leonhardt, 2016. "The American Dream, Quantified at Last." New York Times, December 8.

6. For a comparative review of the regulatory environments of children's homes in six states, see Margaret Wright McFarland, "Who Will Mow the Lawns at Boy's Town: Labor Laws in an Institutional Setting," in Richard B. McKenzie, ed., *Rethinking Orphanages for the Twenty-First Century* (Thousand Oaks, CA: Sage Publications, 1998), chapter 12.

7. J. K. Rowling, "Isn't it time we left orphanages to fairytales?" The Guardian, December 17, 2014.

8. Sarah Ruiz-Grossman, J.K. Rowling Breaks Down Why Volunteering At Orphanages Can Cause More Harm Than Good, Huffington Post, August 25, 2016,

9. Personal correspondence with Kate Whitton, August 30, 2016. For more on Kate Whitten's orphanage research, see "The Global Health Initiative at Duke University."

10. Shenandoah Chefalo, Garbage Bag Suitcase: A Memoir (Traverse, Mich.: Mission Point Press, 2016). Statistics compiled by the Anne E. Casey Foundation.

11. Kristen Turney and Christopher Wilderman, "Mental and Physical Health of Children in Foster Care," Pediatrics, October 16, 2016.

12. Aaron Blake, "The American Dream Is Hurting," Washington Post, September 24, 2014.

Additional Notes

Orphanage Alumni Believe in the American Dream was published under a different title *The American Dream Is Alive and Well—among Orphanage Alumni!* December 15, 2016 by National Center for Policy Analysis, Dallas Headquarters: 14180 Dallas Parkway, Suite 350 Dallas, TX 75254. It can be viewed at this site: http://www.ncpa.org/pub/the-americandream-is-alive-and-well-among-orphanage-alumni

Free Will Baptist Orphanage, Middlesex, North Carolina is one of six orphanages in data published by Dr. McKenzie. Author, J. Andrews Smith, was a child in Free Will Baptist Orphanage 1949–1960. The author is submitting for readers' information. Free Will Baptist Orphanage name changed in the 1950s to Free Will Baptist Children's Home.

American Dream Survey
Summary Statistics
(Alumni from Free Will Baptist Children's Home, 2016)

1.	Total respondents	71
2.	Average age	71
	Age range	28-97
	Under 50	3%
3.	Average year of arrival	1953
	Range of arrival years	1925–2003
	Average years in orphanage	8.7
4.	Lived in foster care	6%
5.	Lower and poverty income classes before home admission	74%
6.	Lower and poverty income classes today	1.4%
7.	Middle and above income classes today	84%
	Top income class today	4%
8.	Very favorable and favorable assessments of children's home experience	63%
	Unfavorable	5.6%
	Very unfavorable	1.4%
	(The rest, mixed assessments.)	
9.	Very strongly agree or agree they have lived the American Dream	73%
10.	Have not lived the American Dream	7.8%
	(The rest, "not sure.")	
11.	Very strongly agree or agree the American dream remains viable for today's generations	90%
12.	Average happiness rating on scale of 1 (not happy at all) to 10 (very happy)	8.83
	Range of ratings	1–10
	Mode	10
	Median	10

2

Paths of the Cousins

A Coal Miner's Daughter

Christine Coleman
1965–1984

MOUNTAIN MISSION SCHOOL
GRUNDY, VIRGINIA

I n 1966, I was one of seven siblings from the Coleman family placed by our biological mother and maternal uncle at Mountain Mission School (MMS), a home for orphaned and neglected children located in Grundy, Virginia. The home encompasses several buildings or residences which houses boys and girls of  all ages, a school, and a church. The school incorporates grades K-12 at the home, and accepts a limited number of day students from the community.

Entrance to Mountain Mission Campus

Our biological father, Ernest Coleman, was a coal miner by trade. In researching our ancestral story, I found that he was of Cherokee decent. He resembled the characteristics found in the Cherokee people, with high cheek bones, and very dark black hair. There were periods, in which he exhibited an aggressive temperament and for many years, he struggled with depression and alcoholism. Until his separation from my mother, Betty Jo Murphy Coleman, they resided in Phelps, Kentucky. Located in the Appalachian mountains of Pike County, Kentucky. Phelps is a small town that lies in Southeast Kentucky near the Virginia-Kentucky border; and approximately a one hour drive to Grundy, Virginia. Our birthmother had three children from

Reclaiming the Child statue—located at the entrance gates Mountain Mission School

a previous relationship; however, they were much older and not eligible or required to attend MMS. Occasionally, they would visit us at the home accompanied by our father. For many years, I believed that the Coleman family consisted of ten children. However, it wasn't until I was much older that I learned the oldest children were actually my step-or half-siblings.

There were three girls and four boys comprising the Coleman sibling group. I was merely a baby; age one, and the youngest of the seven children who entered the gates of MMS. While growing up at the home, during my teenage years, children teased me with the nickname or call me "Chris Coalminer".

This title seemed so ironic because my father was actually a coalminer by trade. Comical too, is that the other children did not know this detail. My next oldest sibling to me was Kenny Ray ('66-'84), age 2. He did not pass the seventh grade, and spent the remainder of his stay at MMS in the corresponding grade with me. My next oldest sibling to me was Debbie Kay ('66-'81), age 4. She later was Salutatorian of her graduating class at MMS and, in my eyes, exemplified the necessary qualities to do well in college and life. When Debbie Kay left the home, she

Chris Coleman - 22 months

moved to Springfield, Illinois, and has maintained limited communication with my siblings and me. To date, it has been almost 35 years since I have seen my sister or spoken to her by phone. My next oldest sibling was Carl ('66-'80), age 5. Carl and I have always had a close sibling relationship, and our personalities and temperament are much alike. At the home Carl was and, to this day is still, a natural versatile athlete. He did well at any sport he encountered. Some of my favorite memories are of Carl teaching me to how to throw and catch a baseball, basketball, and football. When he played sports, he made each one look easy to play. While at the home, no one could defeat him in the game of marbles. He was the marble champion. My next oldest sibling was Sue ('66-'78), age 6. Sue was characterized as a tender- hearted and a fun-loving person. She was very protective of me, and from all accounts was the "big sister" who took care of me as a baby.

Chris Coleman – age 3

After many years, some of what I have come to know about my family is that Sue endured a difficult childhood; and was forced to "grow up" before her time. At the home, Sue was often observed to be a very nervous teenager, a deeply caring individual, and a hard worker. Recollections of my big sister, depict her biting her nails to the quick, crying periodically, and very resistant to talk to anyone about her problems. However, it was understood by all the girls at the home, that no one would challenge her or cause her any problems. Sue was recognized and known as a straight shooter, and she was very protective of her siblings and friends. Sue did not graduate from MMS but left when she was 18 years old. A few years later, she married and had two children.

My next oldest sibling was Doug ('66–'77), age 7. After he left the home, he often told stories about getting into trouble practically every day at MMS. He described getting 'whippings' even when he had not done anything wrong, because he often associated with other boys who were ill-behaved and enjoyed fighting. What I remember about Doug that would suggest trouble was his mischievous grin. Compared to other boys his age, Doug was shorter in stature; nonetheless, he was strong. He could walk on his hands with his legs vertical in the air, the full length of the gymnasium. At the age of 18, he left MMS and enlisted in the Navy. After serving for well over 20 years, he retired from the Navy and now resides in Reno, Nevada. The oldest of the Coleman sibling group placed at the home was Glen ('66-'76), age 8. Most of the older teenagers at MMS referred to him by his nickname, "Tex". As far as physical features, Glen most resembles my father. He did not graduate from MMS either, and as a child, I did not have a lot of interactions with him. Presently, Glen resides with my brother, Doug in Reno, Nevada. As of the writing and submission of this story, the only sibling with whom I have frequent communication and contact is Carl. As siblings, our relationship remains close.

I was not informed until my early teenage years that I also had a younger sister who was not ever placed at the home. Her name was Darlene. She was three years younger than me and reared by my birth mother. To this day, I still do not know the reasons why Darlene was not placed at MMS to join her brothers and sisters. For many years, this fact was confusing to me and I never had the opportunity to ask this question of my birth parents.

"She Gave Them Away"

Being placed at the children's home or "orphanage", as it was once recognized; at such a young age can

Coleman Children
Front (L-R) Chris -age 15 and Kenny;
Back (L-R) Carl and Debbie Kay

have its advantages and disadvantages. Some might portray it as a blessing, while others may depict it as a curse. It is uncommon and no longer prevalent in this present day for children's homes to carry the label of an orphanage. Having worked for many years in social services, it is honestly difficult to acknowledge that as a very small child I was placed at a home with my siblings. Like anyone else, there were those times when I felt sadness, that this would be my fate. During our adult years, my brother, Carl told me a story of his recollection of our first day at the home. His version noted a memory of playing on one of the playground swings for hours while we were being acclimated to our new environment and surroundings. When he tired of this, he sat intently near the entrance gates of the home and waited anxiously for our mother and uncle to come back for him and his siblings. I cannot imagine the loneliness, hurt, and confusion he must have felt on that fateful day. Although I did not ever experience his particular feeling of disappointment in that manner and on that specific day, I also would later come to know those feelings in my own way. As it is, if you are one of those children who need any stay, especially a lengthy stay, at a children's home, you are undoubtedly introduced to and experience enough disappointments and heartache for a lifetime. Indeed, I would come to know the same hurt, pain, and betrayal in other forms. Yet, I unequivocally believe that I was protected and safeguarded from a childhood and potential life of pain or misery like none other. I am certain as well that I was part of the majority who often wondered why I couldn't live in "a house that had a white picket fence" with my brothers and sisters. Having said that, I am sure that at the age of 12 years old, I acknowledged that having any hope or expectations of a life outside of the children's home was simply a pipedream. Once I accepted the fate that I would be staying at the home until I graduated from high school and moved away to college, I no longer expected my family to be available or to visit me. Some may refer to this mentality as a form of acceptance; yet for me it was self-preservation.

Since I was so young when I entered the children's home, I did not know or relate to any other 'home life" and consequentially had no other comparison. To many, I epitomized the very definition of an institutionalized child. It was not what I sought, but it happened, and I feel that I carry some scars, as would anyone, who lived for 17 years in a home with many other children. Much of what I have come to know and accept about my family and our lives before we were placed at the home has been through stories from older siblings, relatives, friends, teachers, and personnel at MMS. Because I entered the home at such a young age, I was neither aware of nor privy to the circumstances for why my siblings and I were placed at MMS. I would not learn of any dynamics or specifics regarding my parents and biological family nor the reasons surrounding my entrance to the children's home until I was in high school.

According to an account from my brother Carl, all of us were very filthy the day we arrived with my birth mother and maternal uncle for placement at the children's home. This memory coincides with an account from a "special teacher", whom I would later call "my mom", that I was very sick and suffering from dysentery at the time.

Throughout my life, I have heard recollections from people about their earliest childhood memory. I often questioned if not being able to remember occurrences and circumstances were considered a cognitive deficiency, a flaw, or simply something more. I wondered if there was something wrong with me because I could not recall vivid recollections that others seemed to be able to do with ease. It seemed that the harder I tried to remember incidences and events about my earlier years, the less likely I could recall any specifics or occasions. Until now, I would come to distinguish that this impasse, is certain, and at times beneficial and necessary.

One particular story told to me by my birth mother and verified by my "special teacher", was that on the day my birth mother took me and my siblings to the home, she placed me in the hands of a kindergarten teacher named, Miss Eleanor Peterson. Her precise directives and instructions to Miss Peterson were to "take care of my baby." Those words alone would come to serve as a life time of comfort for me. Rightly so since Miss Peterson ('62 -'01) was a special teacher, friend, and indeed even a "mom" to me. I don't recall that I ever referred to her as Miss Peterson while at the school. For as long as I can remember, she was my "mom", the special person assigned to take care of me when I was a baby, and she never shunned or evaded that duty.

Throughout my lifetime, my newly established "mom" and I remained very close. Even so until her death, she remained my mom. During the last years of her life, there came the time that I was able to give back and care for her. I thanked her for the love and care she showed even when I was not a loving person. I told her many times that she would always hold a special place in my life, and I thanked her for being my guardian angel. I was with her as she lay dying and unable to recover from a lengthy illness. Although she did not open her eyes, I know she felt my presence. As I sat near her, I held her hand and I told her that any redeeming quality I possessed was gained from her presence and existence in my life. I cried as I told her that my life would never be the same without her. I simply thanked her for loving me.

Around the same time I was to graduate from high school, I would be told a very different version of the day my birth mother took my siblings and me to the home. This faculty member's account conveyed that my mother stated in the presence of her own children, "that she did not want us when she gave birth to us, and she sure did not want us then." I have struggled for many years with these cruel and harsh words, unable to understand that concept. I have contemplated how any parent could say such very unpleasant comments to their child or children, and dismiss or dissolve a family network so easily. Perhaps this explains why I pursued and flourished for many years in the social services field. Seemingly, my sacrifice in this profession is instinctive and gives me a sense of accomplishment and satisfaction. Even so, I have accepted that it is more important, meaningful, and healthier for me to believe that while my birth mother may have abandoned her children by giving us away, nonetheless, she put us in a safe place, and asked that a very special lady to take care of her baby. For that I am eternally grateful.

L-R: Debbie Kay, Sue and Chris - age 14

"Little Girl in a Big Dwelling"

At Mountain Mission School, it was the responsibility of the older girls and female teachers to care for the younger children. I would learn later that I was cared for by my older sister, Sue, and Miss Peterson, or 'mom'. When I was four and a half years old, a new building was erected for placement of infants and preschool children. This building was named Toddler Hall, also known as "The Little Kids Dorm." This structure was utilized to house children ages 5 and under, three teachers, and two older girls who were solely responsible for the toddlers care. The three teachers who had a dual role of teaching different classes at the school and whose responsibility it was to care for us were: Ms. Janice Whitaker, who taught sciences and some math courses to all high school children; Ms. Shirley Cash, who taught seventh grade; and Ms. Mabel Abbott, who taught typing and clerical classes, and also coached the junior varsity boys basketball teams during the early years. Throughout my entire stay at the home, these teachers were on the staff. Currently, only Ms. Whitaker remains at the home. The laundry amenities would also be located within this building. Through the eyes of a child, everything appears big, and Toddler Hall was no exception.

Chris – age 4

My earliest childhood memory at the home was being officially placed and reared in Toddler Hall. I, as well as others my age were the very first children to live there and this structure did not resemble any other dormitory. When viewing Toddler Hall from outside, it appeared to be a one level story building. However, once inside there were steps leading down to a large playroom for the children. Adjacent to the playroom was a large laundry room, and several individual rooms for the staff of Toddler Hall. Upstairs, which was also the main entrance presented a huge living room. This is where the children would sit on large, colorful oval rugs and listen as the staff members read a story or gathered with them to watch television. Within these premises, there was also a kitchen used to feed the children and staff of Toddler Hall. The younger children who demonstrated attempts at climbing out of their baby beds would be placed in a bubble top bed. Likewise if a child threw a tantrum or misbehaved, they would also spend time in the bubble top bed. Even as a young child, I knew that the bubble top bed was no place for me. I was afraid of the appearances of this bed, and made sure that I never had to be placed in it.

Some of my chosen memories at Toddler Hall were of times spent in the large playroom as it was filled with an infinite number of unique toys. One of the toys I recall was a large red rubber bouncy ball with a handle. This giant red ball appeared to be equal to my height. As children, we would sit on the ball and bounce. This big red ball could and would bounce us a few inches, and/or if you were really good, a few feet. I can still picture us racing from one side of the playroom to the other. As children, we would play until we were all exhausted. There was never a dull moment in the play room.

On the Toddler Hall premises, there was a playground with monkey bars and swing sets. Along the boundaries were paved sidewalks that served as a road course of sorts for daring thrill-seeking children who enjoyed racing their big wheels or little yellow flat racer toys. These toys can simply be described literally as flat seats on wheels with existing handle bars. A child would sit down on the toy with their legs and feet at a 90 degree angle. The child would get a tight grip on the sides of the yellow seat, request an adult to give them a push, and they held onto the seat for dear life. Using their feet solely to guide and steer their way through the course. As a child, this paved concrete course brought us a lot of fun; and for many, it was our initial introduction to the first but not last of many bright red skinned knees and elbows.

While living in Toddler Hall, it is my recollection that I was a well-behaved child. I possessed a sense of fear of getting into trouble and of having to face the teachers. I don't believe that I was a mischievous child. I can remember only two distinct "whippings" that I received and who administered them to me. While I believe one whipping was probably warranted; the other was definitely not necessary. One whipping occurred at bath time. It was in the evening and the staff was preparing the children for baths, story time, and bed. In the bathrooms, the old tubs were made of acrylic; they were large and displayed a high-end near the back of the tub. I, and several other children were bathing in a freshly cleaned, shiny bathtub filled with

Kindergarten
Graduation
Chris - age 5

water that made ideal conditions for a perfect slippery slope. What great fun we had as we lathered and covered our bodies from head to toes in soap and slid down the slippery slope. This was very entertaining until one of the staff came into the bathroom and noticed that most of the water from the bathtub was now puddled on the floor. I can only imagine the looks on our faces at that time when she asked how all of the water got on the floor. She whipped each of us with a belt even as we were still bare and wet from the bath. I remember sitting down and squirming, struggling to protect myself as she tried to whip me. My words to her were that, "I don't want a whipping, and I will be good." Nevertheless, I still got the whipping, and I must admit it hurt. However, I never tried that escapade again.

There were a lot of children who lived in Toddler Hall, and I was one of a few who were introduced to the younger children as the "older kids." With that title, came my first responsibility as a leader. As an "older kid", the duties were to help guide and instruct the younger children to the general routine activities of the day. When we awoke in the morning, my job was to help make sure all the girls were up, their beds made, waiting in line to brush their teeth with their hair combed, and to be given clean clothes or be assisted in getting dressed. This same routine occurred at various times throughout the day such as before each meal, periodically for a bathroom break, bath time, and at bedtime. The adults in Toddler Hall depended upon 'the older kids' to help the younger children adapt and manage a routine.

It was not unusual for very young children who knew no English to be placed at MMS and into Toddler Hall, and thus depended upon the adults or "older kids" to help them learn simple key words, daily routines, and eventually English as a second language. As a child, this was easy enough because learning could be done by pointing and naming objects, simple observation of actions or repetitive requests. Naturally, children repeat themselves so learning is certain and inevitable to occur.

As a leader in Toddler Hall not all experiences were pleasant. On one occasion, I was given the responsibility to shadow a special needs child and to inform one of the teachers when he had to use the bathroom. The only problem with this responsibility is this child did not speak or verbally communicate, and only grunted when he wanted to connect. Reflecting on this story, I still wonder how a four and a half year old child was to know when a younger special needs child needed to use the bathroom, especially when he could not communicate this appropriately. As a result, this child used the bathroom on himself, and one teacher summoned me to get a switch from a tree, as she was going to whip me. I asked this teacher why I was to get a whipping when I did not know that this child had to use the bathroom. The teacher stated that it was my responsibility to pay attention, and to inform her when this was to happen. She whipped me five times with a switch that hit my lower back, buttocks, legs and upper thighs. The switch broke during the whipping so she got another one.

It was also during this time, that I was beginning my official transition to the Girls Dormitory. There was a standard rule that the girls had to wear a skirt to all meals during which all siblings sat at tables together. I arrived at lunch after the whipping and I refused to sit down in a chair, because I was in so much pain. My sister Sue noticed that I was quiet and not wanting to interact with anyone. She took me to a bathroom near the dining room and questioned me about what was wrong and why I would not speak to anyone. I refused to answer her, and she began checking to see if I was hurt. I started crying and asked her to stop as it was only making it harder for me. Sue saw the red marks and welts on my legs, buttocks, and lower back. She became furious and demanded to know what happened. I told her what had occurred, and she summoned our sister Debbie. The two of them looked over my marks again, and assured me that this teacher would never hit me again. I was very scared as I knew it only meant more trouble for me. Sue waited for the teacher to come to the lunch meal and confronted her for the whipping she gave me. Sue told her that she was to never lay another hand on me or that she would deal with her. To my best recollection, I never received another whipping from this teacher during my stay at the school.

"The Bell Tolls for Thee"

In August of 1970, I had officially made my transition to the Older Girls Dormitory, and was now living on the first floor with girls, ages 5-13. My sister Debbie lived on the same floor with me, but we were not placed in the same room. Sue lived on the second floor with girls her age. In this dormitory, I was made aware that a bell was rung and could be heard around campus throughout the day, and this is how you would know what was to occur and where you needed to be at the specific time. At six o'clock in the morning, the head dorm parent, Mr. Paul Platt, would ring the bell for the first time which was to wake up everyone. At 6:20 am, a second bell would ring indicating there were five minutes left before breakfast time. At 6:25 a.m., a third bell would ring as it was now time for breakfast and all children needed to make their way to the dining hall. Being prompt was consistently reinforced at MMS, and meal time was no exception. Punishment and consequences ranged from whippings, sitting or standing for periods of time, exclusion from events, extra chores, or lectures for children who were late for meals, school, church or other events.

The next bell rang at 8:00 a.m., and this was one in a series of three to notify all students that school would begin. The school was located on the campus of MMS and less than a hundred yards away from the girl's dormitory. The next bell was rung at 8:20 a.m. when all girls would make their way to the "yellow line" to wait for the final bell. The yellow lines were understood defined boundaries divided by an actual road in the middle of the campus that separated the boys from the girls. Neither girls nor boys could cross over these lines without permission, unless accompanied by a staff member, or unless making their way to school. The third bell rang at 8:25 a.m. Students not in the school building by the 8:25 a.m. bell were considered late. Tardiness for school also carried strict consequences. Every class was an hour long, and bells would ring to begin and end each class with the final bell to end the school day at 3:55 p.m. The bell to signal cleanup for the dinner meal rang at 5:30 p.m. The next bell was at 5:50 p.m. and the final bell at 5:55 p.m. This schedule was followed daily, and the bells for all meals occurred even when school was not in session. It is reasonable that when I left MMS for college, I was lost without the bell to keep me on schedule. At the home, there was no need for a watch when the bell could keep you on task as a constant reminder for every assignment you needed to engage, encounter, and accomplish.

One common and consistent practice with the reliance and routine of the bell ringing was mutual and accomplished among the older girls. In the early morning of every day, the older girls had a habit of yelling out after the first bell, "What bell is it?" Some older girls would randomly yell, "First bell", while others would yell "Second bell." For those younger girls who did not care about what bell it was, there was an automatic, "Be quiet…" A few minutes later, someone would continue the succession by yelling, "What bell?" This practice occurred daily until the last bell. It seemed the older girls enjoyed this routine as they would chuckle when a younger girl would end the conversation with "Shut up and go back to bed."

As a young child in the older girl's dorm and while living in a children's home, initiations are a common occurrence as it is expected that everyone will be acquainted with them at some time or another. One of the more common and funny initiations is the one played on the younger girls after they have been sent to bed. As that, the younger and smaller girls had to go to bed at 8 pm and the older girls at 9 pm. One of the more common chores for the younger girls was to set the tables for the breakfast meal. It was considered a favorite prank among the older girls to awake the younger girls after they had been sleeping for a while and advise them that it was morning, and they were late for setting the tables. As you might imagine, panic, fear, and sometimes tears began as the sleepy young girls hurriedly climbed out of bed, put their clothes on, and ran down the stairs only to find all of the lights out and no one in the dining hall. This was just one of many jokes the older girls enjoyed playing on the younger girls.

There were a few siblings whose families were also reared at MMS. My first roommate, Marlene ('66-'82), who later became my life long "sister" and friend, and her siblings Carol ('66- '80) and Ralph Blankenship ('66- '80) remained at the home until graduation. Marlene and I used to get in trouble for talking when we were supposed to be sleeping. Marlene would talk into the night and would always ask if I was still awake. If I didn't answer, she would keep asking the questions until I answered or until I woke up. There were a few times that Ms. Riner would get us out of bed and make us stand in a corner. One night she forgot about us standing in the corner and went on to bed. Thankfully, she did come back to get us in the wee hours of the morning. At Homecomings, Ms. Riner would often tell the story that she found us lying on the floor sleeping. I would like to think that this taught us from that point on to be quiet and go to bed, but I am not sure that the lesson was learned in that manner. I still love to visit and spend time with Marlene and her siblings. We share a history and a past in which we all have a common ground.

"The Games We Played"

The grade school years at Mountain Mission School were filled with memorable games, team sports, and many firsts. It must have been very challenging for the teachers and house parents to keep 300 students engaged, busy, and out of mischief. It was not unusual to find many children outside on the campus grounds playing various games such as: jacks, marbles, hopscotch, Red Rover, skipping rope and/or playing Double Dutch, Simon Says, Red Light-Green Light- Yellow Light, and Foursquare. The older boys and girls played tether

All Star Third baseman
Chris - age 11

ball or a pickup game of football, softball, dodgeball, or basketball. These playgrounds were where I fashioned my competitive nature, received an official introduction to and developed an avid fondness for team sports.

A simple challenge of racing one child extended into a race against many others. My attitude reflected that of most of the children in that I could do what others could do, and was not to be outdone by anyone. While the teachers walked around the campus fulfilling their duty to supervise the children, it was not unusual to find various games being played on the playground.

One title that I will always cherish and was my claim to fame is that I was the first female to ever make the Little League Boys baseball team. I absolutely loved those days of batting practice, running bases, perfecting a proper slide, and being peppered with hits as fielding practice was in session. I played third base and was a fearless little leaguer. My nickname during those years was "Chis". I received this as a nickname when a teammate could not properly enunciate my name and called me "Chis". Thus Chis was the name I kept for many years.

One of my favorite memories of playing Little League baseball was captured in my first year. It was the bottom of the third inning; there were two outs with the bases empty, when the pitcher for the Grundy Golden Wave came to the plate. He was very tall for a 12- year-old and taller than most all other players. He was a very good baseball player and knew it. The first pitch by the MMS pitcher, Angel Lopez ('75 -'81), was a fast ball down the middle of the plate, to which the batter sent the ball into left field. Angel ran past the relay player and retrieved the ball. He could hear from his teammates that the runner was rounding second and heading for third. Angel fired the ball to me and as the runner was sliding into third, I applied the tag and looked up as the umpire called the runner out! My teammates ran to me at third base. There were cheers and high- fives as they yelled, "Way to go Chis!" I was so ecstatic that I threw my glove up in the air, quickly grabbed and pounded it, as if getting the out was supposed to happen that way. I knew then, that I had truly arrived at the Little League Boys league and that I would be fine.

Whether it was getting hit by the opposing pitcher while at bat, or getting beaned in the forehead by a ball that took a bad or awkward bounce, I was never going to quit the game I loved to play. As an elementary school adolescent, I often remember praying for nice weather so my baseball games would not be cancelled. In my final year of Little League baseball, I was nominated for the county All Stars. Unfortunately, I was not able to play on the All Star team because I could not produce an official copy of my birth certificate. I was very disappointed that this requirement seemingly out of my control could cost me an opportunity to play the game I loved.

As I entered into the middle school years, I was also involved in cheerleading, Brownies Girl Scouts, and band. I played the clarinet and just loved when we played songs such as *"Caissons Go Rolling Along"* or *"Victor"* (University of Michigan fight song). There was never an absence of extracurricular activities, clubs, or team sports. When not playing team sports, my friends and I found time to ride bikes, roller skate, and try to perfect our balance on our skateboards. As one could imagine, this was during a time when there were no helmets, knee or elbow pads, so skinned knees and elbows were a common occurrence among all of the children.

When I entered high school, I played softball, basketball, and ran track. I was very competitive and the summers at the home, were spent perfecting my skills and staying in shape for sport in the fall.

During summer months, many students went to their families' home, but that was not an option for me. I stayed at MMS and enjoyed summer recreation as well as being on campus with a reduced number of children. Some faculty members-Miss Peterson, Ernie & Patti Hertzog & Mrs. Ruth Smith- invited me to the homes of their childhood concurrently while they took a vacation. These times were very enjoyable; and allowed me to understand that others wanted me to appreciate their families, and be surrounded by people who were willing to accept me for who I was.

I never lost my love of baseball as I would turn my radio to a low volume, and stay awake

MMS Little League Baseball Team — First (L-R): Fifth Player - Chris Coleman

many summer nights listening to the Cincinnati Reds broadcasts with Reds baseball announcer, Marty Brennaman on WPKE 1240 AM radio broadcast out of Pikeville, KY. I can still remember that when the Reds would win, Marty would state, "And this one belongs to the Reds." I could recite the names of all the ball players, their positions, and RBI totals. George Foster and Joe Morgan were my favorite baseball players.

Religious Activities

During the course of my years at MMS, attending church and involvement in church sponsored activities was very much a part of everyday life. There was prayer before every meal; devotions and the pledge of allegiance to the flag before school began; Bible class as part of the school curriculum; devotions with singing every evening in the dorms before bedtime; and attendance at church services every Sunday morning and evening, as well as Wednesday evening.

As with any other event at MMS, being prompt to church was not only encouraged, but expected. The home conducted church services very similar to many that we visited as part of the concert choir. I remember very well the given instructions of no talking, whispering, sleeping or interruptions in church services. If a child did disrupt or not abide by any of these rules, then discipline was guaranteed. Usually, a child was whipped and had to spend following church services sitting by a faculty member who monitored the child's behavior.

There were enjoyable and fun times within the church services as Bible Bowls were conducted allowing students to showcase their memory of the verses and events in the Bible. Also, there were some church services that featured speed reading or finding a certain verse that detailed specific events. There were also services that permitted certain older students to give a personal testimony of when they accepted Christ into their lives, and the particulars that surrounded this event.

Youth groups were formed according to ages/grade levels, and these met every Sunday afternoon and early evening, to allow students to participate in an extracurricular activity that featured fellowship and the teachings of the Bible. The junior high school youth group was called J.C, which stood for Joyous Christians, and the high school youth group was called A.C, which stood for Adventurous Christians. I was a member of these two groups throughout school. I enjoyed the AC youth group the most, as it seemed that they were permitted to do more entertaining and satisfying activities. It was also during this time that I had the most memorable time while white water rafting.

The Adventurous Christians embarked on a weekend trip to Unicoi, Tennessee. The weekend was filled with camping, canoeing, hiking, rappelling, and white water rafting on the Nolichuckey River. This trip involved only the high school aged females. Our leaders for the weekend were teachers, Patty and Ernest Hertzog. The Hertzogs brought one of their small children, Jeffrey approximately age 8, along for the weekend trip.

Our youth group was divided into groups of six girls to each raft. My particular raft had one girl who weighed approximately 90 pounds soaking wet. This girl had some fear of the water, but chose to get in the raft to overcome her fears. Another girl in the raft attempted to tell everyone what they could and/or should be doing. She was somewhat bossy, so many girls tried to ignore her demands. One other girl spoke very little English and she rattled off sentences in Spanish to what seemed to be mania mixed with cursing. There was one who paddled the raft consistently and intently. I, on the other hand, when nervous or anxious, have a bad habit of laughing. I sat in the back of the raft and laughed to the excitement and fear of others, all the while attempting to paddle and steer the boat. The skill level was deemed intermediate on the waters. I laughed so much at our foolishness, and reticent attempts to navigate the waters, as well as other's excitement and hysteria, and their commands to tell me to be quiet, that I did not realize that we had hit a large rock and many in the boat were now falling out. The boat was displaced at an angle and I was pinned against the rock and the boat. The petite girl was screaming and her eyes were big as saucers. I reached into the water and grabbed her out telling her to calm down. The girl who spoke no English was at this time, I am sure, cursing and crying. The demanding female sat on the rock in disgust. Everyone else clung to the boat until they were pulled to the large rock that offered stability. As you might surmise, after that weekend, there were many girls who rededicated their lives, others who were thankful for grace, and many others who had a personal tale for purposes of witnessing to others. The weekend could have been catastrophic, but God had a better plan. The Hertzog's young son told his daddy that he lied. When his father asked what he lied about, he stated, "You told us this would be fun; that was a lie, this was not fun." We all had laughs for many years as we remembered the weekend while camping and rafting on the Nolichuckey River.

One of the unique and special benefits of religious activities upon our lives at the home was learning and memorizing scripture that seemed to be embedded in our minds and hearts. Recalling these has helped me numerous times when times were tough and disappointments seemed to be countless. What to most people was repetition, formulated a spiritual foundation and a blessing that is unparalleled.

For many years, the Sunday morning church services were directed by the President of the school, Charles M. Sublett. Every year, as Mr. Sublett became more involved in visiting other area churches to conduct fundraising and speaking engagements on behalf of the school, the preaching duties were shared among the faculty men. Mr. Sublett was very kind, knowledgeable, and often told many stories about the origin and foundation of the home. He would walk up the aisle singing "Victory in Jesus," and he knew every word to the song. His wife, Mrs. Berniece Sublett was the daughter of the original founders of MMS, Pa and Ma Hurley. When Mr. and Mrs. Sublett retired from MMS, their daughter, Mrs. Charliece Swiney and her husband, James assumed the president's title, role, and duties. These responsibilities eventually were passed on to their daughter, Cynthia Rodda.

"The Value of an Education"

Junior Year High School
Chris — age 17

At MMS, education was always paramount and foremost as this is the precedent stressed by all teachers. To this day, the home is known for this core value received by many students. MMS also served as a day school to some students who lived in the community. Their families chose MMS for its high standards, supportive faculty and academic achievement.

The home has the capacity and capability to serve infants, toddlers, and is comprised of school grades K-12. There was never any "missing school" or cutting classes due to being sick as the teachers brought the homework to you.

A flood in 1979 wiped out many homes and businesses in the town of Grundy, Virginia. MMS students waded through flood waters that were waist high to get to school. Classes were still held, schedules kept and life as we knew it carried on. Children, who lived at MMS, would see the same faculty teachers during school hours as you did in the dorm life. Their job was 24 hours a day, 7 days a week, and 365 days a year. So, a student had to believe if they got into trouble at school, it carried over to the dorm home life. Even now, I am amazed and often wonder - How did the staff have the stamina and perseverance to do their jobs?

The academic curriculum was comprised of all the prerequisite courses and compulsory work by the authority of the state of Virginia. At MMS, there was mandatory daily study hall for one hour every night after devotions. These years of studying proved well for me as I was Salutatorian of my senior class, and I was very proud of this achievement. The discipline and study habits imparted in me at youth, allowed me to truly appreciate the value of an education.

There are many reasons I owe a debt of gratitude to MMS, and its value on education is only just one of them. There were students who graduated and later became doctors, attorneys, police officers, and corporate businessmen and women. Also, there were some who devoted their career and service to the military, as well as, those who were employed within the government and others who worked in the social services field.

The value of an education instilled in me at MMS has proven noble for me throughout my life, and was one of the things that influenced me to attend college. Leaving MMS, I knew there was no room for failure. Where would I go? Many of the teachers influenced me to pursue college. I recognized, understood and concluded that would prepare me for a better future. My career in Social Work was influenced by my childhood. My management style was influenced by awareness of each adult child's management system while at the home. I can attribute my manner of studying systems from observing teachers and house parents as well as other adults' ways, and I learned how to get into and around their systems, and find a way for their system to work for me while at MMS. This unique learned skill was huge when I was placed in positions of managing people in my professional career.

Senior Year, Milligan College, TN
Chris – age 21

Finally, living successfully with 300 other children prepared me for forming and maintaining relationships throughout life. While at the home, I learned that some relationships were not healthy and could be a barrier for my overall well-being. This concept has carried over to my adult life and I have avoided relationships that might not bode well for me or my career.

"Chores…Prepping for Life's Duties"

One of the attributes of which I am proud is my work ethic. I feel it was developed, enhanced, and perfected at Mountain Mission School. Chores were a part of daily life and were given congruent to your age, maturity, and ability to accomplish them. All chores had to be done every day. The younger girls would set the table precisely for every meal, while an older girl would clear the tables after every meal and sweep and mop the dining area. Other chores included cleaning plates, bowls and silverware, running the dishwasher, peeling potatoes, snapping beans, shucking corn, sweeping porches, cleaning the bathrooms to their entirety, and sweeping and mopping floors on every level of the dorm as well as the kitchen. Given that there were three hundred children at the home, these chores obviously took some time. The older boys worked on a dairy farm owned by community members who bartered- Work from the boys and, in turn, the home reaped the rewards of what food/benefit they would produce.

Two older girls would be awakened at 5 a.m. by a staff member and expected to cook breakfast and dinner meals for everyone. For the dinner meal, they were expected to report to the kitchen by 4:30 p.m. to help with dinner preparations. After nine weeks, all chores would be switched on a rotational basis.

If there was something to be done around the home, you could bet it would soon become an assigned chore. If you complained about how much you hated it, you kept that job longer than others. If you misbehaved or fought with another child, you were assigned a chore that took many days to complete. This was the staff's way of discouraging fighting. By the end of the assigned chore, you were friends again with the same child with whom you fought.

If you failed to do your chores, there were consequences. Part of our daily life at MMS was learning that hard work was expected and everyone had a specific job to do. The precise manner was set for our lives, to keep us busy. If a child did not do their job correctly, then they were told to do it over and over until it was up-to-par. I learned very early that it is much easier to do a job right the first time than to have to come back and do it over. I developed pride in any job I had to do, and to this day, my motto is still "Do it right the first time." What was important was that we all learned life lessons such as the significance of a job well done and respecting elders. These values shaped us into who we are today. My work ethic still remains very strong. It is ironic that on my performance evaluations, I am often told that I have a strong work ethic. For that I am very grateful.

"Orphan meets the World"

As I entered high school, there were many opportunities for myself and others to appreciate various social experiences, outlets, as well as trips that would otherwise not have been possible. There were noted events such as: the Winter Joust Queen (equivalent to Homecoming Queen), and I was fortunate to win this event when I was in ninth grade. We established and participated in regular fund raisers to support our current cause that also taught us the value of working hard and developing skills such as preparation, presentation, and entrepreneurship.

Talent contests by students were held once a year to showcase their sort of talents. Rewards for good grades included: Permission to stay up later than others two weeknights (of your choosing) per semester and permission to visit with your girlfriend/boyfriend within public vicinity. These rewards meant that you had to be quite trustworthy, too.

If you were chosen to be in the concert choir or were enrolled in this class when you became a high school student, then you were able to: travel to many and various churches across the United States, sing at major events such as the Wolf Trap Gala in Washington, DC, be on stage with the Vienna Boys Choir, and visit seven different counties. These trips also included traveling across the United States to major sites and popular locations. At times the choir was recorded for purposes of making albums and tapes to sell to those people who had heard of the MMS Children's choir. I was blessed and fortunate for the opportunity to travel with the choir. It afforded me an experience that many others would never see in their lifetime.

Another occurrence that came with traveling with the MMS Children's Choir was staying with church folk who were kind and gracious to have us in their homes. There was a certain anticipation of waiting to have your name called and meeting "the family" who would take you in for a few nights to entertain and show kindness to you, even when they didn't really know you. Just as they were looking among the many children to scope out those who would be staying with them, we were surveying the crowd to determine if we could pick out our "family for the next few evenings." I have fond memories of staying in the homes of some wonderful people.

"You Have Done It Unto One of These"…

Since its inception, MMS has predicated and relied on the contributions from Christian churches/Churches of Christ as well as monetary gifts from former alumni, special interest groups, individuals, as well as endowments and trust funds.

For many years, before the old girl's dormitory was torn down and a new one rebuilt in its place, a Bible verse was inscribed high on the brick of the girl's dorm. The scripture from Matthew noted, "Inasmuch as you have done it unto one of the least of these my brethren, you have done it to me." This scripture served as the motto for many who passed through the gates of the campus. Giving financially, showing kindness and mercy to the children at the home was not only necessary; it also served a purpose for self-sustainment.

The children's home has always predicated their services on operating without any reliance on federal dollars. The dependence was based upon churches who gave not only monetarily, but by the truckloads: food, clothes, school supplies, and toiletries for the home to continue in its usual operation.

What a powerful message is presented in the home's motto. Throughout the years, many people have donated their time, finances and material possessions to the home, all within the interpretation of- "You have done it unto me."

An example of such giving could be found at Thanksgiving time, when members of churches in Indiana and Ohio who would come to the home and spend quality time with all of the children. They would do maintenance work at the school, and schedule periods for recreational games, and activities such as ice cream socials, and opportunities for treats such as cotton candy and popcorn. I looked forward to every Thanksgiving and Christmas as these were my two favorite holidays and special events of the year.

Many people from these same churches would receive a child's name for Christmas and bless them with plenty of clothes, and toys. I always enjoyed Christmas, and there was never a time that I thought that I was missing out on anything. I may have wanted or desired much, but I TRULY was never without anything. The school did their best to ensure that every child had a great Christmas. There was never one child who did not receive an abundance of Christmas gifts. The perception of many was that we as children had nothing, but most children were blessed far more than those in a "typical" family home. I for one was blessed far more than I deserved.

"Shaken…Dealing with Grief and Loss"

Just like any other child, I experienced and endured true loss while attending MMS, and I had to work hard to manage this pain. When I was 16 years old, I experienced a hurt and loss unparalleled. I was informed that in the early hours of one Thanksgiving morning, my ex-roommate named Teresa Thomas, who was merely 19 years of age, and a sophomore at Hanover College in Indiana, was on her way home to Virginia, for her Thanksgiving break. Approximately, one mile from her home, she was in a fatal car accident. She was thrown from the vehicle and her life tragically ended. The gentleman who was driving sustained serious injuries, but lived. I lost a dear friend that fateful day. Teresa was a kind and gentle soul, beautiful, smart, and well on her way to accomplishing great prominence in her life. She had everything to live for. Losing Teresa that day was very tough for me.

In December of that same year, and four days before my 17th birthday, my father committed suicide. I was still trying to comprehend and deal with the loss of my good friend. I never had the chance to say good-bye to either of them. I was tormented and grief stricken by that fact for a very long time. There were nights of insomnia, grieving with loud sobbing, and being in a fog for weeks. I felt broken and shaken. At MMS, you dealt with loss the best way you could: You either spoke to a teacher and house parent if one was available, talked with your own peers, or dealt with it and managed the pain on your own. I remember being numb and not knowing how to recover from this grief.

For years I had many mixed feelings regarding my father. I was entreated and taught to love my father and mother, no matter what precipitated their past actions. I loved my father, but I was confused and haunted by his actions. I did not understand or comprehend how he could leave me in such an extreme and painful manner.

Indeed, I wanted to love and understand him, but I did not love his ways. My father repeatedly crossed boundaries with me. He continually failed to keep his word. He violated my trust, and then there were times when he violated me. However, I was told to forgive him, and love him in return, no matter his faults or actions. By doing this, it seemed I was making concessions, and I struggled with this concept for many years.

I truly wanted to love my father and to have a healthy relationship with him. Yet, with his suicide and death, I was angry with him for leaving me yet again, and for making this decision so final. To this day there are still so many unanswered questions and so many feelings and thoughts still left unsaid.

I was shaken about those events for many years. Grief, denial, and pain typically have their stages, but for me, it seemed as if these phases took years to overcome and understand. I never really understood how grief and loss could be internalized and evolve into more deep rooted problems until I dealt with it further as an adult. Within my own personal life, I have had a difficult time dealing with loss, abandonment and trust issues. I expect people to do exactly what they state they will do, and anything less than their word is a disappointment to me. I expect that people I love will eventually abandon me and skip out on their word, because most people do, in a matter of time. For many years, I blamed myself for losing those I love, yet the realization that it had nothing to do with me was difficult for me to understand and accept. I pushed them away, they stopped loving me for a reason; it had to be me. How liberating to learn that it was not my fault, it had nothing to do with me. I cannot make people love me. I can only be true to myself. Loving and letting go is not easy, but for my own happiness, well-being and peace of mind, it is a must. I am a whole and complete person...I can love and be loved.

Recollecting upon my years at MMS, I cannot help but feel blessed and highly favored to be a part of a school that loved me when I was not always loveable, displayed care when I needed it, even when I did not always deserve it, and furthered my capacity to grow spiritually. MMS strengthened my resolve and character by influencing my life with Christian values and opinions aligned with God's Word.

Living in a dorm with 150 girls, taught me at an early age the meaning of love, sharing, acceptance, responsibility and accountability. In this environment, I learned the concept of contentment and survival within various managed systems. This experience prepared me for forming and maintaining relationships throughout life.

I fully believe that those who had a part of shaping my life also gave me a solid foundation of morality and principles that I can use as a measure for the rest of my life. Because of MMS, the possibilities are many and my future is endless. I recognize that I am forever indebted to their devotion and sacrifice.

"Leaving the Nest"

Mountain Mission School has always predicated its mission in regards to giving their children two great gifts - these are roots and wings. Through the sacrifices of many these gifts form a solid foundation in children.

I graduated from MMS in 1984 and attended one year at Cincinnati Bible College (CBC) in Cincinnati, Ohio. As I approached my high school graduation, fear and doubt were prevalent, since I was unsure of what I wanted to do with my life. The opportunity to attend CBC seemed inviting to me. After attending one year at CBC, I transferred to Milligan College in Johnson City, Tennessee from which I graduated with a Bachelor of Science degree in Health and Physical Education. For much of my high school years, I assumed I would be a teacher, but somehow after completing my undergraduate degree, I did not have the passion to teach that was needed or I had witnessed in others before me.

Likewise, the availability of teaching positions appeared to cycle every five years in Tennessee. So, I did not foresee a bright future in teaching.

When applying for jobs, there were ample positions in the mental health field, so I became persuaded to give this arena a chance. After ten years of working in the mental health field in psychiatric hospitals, as a Case Manager, liaison, social worker for the mentally ill, and working in residential group homes, I applied for various positions with the Department of Children's Services (DCS) with the state of Tennessee. For the next 25 years, I would be employed in various positions in capacities in the social service field. Some positions were in the child protective division of the DCS in Johnson City Tennessee, and in various counties in North Carolina. During this duration, I was hired by the DCS as a top level supervisor for the Child Protective Division and served in this capacity for eight years.

In 2010, I moved to Franklin, North Carolina after learning that the annual income and benefits for this state were enhanced and

Milligan College, TN. Graduation "Orphan Sister" Marlene Blankenship and Chris

upgraded. I worked for one year as a CPS investigator in Murphy, North Carolina. Next, I was hired as a supervisor by another county DSS, in a small town near Sylva, North Carolina. After two years, I was promoted and became a Program Manager for this same DSS. This was my first introduction to upper level management.

I served as a Program Manager for three years while employed at this county DSS. In the course of my employment, I was introduced to Jerry Smith, director, and author of *The Family* and existing author for this book. While serving under Jerry's guidance, I learned about principles of management, how to co-exist under different managerial styles, and I learned about myself. Jerry has my utmost respect and gratitude. He invested in me and saw my worth as an employee. I could never thank him enough for all that he has done for me. To this day, we remain very close friends.

In January of 2015, I left the DSS agency to complete the compulsory requirements for a Master's degree in Public Administration. I graduated from Kaplan University in 2015 with an MPA degree while maintaining a 4.0 GPA. After earning my MPA degree and afterwards exploring the job market, I did manual labor for approximately six months by deep-cleaning homes and cabins in Western North Carolina. While this period in my life was good for self-reflection and allowed me to become physically fit, this time in my life was also very lonely. In my lifespan, I had always had stable employment so these circumstances were new to me. There had been the usual highs and lows and second guessing. Now I had to take a long, hard, tough look at who I was and account for my faults and inadequacies.

In July of 2015, I was invited to speak at a Homecoming celebration for the Free Will Baptist Children's Home in Middlesex, North Carolina to articulate and describe what it was like to be reared in a children's home. In doing this, I witnessed a most humbling and grateful experience. For the first time in my life, I had to face the demons, fear and the weight of uncertainty that held me back from truly succeeding. The truth of the matter was that I had not obtained the high profile job I expected since receiving my MPA degree.

A few weeks before I spoke at the Homecoming celebration, I became somewhat at peace with my life and the direction it was headed. Many would portray my experience as an epiphany. I simply vouch that it was God working in my life. On one hot summer night in June of 2015, I laid awake late at night tired and trying to fall asleep. I had the television on but was not watching it.

Just as I moved to turn off the television, an evangelist came on. I had never watched this man before, but the title of his sermon caught my attention: "Being a Bounce Back Person - Power of Positive Thinking." I decided to listen further.

He announced: *"Every Setback is a Setup for a greater Comeback."* He reminded me that God stated there will be storms in our lives, but just as a palm tree withstands a storm, IT will bend but not break; so too, we can withstand the storms of life. We will be stronger because of it and ever so stronger than before…. as God promises that "No weapons shall prosper against us."

I took solace in the fact that God had me in the right place for this day, and I know he would faithfully guide me throughout this time in my life, just as He had always done. Psalm 91: 1 reads, He who dwells in the shelter of the Most High will abide in the shadow of the Almighty.

For we know that our Father is a loving and sovereign God, and that he will cause all things to work together for the good to those who love him and are called according to his purpose (Roman 8:28). So I had to thank God for each disconcerting or humbling situation, for each problem or hindrance, for each obstacle or disappointment that triggers in me anxiety, anger, or pain. All of these are opportunities to see Him work in His time.

I became confident that God would bring me to a place of abundance. He would enrich and beautify me through each problem, conflict, and struggle. My momentary troubles were not too big for him. God would enable me to know in a personal experience the incredible blessings He had in store for me.

Essentially, I would need to be mindful that Christ is not a weak person outside of me, but a tremendous power inside me…that through Him, I am competent to cope with life, and to love with His love.

For it is only Christ that helps us deal with the realities of living in a fallen world with its disappointing relationships, unfulfilled longings, and shattered dreams. Only God will meet us at the midst of your pain and turmoil, and allow us to see things from a perspective that is true. As a result, even in the face of heartache, there is joy and praise.

I resolve and rejoice that I can grow, develop my gifts, and enlarge my capacities…that I need not be forever shackled by my past. I am not a victim, but a victor. With confidence and joy, I can look forward to becoming all that HE has in mind for me.

Note: In April 2016, I accepted a position as Vice President for Programs and Services at the Free Will Baptist Children's Home, Middlesex, North Carolina. I currently reside on campus at the Children's Home.

I Owe a Lot of Love

Archie Thomas Rahmaan
1953–1965

THE COLORED ORPHANAGE OF NORTH CAROLINA
OXFORD, NORTH CAROLINA

During summer, 1953, my younger brother Ernest, age five, my older brother Fountain, age seven and I were admitted to The Colored Orphanage of North Carolina, Oxford, North Carolina. I was age six. Two years earlier our father murdered our mother and we were placed under the care of the Rockingham County, North Carolina, Department of Public Welfare. We witnessed our father murdering our mother. There were five of us boys and Evelyn Rudd, our aunt, took us in. My two younger brothers were not placed in the orphanage. They remained with our aunt after our arrival at the orphanage.

When we arrived on campus that hot summer day with our social worker around 1 o'clock, there were over 150 boys and girls in care. Two weeks earlier our social worker picked us up and we met with Dr. Theodore Brook, Superintendant of The Colored Orphanage of North Carolina, at the Rockingham County Department of Public Welfare. He told us it was a good

100

place and we would like being there. He told us about what they had at they orphanage and what we would be able to do. He and our social worker did their best to help us understand our placement. My oldest brother Fountain did not want to go to the orphanage. Neither did I want to go.

We were picked up from our Aunt Evelyn Rudd's house and taken to the orphanage by the social worker from Rockingham County Department of Public Welfare. On our arrival to the campus, we were taken to the younger boys' dormitory to meet our matron. Two female matrons, each responsible for 30 boys, lived in our dormitory with boys ages 1-11. There were many children on campus as we walked to our residency. After being greeted by our matron, my older brother and I had a fight shortly after arriving at our dormitory. It was broken up by our matron. Fountain never did adjust to the orphanage and three years later left campus to live with our Aunt Evelyn Rudd.

Around dinner time we heard the campus bell ring for the first time. The bell was rung thirty minutes before dinner that day to alert us to get clean. Second bell rung signaling every child and their matron to walk to the dining hall and younger boys to lined up, and then enter the dining hall and go to our assigned tables. My brothers and I sat at the same table. We all stood for the blessing before we sat down. Every child sat down the same time. Our tables were already set and food in plates for our meals. The food was good. The boys sat at tables together and girls sat at their tables. Between 1961- 62, the orphanage begin allowing boys and girls to sit at the same table.

Our first night was sleeping in the same room with double-decker beds. I remember being happy my bed was on the bottom that first night.

My younger brother Ernest and I began adjusting to campus life. By the start of elementary school that fall, we had friends and looked forward to attending The Colored Orphanage Elementary Public School on campus. The school was not only for orphanage children but, too, served children from the community.

We begin making friends and fitting-in with other boys in our dormitory. Each Wednesday the entire campus had a worship services together. On Sunday mornings after breakfast we had Sunday school at 11 a.m. On Fourth Sunday, a minister or sometime a community leader would be invited to come to campus to speak to us for our Vesper services in the chapel at 2 o'clock.

Our holidays were always on campus. Children did not leave campus for any of the holidays. During Thanksgiving week we sang songs and talked of things we were thankful for. Christmas was different. The previous year

Christmas with Santa at The Colored Orphanage of North Carolina 1952
Photo provided by Archie Rahmaan

before I arrived on campus, I was told about a helicopter that flew in with Santa meeting the kids and passing out gifts. It seems the helicopter with Santa visited many of the orphanages in North Carolina that year.

Christmas was the best time of the year for me and other children on campus. Different woman organization's groups came to campus and gave us Christmas parties with Christmas gifts. Most of the organizations were from white churches and groups. During my Junior and Senior years African-American women groups came on campus and gave us Christmas parties.

Easter each year was always fun and with a special service on Sunday with an Easter egg hunt afterwards. On Easter Monday, all the young children received Easter baskets. On this Monday there was always a baseball game with boys from campus playing off- campus teams. We usually beat anyone we played. I do remember a team from Durham, N.C. Their coach would get so upset losing to us.

We were not allowed to play on the public high school sports teams. The orphanage did allow two boys to play each year on the school football team. There was a rule to play which we had to abide by … if one of the two boys had bad conduct, neither of the boys could play on the team at Mary Potter High School, Oxford, N.C. There was close to 100 students in my senior high school graduation class.

On campus, boys could have a girlfriend. Our junior and senior years in high school, boys could visit with the girls at their dorm under supervision. No chance of us being too cozy with each other. There were socials on campus once a month, on Friday night, for high school teenagers. Often we had dances at our socials.

We all had assigned chores on campus. My junior year I was assigned to help clean the dormitory. The matron to the older boys' dormitory was Ms. Bessie Davis. I'd had a rough day at school before starting my chores after arriving home from school that day. Ms. Bessie Davis assigned me work and before I completed she assigned me something else to do; then she assigned me something

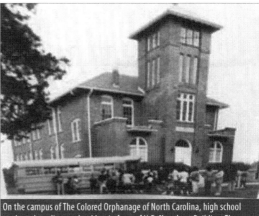

On the campus of The Colored Orphanage of North Carolina, high school students boarding a school bus in front of H.P. Cheatham Building. The bricks used for building the structure were made by boys of the orphanage and the building still stands today. Photo provided by Archie Rahmaan

else before I completed the chores I was working on. It just bothered me. I finally got Ms. Davis attention. I told her one day that I would own a chicken farm and I was going to hire her to come and work for me. I knew I would be in trouble afterwards … at least I thought I would. Not at all, Ms. Davis started laughing and my offer of employment at the chicken farm soon spread all over the campus. Everyone was laughing over my offer to her. I still reflect and laugh until this day.

Many of the children had nicknames. For a while I was called 'Red'. It came from my complexion when I restrained from saying or doing something. We did have runaways from time to time and usually all were returned to campus. I never spend a night away from the orphanage my entire years there. I did leave the orphanage once to attend the funeral of my older brother Fountain's funeral his junior year in high school. He died in a car accident. He was an 'A' student in school.

While at the orphanage I found myself observing Mr. William Easton, our 8th grade teacher, parenting his own children. He, too, was our baseball and basketball coach on campus. I watched how he related to his wife and children and I've never forgotten. It impacted my parenting with my son. We were taught to be good citizens and be productive.

After leaving the orphanage I attended college and later became employed by Kirby Vacuum Cleaners. Within five years I worked my way up as the Area Distributor opening my own office in Chapel Hill, North Carolina. One day I called my former matron, Ms. Bessie Davis from the orphanage, and reminder her I had offer her a job to work on my chicken farm. I then told her, she barley missed the chicken farm. I told Ms. Davis I was self employed and 4-5 people were working for me. It was not a chicken farm, but she could come and work for me in my business, and offered her a job. We both just laughed and laughed.

After talking with Ms. Davis, my business had a break-in and I could not recover for lack of insurance and found employment with the Orkin Pest Control Company. I left Orkin Pest Control Company and founded my own pest control business... Rahmaan Exterminators, Chapel Hill, N.C. and have been in business for the past 40 year. I am past President of the Alumni Reunion Association and have served on the Board of Directors of Central Children's Home, and now I'm an Honorary Board Member for life.

I am thankful for The Colored Orphanage of North Carolina for being there when we lost our mother and our father was sent to prison. My parenting skills, religious life, civilian life, being a husband to my wife and professional career I owe a lot of love to the staff from the orphanage.

Note: Posted on the website to my childhood home is the orphanage history. The 'Grant Colored Asylum' was renamed and incorporated in 1887 as 'The Colored Orphanage Asylum of North Carolina.' In 1927, the orphanage was reincorporated as 'The Colored Orphanage of North Carolina,' and in 1965 was renamed 'The Central Orphanage of North Carolina.' In August of 1986, the facility became known as the 'Central Children's Home of North Carolina, Inc.'"

A New Chapter

Zbigniew John Jalocha
1954–59

CARMELITE HOME FOR BOYS
HAMMOND, INDIANA

I was born May 25, 1948 in Wildflecken, Germany to Polish parents, Chester and Lottie Jalocha. My parents stepped off the SS Marine Jumper and onto American soil in Boston, MA, the 1ˢᵗ week of May, 1949, with my father holding me in his arms. I was 11 months old. My good fortune in being born in a Displaced Persons camp in the American sector in Germany after WWII, and thereby having the opportunity to come to the USA, comes with a back story. My dad grew up in a little village, Kalonka, about 50 to 75 miles west of Warsaw, the capitol of Poland. One day late in the war, the Nazi soldiers rounded up all the men of the village into the large courtyard in front of the Catholic basilica for a work detail. Each was asked to state his name. The men were then separated into 2 groups depending on whether or not their names were on a Polish underground list one of the Nazi officers had.

John and his father
Wildflecker, Germany

The group my dad was in was told to go home. Those on the list were executed right there in the square. It turns out my dad's name WAS on the list. In Slavic language countries people are often referred to by their lineage rather than their proper surname. Romanoff is a classic Russian example. My dad was on the list as Cheslaw Ignacow (from the line of Ignac) rather than Cheslaw Jalocha. My father escaped death only because the soldiers asked everyone their names instead of calling out the names on the list and having them step forward. My father had extremely poor vision from birth. Even with glasses, his vision was 20/200 (legally blind) so there was no way he could have actually been in the underground. With the Nazis looking for him in Poland, he fled to the south of Germany where a Catholic farmer gave him food and shelter for working on his farm. By that time all German men between 16 and 60 were being conscripted into the army so there was almost no men left to work the farms. Fortunately for me this was the sector of Germany being administered

SS Marine Jumper

by the American army after the war. My father met my mother in one of the DP camps they were running. Besides bringing us to the U.S., the SS Marine Jumper brought many refugees from the DP Camps to the U.S. in the years after the war, among them many Jewish refugees, mostly women and children.

The job that my dad had waiting for him on a farm in Fair Oaks, Indiana (near Rensealeer, the Jasper county seat) only lasted until the following Summer. There was a large Polish community in East Chicago (a factory town of ethnic enclaves) in Lake county, 2 counties away. My dad found work there and some measure of comfort in a Polish speaking community. My mother didn't fare as well. The brutality of the war, now being pregnant with my sister, living in a foreign country and unable to speak English, a husband who was now doing odd jobs and cleaning the bar downstairs from the room in which they slept for food and a place to stay took its toll on my mother. She went into severe depression and paranoia. He'd come home and find that she'd hardly moved. I hadn't been changed. Neither she nor I ever got a washing. Nothing had been straightened or cleaned. Dad went to the authorities for help. A judge remanded her to the state mental health facility in Logansport, IN. My sister Mary Louise was born there, January 17,1951. My mother never got better. My dad would take my sister and I to visit her on a regular basis those 1st few years hoping she would, but it didn't happen.

My dad landed a regular factory job and was able to get a 1st floor apartment in a home across the street from St. Joseph Catholic Church on Kennedy Avenue. An old Polish couple, who lived in the back basement apartment, would watch my sister and I while he went to work. I remember standing on the front steps looking the 3 blocks down Kennedy Avenue, waiting for him to round the corner walking home from work. By that December we were being cared for by the Carmelite Sisters. The Home for Girls was 2 blocks east of St. Joseph's back parking lot, across a set of railroad tracks and an open field and Euclid St.

I would end up at the Carmelite Home for boys in Hammond. I remember the beautiful Christmas lights as we rode in the cab that night. I also remember the round tables in the gathering room and Christmas tree and the beautiful decorations. A new chapter was starting in my life. I would no longer be able to look down Kennedy Avenue waiting for my dad to round the corner on his way home.

We boys were divided into 3 groups according to our age, with our own gathering room and a group bedroom upstairs. I started in the A labeled group, the youngest. Sister Mary Angelus looked out for us; or, more properly, was primarily responsible for our care. The cubicle that accommodated her small bed was behind a door off one of the corners. I became aware of hospitals and sickness while in that group. I was circumcised and had my tonsils taken out with some of the others for our health. There was a bell to wake us each morning. If we did not like the food at meals, we'd hid it behind radiators.

One morning when I awoke I couldn't walk for a few minutes. It happened again but then went away. And then, one morning, it didn't go away and I tumbled down a whole flight of steps going downstairs to the dining room. I remember looking up at the doctor while in bed in the sick room. They said I had growing pains and not to worry. Until then I didn't know I had to worry. Things must have fixed themselves pretty quickly because I don't remember any recuperation. Talking to my dad after I left the home I found out that it had something to do with polio, perhaps a reaction to the vaccine they gave us.

Sister Frances Therese took care of us when I moved to the middle group of boys. She was special to me from the beginning; even her name was different. There was Sister Mary Lucy, who played the organ and was in charge of the church music. There was sister Mary Ida, who was in charge the older group of boys. There was Mother Mary Cotilde who was in charge of all the Sisters. She was the only one without a form of Mary in her name. She must have thought I was special too. I learned of love while in this group. Music was a big part of living at the Carmelite home. It was a major part of the Catholic liturgy. It was a large part of whatever presentation we would do for any benefactor or organization that would give money to the Home. If there would be a new song to learn, I'd often have it memorized after 2 or 3 times through. She would then ask me to teach it to the rest of the group so she could catch up on some sewing or other care task for the group. We often had our eye on each other. One time the tooth fairy left a little army man under my pillow. I had to pull her aside and explain that I knew she was the tooth fairy because I had seen that toy in a box of other knickknacks on the shelf in her sewing closet. Our personal talks were what I imagined a mother son relationship was supposed to be like, not secret, but private and special. One night I woke up to catch Sister Frances Terese crying. I don't remember if it was then, or later, that I found out, but others in the convent were finding fault with her, Mother Ida in particular (she had been promoted). I tried to comfort her even though she told me that she was fine and not to worry.

I got a lesson in meanness and ethnic bigotry when I moved to the older group of boys. We had an out break of measles once at the Home. Those of us that had it were quarantined in a sick room. One day Mother Ida spotted me walking down the hallway and demanded to examine my chin. I was put in with the rest of the sick kids as a precaution. After 3 days I was released because when the doctor came to examine us I apparently didn't have the measles. 2 days later I had the measles.

L-R, John, Chester and Mary Louise Jalocha

My dad would take the same 2 weeks off every year in July, the plant shutdown. When he came to get me one year I wasn't there. Mother Ida had allowed me and 3 other boys to go on vacation with Fr. Melvich, the resident priest on site, and his sister to the family cottage at Koontz Lake for a week. Sister Frances had confided in me, a little Polish kid, that she was French Canadian heritage from Saulte Saint Marie in Michigan. I remembered being moved from Saint Casimir's grade school, where the Polish congregation worshiped, after the 1st grade to St. Joseph's a German heritage congregation grade school. Somewhere along the line I learned that most of the Sisters from this order were German, many having been born in Europe. Rightly or not, I began to make the connection.

I got to leave the Carmelite Home and live with my dad as a present for my 11ᵗʰ birthday. It really wasn't a birthday present. My birthday just happens to be close to Memorial Day at the end of the school year. This only happened because now Mother Cotilde was in charge. Sister Ida had been demoted. Sister Lucy loved my dad and me and would spend a moment or 2 talking with him when he came to visit or take me home for a weekend. It probably didn't hurt that she had someone who could learn some new music at a moment's notice if necessary. I often wondered if the vacation incident got reported to the higher ups through Fr. Melvich, who happened also to be a music teacher at Bishop Noll High School as well as the one who celebrated daily mass at the home; and, of course, he had a working relationship with Sister Lucy. I was given a couple of trial runs to see if I could be depended upon. I would be allowed to walk down Homan Ave. to the South Shore train station, board the train, and get off at the Roxana station in East Chicago and walk the few blocks to my father's house. I can still see him looking up from his work in the garden as I opened the gate. After church on Sunday, I would board the train again and return to the Home. My sister, who had been staying at the Carmelite Home for girls on Grasselli Ave. in East Chicago, my dad, and I were now a more typical family. I was in charge and responsible for anything that might go wrong while my dad was at work. The Gajdas and the Rossis across the street had boys and they invited the new kid on the block to join them. My sister found a friend 2 doors away in the milk man's daughter. That Fall we would walk to the end of the block to pick up the bus to St. Stanislaus Catholic School. 1959 was such a great year that the White Sox even brought a pennant to the Chicago area.

I was fortunate to have had few Sister Idas and many Frances Tereses during my childhood, not only at the Home but also at St. Stanislaus afterward. I visited Sr. Frances Terese the 3 Summers before I went away to high school with the Franciscan Friars in Sturtevant, WI. My sister and I would ride our bikes, the 1ˢᵗ summer to the Boys Home, and the 2ⁿᵈ and 3ʳᵈ to the Girls Home where she had been transferred. By the time I was in the 8ᵗʰ grade, I was beginning to question the textbook brand of Catholicism. I practice the Way of Catholicism today rather than adhere to all its Theological mysteries;

the important word being practice. The Catholicism of my father was one of looking ahead, past hard times. It was a Catholicism of acceptance, knowing that refusing to carry a small cross would only earn you a larger one down the line. It was a Catholicism of tolerance, knowing not to be afraid of people who are different from you because we are all the children of the same Creator. The Catholicism of all those women that loved me was one of caring for the less fortunate and being willing to do with a little less so that a young person at the beginning of life's journey might have a chance at a little heaven on earth, rather than be in the throes of conflict and on the road to Hell. They didn't want life to teach him that there is not enough to go around. My Catholicism is a Catholicism that believes that if you try to get your heaven on this earth by accumulating all you can and enjoying all the pleasures you can, it will surely end in your death; or you can believe, as Jesus invited us, that a life of caring will merit an eternal reward because the world will not end with our death and the goodness we've created will continue on and we will somehow be a part of that. Not having spent a lot of time in a small family unit has sometimes made me feel inadequate in specific situations but I somehow feel blessed that, without trying, I seem to treat everyone as my brother or sister because my family was so large and my mothers were so many.

Today, my sister, Mary Louise and I live with our spouses within a mile of each other, in the mountains of Western North Carolina.

Note: John graduated from St. Joseph Calumet College, Whiting Indiana — BA English and Secondary Education. His father remarried and John has a step sister, Carmen Yvette and half sister, Helen Josephine.

We Shared the Bond
of a Family

Nancy Frady
1975–1979

ELIADA HOMES FOR CHILDREN
ASHEVILLE, NORTH CAROLINA

M y parents are Robert and Roberta Frady. My father died when I
was four. My memory of dad is him coming home from work and
sitting on the couch and putting me on his leg, and bouncing me
on his leg. It is a good feeling I still cherish today.

My other memory of my dad is not a good one. It is the night he died. My mom
was in the kitchen and my dad pulled up and then I heard yelling. My mom ran
outside and told me to stay in house of course. I didn't listen, but I was standing
on the front porch as my dad and two other guys fought. I remember my mom
tried to stop the fight and getting stabbed. I saw my dad fall to the ground, and
heard mom screaming. Dad was murdered from a knife in his heart. Mom didn't
take us to the funeral. I guess it was too hard on her. After the funeral, I remember
mom going though a trunk and her pushing it across the room and saying, "Bob
why did you leave me?" My mom was left with raising three girls by herself.

L-R: Sister Susan, Nancy and her father in 1962

I remember my mom working all the time. We moved more then anyone I have ever known, never really had any friends because we did not stay anywhere very long. My life went from school to school and place to place. I never remember having a birthday cake, let alone a party. For Christmas each year, my mom would have to put things on lay away and get help from churches. I remember them bringing us gifts to the house.

Five years after my father's death, around 1969, my mom met my step father. He was good to us kids, but very mean to my mom. He would drink all the time, and they would fight and the cops would always come and take him to jail, but he always came back.

In March 1970, my little sister Kathy was born and I was age nine. Also, in September 1970 my older sister Susan had a baby and her name is Jensie. Since my sister was very young, age 14, at Jensie's birth, my mom raised Jensie for a while. But once again we moved to a new house and area to keep everyone from knowing about my niece Jensie. Everyone thought she was our sister including us. My mom and older sister started arguing and fighting with their sharing parenting responsibilities' of Jensie. Soon, my older sister Susan left home, leaving Jensie with mom. This left me and my sister Julie to take care of

Eliada Homes for Children

my younger sisters and niece.

In July, 1975, my mother took me and my two sisters Julie and Kathy and my niece Jensie to Eliada Homes for Children, Asheville, North Carolina to see if we would like it. We told mom we didn't like it; that it was a weird place. But, a week later we were living there.

My life at Eliada Homes for Children began when I was 15. My niece and one of my younger sisters, because they were younger were separated from me and my other sister Julie. We were placed in Cummings Cottage. That was really hard because we had never been apart. Me being the oldest, I really worried about them. I would try to see them everyday in the dining room or church just to let them know I was still there and loved them. My sister Julie who was with me in Cummings Cottage ran away after being there two days and she got to stay home. To this day I have never understood why she could stay at home with our mother and we could not.

My first night at Eliada I was confused and scared. I was worried about my sisters, and also my mother. A girl told me it would be okay and not to worry; later that girl became my roommate and very good friend. Learning the different ways they did things was different than home. My bed time was at 10 p.m. and we always ate three meals a day (something I had never had). I learned to do my homework and get to school on time. We were always in our cottage when lights would come on at dusk. Learning to call staff members Aunt and Uncle took me a while, but I got used to it.

I was in the 9th grade when I begin high school on campus at Eliada. School was hard for me; they expected us to maintain a C average. We had bible classes there and I remember when they told me we had to memorize not just versus but chapters from the bible, too. I struggle for awhile in school, but I finally got into making A's and B's all through high school. When I was home nobody was there to check to see what or how our school was going.

At Eliada, we had to play sports. I was on the basketball, volleyball and softball teams, and I participated in gymnastics. I had never played any of the sports before.

I remember my first breakfast was cream of wheat and the evening meal was liver and onions. Of course I did not like any of the meals but we had to eat everything on our plates or had to sit there until it was gone. Today, I eat liver and onions and cream of wheat with no problem.

One of my jobs at Eliada was the dish room. After the evening meals I would stay with other girls and do the dishes. I remember young children sitting there struggling to finish their food and talking to them. I told the children if they would not tell on me I would throw the food away. To this day, no staff member ever knew I did that. A couple of things I remember are getting a cake on our birthdays in the dining room and Christmas was a big

Kapelle Singers: L-R: Randy Carson, Polly Hubband, Nancy Frady, Willie Teague, Helen Teague, Diane Farmer, Jamie Sinard; (in back) Alethea Harris

thing. They would put a huge tree in the gym. We would sit there until our name was called to come up and receive our gifts. I still missed being at home and being with my family, but I knew I had to make the best of my situation. I joined one of the singing groups called the Kapelle. We traveled the eastern part of the U.S. and Canada and went to Florida in the winter during Christmas break. We got to sing in missions and churches, and visit different places.

After my first tour, my mom came to Eliada to get us out and take us home. I told mom I wanted to stay at Eliada because I really liked it and I had lots of friends. So she took my niece and sister home. I would see them once a month when I got to go home and visit. Sometimes that was hard, because everyone was home and they wanted me to stay, but I always went back to Eliada.

One of the best memories I have of Eliada was meeting my first boyfriend. He was one of the older guys that had lived at Eliada and had left to go live with his dad. He would come up with some of the older boys that had also lived there. They would come up and play basketball, and talk to us about living there. The staff told us girls not to talk to them, but of course being teenage girls, we didn't listen. So, the first and only time I got in trouble, all five of us girls had to go see Mrs. Cameron (the head lady). She put us all on a month restrictions before and after school and also Saturday's after all our jobs were finished. Anywhere the house mother went, we had to go with her and that included sitting on the front pew in church. I still continued seeing my boyfriend on weekends when I got to go home. After about a year he moved away from Asheville so we called it quits. We still remain friends to this day.

I stayed in the Kapelle for another year; I loved the traveling and meeting new people. By this time I was a senior in high school I was really missing living with my family. So after high school I returned home. It was strange being home and I found myself missing my Eliada family.

Years went by after leaving Eliada. I always felt like something was missing in my life. Years later I got married and had two children and later divorced. I continued feeling something was missing. I met another man and stayed with him for 18 years and I had another child. In 2009, I married for the second time. All my children were in the wedding.

Nancy with her children at 2009 Wedding
L-R: Mandy Moses Smith, Christopher Moses, Nancy, Shawn Munro

Diane Farmer (1971–83) and Helen Teague (1972–81) are the friends from Eliada I have kept in my life after leaving the Home in 1979. All three of us were in the Kapelle singing group. They're pictured in photo of the Kapella Singers with this writing. We all have a special bond of a great friend ship. I met these girls when we joined the Kapelle. We all enjoyed traveling. I remember one time we got Diane down in the van and took her bra off and

Nancy's Wedding: L-R: Helen, Diane and Nancy

put it on the antenna of the van. Aunt Candy, Kapelle Director, saw it and we got in trouble. Our punishment was we couldn't go swimming that evening after church. That punishment really didn't bother me. I couldn't swim. After we all left Eliada, Helen married a man in the military and moved away. Diane married a man in the military and move to Germany. Diane came back before Helen did.

Diane and I continued our wonderful friendship again. Our children grew up together we took them trick or treating, baseball practice, and they played together in my front yard. When Helen came back we never missed a beat with all of our friendships. Helen was my matron of honor in my last wedding.

L-R: Diane and Nancy

Helen has since moved away again to live at the beach. I miss her very much. We talk as often as we can. Diane and I are very good friends to this day. We have been through so much together. We've had our disagreements but we have remained very, very close friends since 1975.

I begin going to the reunions at Eliada. It was so nice to reunite with my old family and friends from my youth. I realized my Eliada Family was what I had been missing in my life.

In 2013, the alumni of Eliada honored me with their vote to be President of the Alumni Association. I have been in charge of getting the reunion together every year as their president. I, too, keep track of the coming and going of the alumni. I truly enjoy this and serving as their president.

In 2016, I was nominated to the Eliada Homes for Children Board of Trustees. As a board member it gives me the opportunity to be involved in Eliada, as an adult, and in the children's lives in the Home today. So you see, I left Eliada Homes for Children, but it never left me. As I think back to my years there in childhood, they were probably the best years of my life. We were all there for different reasons, but no one cared or knew why the others were there. We just bonded and became the family that we still are. I try my best to stay in touch with my "Eliada Family". We shared so much while we were there. I will always remember the love, the laughter, and the tears—but most of all; we shared the bond of a family.

I still do not know why my mother put me in Eliada Homes for Children. But, I'm glad she did. Today, I have another wonderful family.

Note: Posted on the website of my childhood home, Eliada, is the Children's Home history:

"Eliada grew out of Faith Cottage, a ministry founded in 1903 by Reverend Lucius B. Compton as a home for unwed mothers. This house was a safe and short-term haven for these girls and women and it was the first of five homes of this kind. The last Faith Cottage closed its doors in 1971. All together, these five homes reached out to help several thousand women.

"It didn't take long for the number of children not kept by their mothers to exceed the capacity of the various Faith Cottages. By 1906 Dr. Compton located a small cabin with a few acres of land located about five miles west of Asheville and opened

an orphanage he named Eliada Home. The name Eliada is a biblical reference. Eliada was one of King David's sons; the Hebrew word means "one for whom God cares."

Dr. Compton and his wife, Edith Van Dusen became known as Dad Compton and Mama Edith to several thousand children. They even adopted a baby girl named Mary Elizabeth when he was 61 and Mama Edith was 55.

"As the years went by more land was bought and donated (including a farm) until the campus swelled to over 1,200 acres. The acreage included Slippey Mountain, upon which a large reservoir was built in 1914; a small lake in which kids swam for years; rolling hills where the hay was baled each year; and a great view of the Biltmore Estate on a clear day.

"Buildings were quickly added: the school and chapel were built in 1911; the first telephone was installed in 1913; a new Main Building — the Big House — was constructed in 1915; a wood-covered amphitheater with seating for 2,500 and used for the tent meetings was constructed in 1917; and the main barn was built along with two others in 1927-1928. The fireproof Allred building, which served as the baby house, was completed in 1930, and is currently listed in the National Historic Register along with the Green Building and the Barn.

"The children and staff maintained the property in a variety of ways. Together they bottled and sold milk from Dr. Compton's prize Guernsey cows. They kept chickens, sold eggs, grew much of their food, canned and pickled the produce, and helped with the maintenance of the land and buildings. This continued throughout the 1970s, and returning alumni still refer to Eliada as "The Farm."

"Since Dr. Compton passed away in 1948, and there have been only five other individuals to lead the organization: Miss Grace Green, Mr. Archibald H. Cameron, *Mr. J. Stewart Humphrey, Mr. Mark Upright, and Mr. Tim Sinatra.

"In more recent history Eliada shifted from the orphanage/dormitory setting to a more family oriented residential care facility. Competitive sports, academics, summer camp, a child development center, an internship program from newly graduated college students, and mental health care were all added to Eliada's continuum of care. Eliada opened the first stand alone Psychiatric Residential Treatment Facility (PRTF) facility in North Carolina in 2006 and now serves the most vulnerable young people in the mental health system. And most recently, Eliada launched the Eliada Students Training for Advancement (ESTA) to serve youth aging-out of the Foster Care System.

*J. Stewart Humphrey was President/CEO of Eliada Homes for Children 1981-2001. Mr. Humphrey worked at the Free Will Baptist Children's Home, Middlesex, North Carolina 1970-72 and President/CEO 1977-81.

All Things Are Possible

Roy C. Page
1960–1969

MASONIC HOME FOR CHILDREN
OXFORD, NORTH CAROLINA

A s the years go by I realize now the memories do too. As I transcribe stories of my life experiences, I will do my best to be honest and accurate.

I have known Jerry Smith for many years. His writings are second to none. I've read his books: "*I Have Hope*" and "*The Family*." I too, was brought up in foster homes and eventually landed at Oxford Orphanage from 1960 to 1969.

I now know it was hard for my mom to let Oxford Orphanage take, educate, and train her children for the future. The experience was difficult for me and my brothers, but oh, so rewarding! My parents had four children: Jeff was the oldest, Roy, Andy, and then Danny, the youngest of the four children.

Jeff retired from the Durham Police Department as 1st Sergeant. I retired as a Fire Captain with the Wilson Fire Department. Andy has worked for 25 years as a truck driver. Danny recently retired as Vice President of Operations of Waccamaw Fuel Company in Selma, North Carolina.

The Beginning

I was born into this world on January 1, 1950, in a home just two miles from the hospital on Tarboro Street, Wilson, North Carolina; however, mom did not make it there. My Mom started having labor pains with me while working in the tobacco fields. My maternal grandfather told my mom to go to the house for my birth. My aunt accompanied my mom to our very old house. I was born in that house, and it is on record that I was the very first baby born in Wilson County that year. The county of Wilson gave my mom a red bicycle because she had been the first to give birth that year.

After giving birth to me, my grandfather came to the house three hours later and instructed my mom to get back to the tobacco fields. My mom never did go to the hospital for follow-up care.

Later on in my life, as a teenager, my mom communicated to me this information of our earlier years. We were very poor, but mom always put a meal on the table.

My dad was a mean drunken man. He beat my mom all the time, and gave her bicycle away to my uncle for a pint of liquor.

My mom communicated to me that we moved around a lot; and especially each time the rent was due. We didn't own a vehicle but moved from house to house with a mule and wagon.

My mom acquired her first public job at Burlington Mills on Herring Avenue in Wilson. We lived on Brown Oil Company road, which was four miles to work for mother. She walked to work each day while my aunt kept us boys at home. My siblings and I drank powdered milk because we were poor.

My mom couldn't afford diapers for us so she would cut up sheets for us to wear. My aunt was lazy and never changed out diapers. During the day, the chickens would always follow us around the yard.

I remembered living in Stantonsburg, North Carolina for a while. My parents worked at Fairfield Diary. Again, we lived in an old house with rotten floors; there were cracks in the walls in which one could see the outside.

This particular time in my life is difficult to talk about. The season was winter with heavy snow. I remember on a Friday night my mom received her paycheck from the Diary and cashed it at the grocery store. My dad had been drinking, and came home drunk and acting crazy. He beat my mom really bad in front of us and demanded her money. My mom told him the money was for food and rent. He grabbed me and held me upside down and threatened to cut my toes off. My mom gave in and threw the money to him. My dad left and told my mom she had better be gone when he came home. My mom called my uncle and he came and got her, but not us. Later on in court, my mom told the judge she thought my dad planned to return to our home. My dad accused our mom of trying to take us away.

The bottom line was we were abandoned that night. My brother, Jeff, told us to go under the house. All of us put quilts on the ground next to the chimney to keep warm during the snow storm. For sixty days, we lived by going to the community grocery store and telling the manager that our mom said to charge the food and milk. We loved Karo syrup and flour for biscuits. For my younger brothers, we mixed Karo syrup and water for their bottle.

The manager at the store finally called Department of Social Services about us. We were placed in different homes. We were now separated from each other. One of my uncles got me and made my life pure hell. He didn't care for me at all. I had to eat in a different room by myself and eat their leftover scraps. He made me clean up their mess while they drank liquor. I finally left and went to a different home of strangers. I was always looked down upon; a nobody. This shuffle went on for four years.

The Judge Rules

The County was awarded custody of all of us, and we had to go to court to talk to the judge. My parents were also there. After speaking to the judge, my brother and I were deemed wards of the state. The local Masons took us to a place called Oxford Orphanage. It was raining heavy that day and we were very nervous because of the unknown. Our ages were as follows: Jeff, age 12, I was 10, Andy was 4, and Danny, 3 years old.

We traveled down Highway 96, and it only took one hour to reach Oxford from Wilson. As we entered the main gate, we noticed all of the big buildings, made of brick, not wood. This place was heaven on earth for us because we were so poor.

Day One at Oxford Orphanage

We checked in at the Administration building and were given new clothes and shoes. The four of us were placed in different cottages. Jeff was in 2-B cottage, I was placed in 1-B, Andy in the Walker building, and Danny in the cottage for babies.

As you enter the campus the boy's buildings were on the left and the girls housing were on the right. The arrangement of the cottages ranged from 1B–4B for the boys and 1G–4G for the girls. The main building was located in front between the buildings.

In 1893, prior to being named Oxford Orphanage, it was known as St. Johns College. There was a chapel, farm, dairy, laundry, dining area and Vocation building with a printing shop, shoe making, electrical and plumbing trades to learn as a skill. Our school, named John Nichols, was on campus and had grades 1-12, under the same roof.

On day two, Jeff and I were assigned to the farm to work after school. Jeff was in the 6th grade and I was in the 4th grade. We got out of school at 3:00 pm and had thirty minutes to get to the farm for check-in with the boss. That day was one I will never forget. The juniors and seniors were in charge of the work details. At break time, the boys got into a circle. I had no idea what was coming! We were made to get inside the circle and fist-fight with another orphan. Then we got water and worked the remaining hour until 5 pm. Jeff and I met back at the farm office to check in and we were both bleeding from fights. The older guys and farm boss said it would make us tough and good for sports activities.

At meal times, the giant bell would ring and we had five minutes to get in line to eat. If we were late, we got put on punishment. Usually, it was extra work detail on Saturdays, our day off. However, if we had to stay after school for poor grades or misbehaving, and were late for work at 3:30 pm, we would get a whipping. This whipping consisted of being hit with a thick paddle as we were tied down to a long drink box by our farm boss. It usually was 25 licks on the bottom and legs. The blood would flow down into our shoes. I hated that man for the beatings. He enjoyed it a lot.

As years went by, I moved from cottage to cottage and changed jobs. I had the opportunity to learn printing from Mr. McSwain which was featured in Jerry Smith's book, "*The Family*." Mr. McSwain was a fine instructor for the kids.

Christmas Time

Each Christmas, all the gifts were given by our North Carolina Masonic Lodges. Each kid would receive fruit bags and one present. This was a happy time for all of the children. The bag would contain a few pecans, walnuts, cashews, one banana, apple, orange and tangerine. The older boys would get wallets, shoes, or a tie with shirts. For us, 14-16 years old, we would get puzzles and school supplies. The girls would get dresses, shoes, make-up, coats and hair dryers.

A lot of children get three days home with their families but the Page boys stayed at Oxford Home every holiday. Christmas was truly a great time of the year for all of us.

Tragedy Strikes the Orphanage

In 1965, the Orphanage was hit hard by a hurricane. We lost over 100 old oak trees. The uprooted oak trees were spread out all over our campus. After the storm passed, the Masons and lots of volunteers from the town of Oxford helped us with cleanup, as it lasted for a couple of months.

Death Came During the Night

Sometime during the night of the hurricane, death occurred to one of our girls. For reasons unknown, Karen McDowell, age 12-15, left her cottage and went to the water tank where our big bell was mounted. This tank was about 75 feet tall. She climbed it and jumped off landing on the concrete. Representatives from the town of Oxford came and got the body during the night. The Oxford Police Department investigated the scene. We were told of the incident by staff at breakfast.

No other facts or reasons were explained to us. This was a hurtful time for us and to her two remaining sisters that were housed in different cottages. The body was sent back to her home for burial. The Orphanage paid for the funeral. What a waste of precious life.

Now at Oxford, there are certified social workers for the children to talk to when needed. Oh, how things have changed for the better.

He Got the Game Ball

Oxford Orphanage has always excelled in all sports. In the 1950's and 60's, we were able to launch our sports programs, thanks to Duke University. The Blue Devils handed down their practice gear for all athletics so we would have the gear we needed for our sports programs. Very few teams that we played had success against us. In the 1960's, Oxford Orphanage was playing 3-A and 4-A schools, and winning against them. An example of this success was a practice game versus Fike High School in Wilson, N.C.. On a Thursday night, Fike boasted with Carlester Crumpler, a big and powerful running back. Our coach, Jimmy Barnette and Fike High School's coach set up this game. Oxford scored seven touchdowns and Fike scored two. The next night, Fike beat Goldsboro for the 4-A state championship. Kudos to both teams!

On Friday, November 15, 1967, I was in the library at school when my teacher requested that my brothers and I go to the office. They informed us that my dad had died in Wilson and we would go there to say our good-byes and to view the body. I didn't want to go because he was an evil man. We left Oxford Orphanage at 12:00 pm, and headed to Wilson for the viewing of our father in his casket. No one was present during those thirty minutes we spent there. We were back at the orphanage about 2:00 pm, on that same day.

That night, we played for the State Championship in football, but my coach didn't want to play me. I begged him and started at linebacker. Oxford Orphanage won 13-0 against Norlina, and I made 18 tackles. The game ball was given to me, which I still have to this day.

Graduation Day at Oxford

1969 Senior Year, Oxford Orphanage

On June 6, 1969, I had made it and graduated from Oxford. All of the senior boys were given new suits and the girls were given new dresses and shoes. There were 13 students in our graduating class. My mother and uncle showed up for the graduation ceremonies. It was a good day for all. I, as well as three others in my class had enlisted in the Navy. Two weeks later, I boarded a plane at RDU for training at Great Lakes.

Military Life

We all arrived in Great Lakes, Michigan at 2 am. We were processed in for gear and given ID tags. For most, the shouting and training by the CO's were difficult; though, not for me. I excelled in all areas during those 16 weeks of training. I graduated as the number one recruit in the unit, among 1,300 sailors, and was offered a United States Navy Ceremonial Guard position in Washington, D.C.

1969 Boot Camp, Great Lakes, IL

Arlington National Cemetery

Military Funeral Arlington National Cemetery

Roy guarding Tomb of Unknown Soldier

I arrived in Washington early one morning and a representative from the Navy picked me up, transporting me to a facility located on the United States Naval base. I was processed in, and assigned to the Firing Party. My training lasted for eight weeks and I was then assigned to a platoon for detail. For the next two years, we carried out about 15 funerals a day because of what was occurring in Vietnam.

In 1970, I was honored, as I was selected to march at the tomb of the Unknown Soldier. One member from each branch of the military was selected by the Joint Chiefs of Staff for this honor.

When I finished my military tour, I received a handwritten letter, personally signed by President Nixon thanking me for assisting with his grandchildren.

Our other assignments were located at the White House, Pentagon, and the War Room. It was an honor to babysit President Nixon's grandchildren, as well as for Dwight and Linda Eisenhower. Former President Nixon and the First lady were always kind to me. This was volunteer duty by me on weekends. I had fun with the children. I had many meals at the White House.

Entering the Workforce

My first job was to marry my girlfriend, Nellie Currence in Washington, D.C. Nellie was from West Virginia, and she was Director's J. Edgar Hoover's secretary. She served in this capacity for nine years. She was the only person with the FBI that could ride the elevator with Mr. Hoover. My wife is the quiet type and reserved. She left the FBI and moved with me to North Carolina. We were married for 43 years and were blessed with four children, three grandchildren, and now one great grandson whose name is Liam.

My first job was wiring electric motors. After my first check of sixty dollars, I had to find something better. Nellie and I were expecting our first child.

I saw in the paper that Hackney's Body Company in Wilson was hiring. I interviewed and the next day was hired. The money was far better, but never enough.

After a year at Hackney's, I stopped by the Headquarters Fire Station on Douglas Street in Wilson and inquired if they were hiring. They were, and I went through the hiring process. I was assigned to Headquarters. Several years went by and I received promotions at a regular pace. The one man that helped me and was a close friend was Elvin Stone with Fire Prevention. He always kept up with me from the various transfers from station to station. To this day, he and wife, Carol are my best friends. Elvin is closer to me than my brothers.

Nellie and I have always loved children and we decided to become foster parents for Wilson County. At the time, Jerry Smith was the Director of Social Services in Wilson County. Jerry is and always will be another close friend.

My wife and I completed the training and classes to become foster parents. We started keeping children and were licensed for seven children. We were foster parents for 13 years and helped over 100 children. We got burned out with our 4 children and the many foster children. This was truly a rewarding experience for both of us.

During my career, I have seen many deaths and tragic accidents to last a lifetime. Looking back on 30 years, I really believe I made a huge impact. Eight years ago, I retired as Fire Captain and Assistant Chief. Wilson Fire/ Rescue Services, Wilson, North Carolina.

Conclusion

I want to say thank you to Jerry and all of the readers for allowing me to share my life events. To do this, was difficult but satisfying. Life does throw its curves but God is still in control. With God's help, all things are possible if it's his will. May God bless everyone.

Daughter of
Polish Immigrants

Mary Jalocha
1954–1959

ST. JOSEPH CARMELITE HOME FOR GIRLS
EAST CHICAGO, INDIANA

Both my parents were born in Poland and immigrated to American after War World II. My father Czeslaw Jalocha was born June 25, 1925. My mother Wladyslawa Hat was born May 25, 1924. Both lived through difficult years surrounding WWII and my father almost lost his life from a Nazi firing squad that killed many friends in his Poland hometown. My parents worked in German worked camps and were required to have identification approved by the German government.

Mother's Work Pass

Both my parents practiced the Roman Catholic teachings and were married after the war by a Catholic priest in the displaced person camp in Wildflecken, Germany. My brother Johnny was born May 25, 1948 in Wildflecken, Germany. Nearly a year later, they immigrated to America and stepped off the ship SS Marine Jumper in Boston, Massachusetts on May 5th, 1949. My father became an American Citizen; my mother never did.

Wedding Picture of my parents

I was born on January 17, 1951 in Memorial Hospital, Logansport, Indiana. I'm not sure if I ever lived with my mother. My only recollection was that my mom was hospitalized for mental illness when I was born. She

Mother's Immigration Green Card. 4'11", Brown eyes, Brown hair

remained institutionalized for her illness until the day of her passing. My dad hoped that mom's depression and paranoid state would improve after having another child. It never did. She suffered with post partum depression and things actually got worse. When looking at pictures of mom from her youth, her flat affect and blank stare is obvious. Did she experience mental illness even then? Dad was legally blind even with lens correction and had trouble with facial features.

My early years were spent with my dad and brother Johnny on a farm in Fair Oaks, Indiana, where my dad worked the fields with other migrants. While he worked, Johnny and I were cared for by "Grandma Geesa" and her family. Grandma Geesa was a small rounded older woman who smiled often. I remember pictures of us playing on the swing set and walking through the tall grass around a big white farmhouse. We seemed happy and content like most young children who are well feed and cared for.

When I was 2 or 3 years old dad, Johnny and I packed our stuff and took a bus to East Chicago, Indiana in the far Northwestern corner of the state. I think at this time, mom became a ward of the state and was institutionalized in a facility in Westville, Indiana, located in northern part of the state. We moved to a small apartment above a bar. My dad swept and washed floors and tables in the bar below. We were not far from the neighborhood Catholic Church, only a few blocks away and within walking distance. The priests and nuns were very influential in my dad's life. Within a year or so, it was deemed better for us kids to live in a different environment and our living arrangements changed again. Johnny moved into the Carmelite Home for Boys in Hammond, Indiana, while I began my life at the Carmelite Home for girls on Grasselli Street in East Chicago, Indiana. Though I was younger in age than those generally admitted to the facility, an arrangement was made because of my circumstances and interception by the nuns and priests at the church. The south shore electric rail system ran through the center of town. This train system become our new mode of transportation and kept us connected to dad and each other. Since I was pretty young when I first started living at the Carmelite home, I don't have a lot of early memories.

Carmelite Home was 1 or 2 stories brick exterior and a huge back yard with a cement pool, swing sets and a small grassy space where we played ball and catch. The yard was completely enclosed on three sides by a faux stone/brick fence with a terra cotta topping. You had to enter the building by the front door. You had to ring the bell and be let in by someone on the inside. The sleeping quarters were two large rooms with single beds along the walls on three sides. A larger corner bed was hidden by a movable curtained room divider. One of the nuns slept in the room with the rest of us girls. There was one room for the younger girls and another for the older girls. A large dining room with an upright piano was just off from the front door.

Carmelite Home for Girls

Shortly after we moved into the Homes, our dad got a job in maintenance at Combustion Engineering, a small machine shop, and then moved into an apartment on Kennedy Ave., not far from the Home for girls. I attended 1st and 2nd grade at St. Joseph School on Kennedy Ave. I started school in 1ˢᵗ grade when I was 5 years old; no kindergarten for me. This was probably so that I could blend in and "catch up" to the daily lives of the other girls' living at the Home. Routines and schedules were important in those days to keep things running smoothly. Since the school was only down the block and around the corner, we walked to and from school in a group. No school memories or pictures from this school unfortunately.

3ʳᵈ Grade

I attended 3ʳᵈ grade at Holy Trinity Hungarian School, on Carey St. in East Chicago, still within walking distance of the Home. Probably was an average student, reasonably popular in so much as never having been bullied and liked school. Was rather shy though and blended in well. On one occasion we had an assignment to write a theme on an inanimate object. I chose to write about a piece of chalk, but instead of writing prose, I chose to write a poem. I got an A for creativity. I was asked to read the poem out loud to the entire class. I was petrified. I must have been as white as a sheet. When I finished and was returning to my seat, I tripped on something (probably my feet) and fell to the floor. Everyone thought I fainted. On another occasion, I was asked to sing a solo for a music class selection and had to climb up two stairs to a platform in front of the room. No incidence of stage fright recalled.

As a young child I used to sleep walk. There was an occasion when I got dressed, walked down the stair to go out, but could not open the door. So came back to the bedroom and heard Sister Teresita whispered, "it's too early to go to school, Marisha (little Mary). It is time for you to go back to sleep." She peeked from behind the partition and helped me unbutton my coat and blouse. Her head was covered with a white bonnet so that her hair was completely covered. She was one of the Carmelite sisters of the Sacred Heart. She was of Polish descent and I believe that I was one of her special ones.

There were two occasions when I had to make use of the infirmary. At age 5 or 6 I had my tonsils and adenoids removed. I remember licking popsicles (root beer was my favorite) and sucking on hard candy and ice cream. On another occasion I got German measles and spent a week in the infirmary feeling miserable. Sally was in the infirmary, too. She was one of the older girls and I don't remember much about her. I just itched and felt so hot. I couldn't eat or sleep. Sister Irene would sponge bathe me with a cool wash cloth and baking soda. I remember hearing the other girls laughing and swimming and having fun while I was stuck in bed on the second floor.

I enjoyed summers at the Home. I would swim with the other girls in the pool and have watermelon and ice cream. We had 2 dogs, one of which was named Sugar. The other dog was a German Shepherd and a guard dog. We did not play much with him. Sugar was black and white of no particular breading and probably weighed 25-30 pounds. My friend Belinda Arceo and I liked to play with Sugar as we jumped in and out of the pool. On one occasion while I was getting out of the pool, my hand slipped and I hit my upper lip on the top wall of the pool. Blood was gushing and Sister Katherine drove me to the St. Catherine Hospital Emergency Room. I was quite a celebrity when I returned to the Home with 5 stitches on my upper lip. When in the "ER", a couple struck a conversation with Sister Katherine about the cute little orphan on the emergency room cot. Apparently they inquired whether or not I was eligible for adoption. A few weeks later, while I was practicing my piano lessons, I received a large red bag full of hard candies; all varieties of red and white striped ribbon candies, and jelly filled orange and green candy drops. There were pink cream filled ones, too. All the candies were my favorites. This was a gift from that same couple from the hospital "ER". Apparently this couple was quite well off financially but could not have children. My dad had been contacted with this request for adoption, but he refused. He was saving

Christmas 1954 with Johnny and Dad

money to buy a house for us to live in when we were old enough to take care of each other. It made me feel very special and valued.

Christmas was always a happy occasion. There was a great party in the dining hall. A gigantic Christmas tree was decorated with lights and bobbles and placed in the corner of the dining room. Catholic charities and other philanthropies as well as personal donors would make sure that we each had a wrapped gift to open. One year I remember receiving a cash register and a stuffed elephant. Through the years I received jump ropes, hula hoops, balls, sweaters and hats. Sometimes we would swap gifts if some girls wanted too. There was always something for each of us.

While I was at the Carmelite Home my dad and brother were always in my life. On Sundays dad would make arrangements to pick us up and go on a picnic. Sometimes he would pick me up and together we would travel the South Shore electric train to Hammond to get Johnny from the Carmelite Home for Boys. We would walk to Douglas Park and feast on Spam and banana pepper sandwiches. We always had Gonnellla Vienna bread, fruit and cookies with tea from an Aladdin Thermos bottle. We would run, play ball and swing. After a few hours we would return "home". On other Sundays we make the run in reverse with dad and Johnny coming from the Boys Home to me. The change of scenery included Riley Park, which had the added benefit of a cannon memorial on which we would climb. Occasionally we would take the South Shore Line to South Bend, Indiana to visit mom. She was a ward of the state by this time and hospitalized in Westville Mental Facility. This seemed like a large facility with multiple 1, 2, and 3 story buildings. We had to wait for the men in white to bring mom to see us. Her affect was always flat. She wore the same gray dress each time we saw her. She would allow Johnny and me sometimes too take her hand, but not talk to dad or even look at him. I suspect that she was well medicated and had received shock treatments while she was there. We would walk the grounds. We never stayed very long. I am not sure what feelings I had after the visits.

The year that I turned 8, my dad announced that he had purchased a house for us to live in. Initially we stayed occasionally on weekends, a trial run so to speak. Had to make sure things would work out and that we could watch out for each other. Dad worked some weekends and did shift work, still at Combustion Engineering, but now working in the machine shop. Our house was a two bedroom Cape Cod bungalow situated in the middle of a tree

Jalocha Home

Jalocha Family

lined street, rows of like houses on each side of the street. It's shaker wood tiles were painted bright Kelly green. It had a black tiled pitched roof, a white front door, and green and white striped awning above each window. A side windowed door opened to a 4x4 foot landing. To the left 4 steps lead up to the kitchen. If you went straight ahead 8 steps brought you in the basement. The kitchen was adequate for a small table for 3 or 4, a refrigerator and stove. The living room was large enough to have a TV, upholstered rocking chair and a small couch. There were two bedrooms. Johnny and dad would share a room, and I, being a girl, had a room to myself. My room had two large windows, one facing the back yard, the other facing the next door neighbor's side door. The other bedroom was at the front of the house with a side widow and a double transom window facing the front yard.

We had a large back fenced yard in which to play ball, and run. It was in this back yard that I learned to ride a bike. Dad would run along side until I learned to balance. In May of 1959, after a few month's successful trial run, we left the Carmelite Homes and moved in permanently with Dad.

I have no special recollections of my 1st day in our permanent home. However, I have early memories of dad, Johnny and I playing cards at the kitchen table. We played "thousand", old maid using a regular deck of cards (joker was the old maid), war and kings in the corner. Johnny made friends with the neighbor boys who lived across the street Jimmy Gadja and Bob Rossi. I played baseball with the boys in our back yard since there was plenty of room to run the bases and field a fly ball. I didn't run as fast as the boys, so I was pitcher. Soon after we moved in, dad planted a horse chestnut tree in the front yard by the front bedroom window. I believe it is still growing there today.

I stayed at this house until I married John Tadey in 1974. We have two grown children. Cathy (36) lives in Joliet, Illinois and works at middle school as a band director. Tony (34) lives in Bloomington, Indiana and works at a university as a multi-media specialist with a focus on distance learning and media preservation. Both children are happy and successful. Both Johnny and I were sent to private boarding schools. My dad wanted us to get a good education and sent us to private Catholic schools. I graduated from St. Joseph Academy (high school), Columbia, Pennsylvania in 1968. I completed ADN, BSN and MSN degrees in nursing from Purdue University. I also attended Calumet College in East Chicago for two years pursuing a teaching degree prior to changing my major to nursing. After 37 years of successful nursing, I am now retired living with my friend and spouse in the mountains of western North Carolina.

Note: Posted on Carmelite Home's website is the Home's history:

St. Joseph's Carmelite Home, originally an orphanage, was opened in 1913 by our Mother Foundress, Bl. Maria Teresa. The poverty in East Chicago was extreme, but faithfulness to this most necessary mission for neglected/abused children has prevailed throughout the past ninety-five years.

Carmelite Home evolved from an orphanage to a group home and finally to a residential treatment center. Over the years, the Carmelite Sisters have cared for hundreds of children. We now provide a fully accredited on-campus school for those girls who need one-to-one academic assistance and a more structured classroom environment. Our children and youth are from many ethnic backgrounds and religions. Our Sisters strive to cultivate a Christian mentality in our residents. In addition to material benefits, social development, and intelligent advancement, we wish to give them a sense of God's Presence in their young lives—to make a difference!

On the wall of the St. Joseph's Carmelite Home hangs a photo from 1913. It shows some of the first children admitted to the organization, standing on the porch of one of its original frame houses on Grasselli Avenue.

For over 100 years, the Carmelite Home has remained a constant in the region, nurturing children entrusted to the care of the Carmelite Sisters of the Divine Heart of Jesus.

…The Carmelite sisters say their mission of helping children in an ever-changing society is unchanged since its founding mother came to East Chicago.

"They serve a very primary role in the work they do," said Lake County Sheriff John Buncich, who chairs Carmelite Home's board. "They're a hidden treasure over there, believe me."

Soon after Mother Mary Teresa Tauscher opened the home, it grew to house about 70 children. A lot of times children came to the home after their fathers were killed in the mills and their mothers could no longer afford to take care of the family.

Now the home – the oldest Carmelite home still open in the United States – serves approximately 65 children, aged newborn to 18, on the same East Chicago street where it began. It has grown to start new programs providing care for teenage mothers and their babies and emergency shelter services.

The home's administrator, Sister Maria Giuseppe, stood recently in front of the 100-year-old picture at the Carmelite Home, recalling the first time she met two siblings who were among the girls photographed.

Then well into their 70s, the two women had come to the home with an envelope of money they had saved over the years to repay the place where they had grown up.

Sister Giuseppe told the sisters she couldn't accept the donation, and the women told her, "Mother would have wanted you to have it."

Sister Giuseppe, who has been at the home for nearly 36 years, said her favorite memories are from reunions when children, who had lived at the home from as far back as the 1930s, gathered to share memories. Even though the women were aged in their 60s and 70s, and most are grandmothers, they're still referred to as girls, Giuseppe said.

Some former Carmelite girls have even returned to the home to work in adulthood. One of those girls is Michelle, who requested her last name not to be used. Michelle came to the Carmelite Home when she was 13, and the sisters put her through Bishop Noll Institute, provided transportation to and from her job and helped her open her first bank account.

He Made a Promise to God

Reverend Charles Anthony Hutchins
1978–1995

PRESIDENT/CEO
EPWORTH CHILDREN'S HOME
COLUMBIA, SOUTH CAROLINA

Charles Anthony Hutchins was the fifth of eight children born to John Sam Hutchins and Carolyn McKenzie Hutchins. He was born in Forest City, North Carolina, but the family soon moved to Walhalla, South Carolina, where he spent his formative years. He attended Tamassee DAR school, which was both a boarding and public school. On his 18th birthday he joined the Army, and when the Korean War broke out he was one of the soldiers headed for combat.

On September 11, 1950, after just 44 days in Korea, he was assigned to a three-man team to go into enemy territory to find some equipment that had been left behind when American troops were pushed back toward South Korea. In the early hours of the morning they encountered North Korean troops. They were hit with a hand grenade. One of them was killed and the second lost a leg. Charles was wounded but he picked up his buddy and carried him back to a first aid station on the South Korean side. Once there, they determined that he was wounded in the left foot and leg. After a month,

Private Charles Hutchins

he returned State-side and spent 21 months in Walter Reed Hospital recovering and rehabilitating. The night he was wounded he made a promise to God: "If You'll get me out of this place, I'll try to make a difference." Charles received the Purple Heart and Bronze Star from his heroic actions in Korea.

While at Walter Reed, he got restless and asked for "temporary duty". He was sent to Camp Detrick in Frederick, Maryland. One day he went into the office where Eva Grey Martin was working as a secretary. She determined to meet that "handsome young soldier". One Saturday (June 26, 1952) she and her sister went swimming at Detrick, and she was surprised to see that "handsome young soldier" working as a life guard. She got his attention, made arrangements for her and her Dad to take him to church with them the next morning, he was invited to their house for dinner, and the rest is history. They were married on June 27, 1953.

Charles received a medical retirement from the Army and was discharged on November 11, 1952. He did not want to be separated from Eva Grey, so he took a job in Frederick as a machinist with Ameritronics, Inc., and Eva Grey's parents let him rent a bedroom in their house in Braddock Heights. He became to my parents the son they never had.

At Christmas that year Charles took Eva Grey to South Carolina to meet his family. That meeting did not go very well, and Charles' mother did not relate to Eva Grey. We knew, however, that she didn't feel that anyone was good enough for her boys, especially one that took him to Maryland. After they went back to Maryland, Charles wrote to her regularly and always insisted that Eva Grey write a note to her. In one of her letters to him, she referred to Eva Grey as "her royal highness." They just laughed about it. In late May, Charles' sister graduated from high school and they went back to South Carolina. That visit went much better, and before they left to return to Maryland, his mother said to Eva Grey, "Honey, I was wrong. I love you." From that time they had a beautiful relationship. (At the end of her life, she thanked Eva Grey for being so good to her and told her she had loved her like a daughter.)

Throughout the months they had dated, Charles always talked about going to college. He said he wanted to be an engineer. On their way back to Maryland after Christmas, as they drove through Greenville, S.C., Charles said, "Let's go by Furman (University) and see what they have to offer." While visiting with the Admissions officer, he asked, "Do you know where a good secretary can get a job around here?" She said, "The Athletic Director is looking for a secretary." She called Lyles Alley to come to her office, he hired Eva Grey and, being a member of the Admissions Committee, he arranged for a special test, and when they left there Charles was enrolled in school and Eva Grey had a job. They went back to Maryland, packed their belongings in a U-Haul trailer, and moved to South Carolina.

Eva Grey had always longed for a college education, but it was more important to her for Charles to get his degree. By the fall semester of that first year, the athletic budget had been reduced but Coach Alley worked out a deal for her to attend classes on a football scholarship. (There was money in the athletic budget for a football scholarship that was not being used so he was able to convince the administration to let her use it.) While Charles went to college he supplemented his income from the GI Bill by selling automobile accessories at car auctions. While Eva Grey worked she ate her lunch at her desk and took a class every day during her lunch hour. After three years of that arrangement, the athletic budget was again reduced and the scholarship was taken away. Coach Alley arranged to get her a job as a legal secretary with Cain, Earle and Boseman. Charles graduated from Furman University and went to work for the Family Service Agency. The executive director was so impressed with his counseling ability that she recommended him for a scholarship to her alma mater, Florida State School of Social Work. After receiving the Master of Social Work degree from Florida State University, he went to work at Holston Home for Children in Greeneville, Tennessee. His life's work was sealed. He began his work at Holston Home as a social worker. There were sixty children in residential care and his caseload was half that number. Within 18 months he became Director of Social Work.

His first assignment was to visit a home where two siblings had been placed in adoption: an 11-year-old boy and a 13-year-old girl. His job was to separate the siblings and return the girl to residential care.

Another of his assignments was a 4-year-old boy who had been discarded into a truck bed. Someone passing by heard his cries and called the Department of Social Services who in turn called Holston Home.

He had to go to the home of a family where the mother had died leaving five children and the father knew he could not care for the children and continue his job. He met the family and got the children ready for the trip. Before he could leave, however, the mother's sister called and asked him to come to get her eight children whose father was absent from the home/ Before he would get to that family's residence, she had committed suicide. He returned to Holston Home with 13 children. Before the week was out, the father of the original five children had taken his life.

He was asked to perform the wedding of the oldest girl from that family of five and a boy who was living at Holston Home. As soon as they graduated high school and were no longer in the care of the Home, they asked Hutchins to conduct their wedding. They were married in the little campus chapel and Mrs. Hutchins gave them a reception in the dining room.

Charles worked with unmarried mothers at a time when girls were placing their babies in adoption. One of those babies he received had a chronic respiratory ailment. It was his practice to always reveal to the adopting family any physical or mental problems of which he was aware, and the couple he offered this baby to was willing to accept him anyway. However, after several days they decided they could not handle it so they called Hutchins to come and get the baby. He tried a second couple, who took the baby at first and returned him in two days. The third couple was different. The mother also had respiratory problems and understood. They were willing to adopt the baby. He kept in touch with the family for several years, but finally they lost contact. One evening we attended the Greene County Fair in Greeneville and they were featuring a rising country music star named Rodney Atkins. Rodney is the child Charles placed with three couples before the adoption became permanent.

Rodney and Hutchins made contact that evening and they instantly bonded like family. He has returned to Holston Home on several occasions to perform for the children. The Hutchins went to his home for a televised fund raiser for the Home. He and his wife, Rose Falcon, continue to write and record country music.

The saddest experience of his work at Holston Home was the death of a 12-year old girl. When he admitted her into care, he was aware that she had a congenital heart problem and he was able to get her admitted into the National Institute of Health in Washington, DC, for assessment and possible treatment. They were unable to do anything for her. She lived less than a year after that trip. Today she would probably be a candidate for a heart transplant.

During his first 15 years at Holston Home he placed more than 100 children in adoptive care and was case worker for an estimated 1200 children in residential or foster care. He was instrumental in initiating admission of African American children and hiring African American staff. Nothing pleases him more than a visit or a phone contact from one of them.

In 1970, Hutchins was named Social Worker of the Year by the Knox Area Chapter of the National Association of Social Workers, Knoxville, Tennessee. In 1973 he received a call from Dr. Alan Broom at Epworth Children's Home in Columbia, SC, asking Charles to join him at Epworth. Charles' mother had once lived at Epworth, and during his years growing up in South Carolina, he had heard much about Epworth, so it was fairly familiar to him. Carolyn McKenzie had gone to live at Epworth at age 5, following her father's death of peritonitis at the age of 27. Two younger sisters were too young to be admitted, and so it separated Carolyn from her family. Nevertheless, she thrived at Epworth. She made good grades in school, and was a stellar "inmate". However, after two years, her mother took her back home to reunite her with her sisters. Charles remembered those stories and happily accepted the position of Associate Executive Director.

The Hutchins moved to Columbia and the children were soon settled in their new schools. They bought their first home, and the neighborhood provided their boys with many friends and playmates. However, there were no other girls their daughter's age who went to public school, so it was not a happy time for her. All of their children were accepted into the activities at Epworth, and the boys played on the Epworth basketball teams. They were included in the Epworth church activities, Christmas programs — anything the resident children did. It was a happy time for the family.

Charles was adamant in insisting that this agency, too, be inclusive, both with staff and children in care. Within six months they admitted the first African-American student.

Epworth Children's Home

Charles and Eva Grey

In 1978, Dr. Broom retired and Charles was named President and CEO, a position he held for 17 years. Under his leadership, the Temporary Emergency Shelter was expanded to receive children into care immediately upon referral, 24 hours a day, 7 days a week. Services to mentally retarded and handicapped persons were greatly expanded into the Parent/Infant Stimulation program and a unique camping program for mentally retarded youth. A Family Clarification program adopted a goal to find a permanent home for every child in care. One of the outcomes of Family Clarification was an adoption program. By 1981, 28 percent of the children were in residential care less than three months. In 1980, Epworth established its Intensive Care Unit for boys' age 6–12 who were considered "high risk", who exhibited signs of emotional disturbances. In 1982, a Parent Support group was begun. A tutoring program was initiated to help children who were behind grade level or who were struggling to keep up their school work.

In 1994 the Health Center was remodeled to meet the requirements of the S. C. Department of Mental Health, designated a "special care" facility to provide specific care for children in need of physical or mental health services. The Trustees honored Hutchins "21 years of tireless efforts as an administrator, a caring professional in child care, a devoted Methodist and a loyal disciple of the Great Physician and a model for stewardship" by naming it the Charles A. Hutchins Special Care Center.

A treat which has become a tradition at Epworth Children's Home is Peanut Butter Ice Cream. No one is certain when it began, although it has been said that during the Depression and the years that followed, peanut butter was a staple that was always plentiful. Ice cream was a treat for the children whenever there was enough cream to spare. One day, someone decided to throw a "dollop" of peanut butter into the ice cream churn, and a tradition was born. Just how accurate that story really is might be open to question, but it certainly is a tradition, however it began.

The recipe was printed in the October 1970 issue of *The Epworth Record*.

Peanut Butter Ice Cream

95 eggs
quarts sweet milk
7 1/2 pounds of sugar
15 tablespoons vanilla extract
2 ½ packages of instant villa pudding (2 pound size)
10 pounds peanut butter

Beat eggs, add sugar, vanilla and 10 quarts of milk. Mix pudding with 10 quarts of milk. Blend egg mixture and pudding. Add peanut butter. Blend well before freezing.

Hutchins retired from Epworth in June 1995 and soon realized that retirement was not what he wanted. Fortunately, Reverend Frank ("Bob") Bostick was President of Holston Home and when he learned of Hutchins' retirement telephoned him and asked him to return to Holston Home as Director of Church Relations. Hutchins immediately accepted the challenge and went to work at his new job. In December 1999, Arthur S. Masker became the President and CEO of Holston Home and asked Hutchins to accept Vice President of Development Resources. He had held that position since January 1, 2000. He has announced his retirement effective January 15, 2015, and will continue as Director of Church Relations part time.

Note: Charles history was written by his wife Eva Grey
In 1986, Eva Grey Hutchins and Dr. Alan Keith-Lucas co-authored The Epworth Story: *Epworth Children's Home, Columbia, S.C. 1896–1985*
Eva Grey "Gay" Hutchins attended Furman University and received a Bachelor of Arts degree in music from Columbia College. She coordinated public relations for Epworth and maintained records of Epworth Alumni Association.
Alan Keith Lucas, Ph.D., is Alumni Distinguished Professor Emeritus of the University of North Carolina and founder of that University's Group Child Care Consultant Services. He has consulted with more than 80 children's homes on three continents, including Epworth Children's Home.
Eva Grey gave Jerry Smith The Epworth Story *book. She wrote inside the cover: To our dear friend, Jerry Smith, a Christian and a major force in pushing for quality child care. Eva Grey Hutchins 4-18-17*

My Life at the Home

Joan Davis
1999–2014

FREE WILL BAPTIST CHILDREN'S HOME
MIDDLESEX, NORTH CAROLINA

I was born and raised in Nash County, North Carolina. After graduating from high school, I got married and moved to Rocky Mount, North Carolina. I am the mother of two wonderful children, and a proud grandmother of four handsome grandsons.

On a lovely day in August 1999, Sabrina (2 years old god-granddaughter) and I went to Middlesex, North Carolina to fill out an application for a job at the Free Will Baptist Children's Home (FWBCH). After completing the application, I began to leave and receptionist Mrs. Brenda Vanderpool asked me to wait. The Director of Children's Service wanted to interview me. I was shocked to have been asked to interview the same day of completing an application. I waited patiently.

At that time, Mrs. Glenda Phillips was Director of Children's Service; she called me in and interviewed me for the houseparent position. In a state of shock still, the interview went well and I was hired. Mrs. Phillips said my start date would be August 26, 1999. As I left FWBCH, I looked over at my god-granddaughter and said to her, "what did Grandma just do", Sabrina just looked at me and smiled.

My first day was Thursday August 26, 1999, at Central Cottage. This was the beginning of a change in my life. There was a lot going on the campus at that time; there was not anyone to train me for my job and duties. I remember Mrs. Joyce Batchelor was working the opposite shift of me; she was so sweet; she left me with all the paper

Photo provided by Free Will Baptist Children's Home

work that goes to each shift during changeover. I took all the papers and began to study them. I decided then that I would learn how the program worked on my own. I worked on that and I did very well, and my part time worker was a help also. I learned fast, I was proud of myself too.

My cottage at that time had nine residents (girls). As I worked with the residents, I began to change the way I thought, way I saw things, and what I would hear also. I was in shock for a while, and then things began to fall in place, meaning, I was not use to hearing people swearing and disrespecting others like that. I fell in love with the cottage, enjoyed working with that group of residents. My stay in Central Cottage was two years.

The Home closed Central Cottage down, and we moved over to Rodgers Cottage. At this time all the cottages had Resident Managers to run the Cottages. Going to Rodgers Cottage was a little nervous at first, but the Resident Manager there welcomed us with a loving spirit. Ms. Euneka O'Neal was the Resident Manager at that time. We had a mixture of ages in the cottage, sometimes it would be hard to keep things calm, but we had a good team of staff that could keep it together. During the time that Ms. O'Neal was Resident Manager at Rodgers, we designed an Educational Center in the cottage, and we set it up like a library area with books, desk, computers, and games. The residents enjoyed it and put it to good use. I worked in Rodgers Cottage for four and a half years.

The residents had a scheduled time for bed. Room time during the week would be until 9 p.m. Monday thru Thursday, Friday and Saturday 10 p.m.

Children would get up for school at 5:30 a.m., breakfast would be at 6 a.m. and then they would catch the 6:45 a.m. school bus. The residents would arrive back from school at 3:15 p.m. They would always get a snack, at 4 p.m. and then have a study hour. There would be some that would have to go to tutoring during that time. If that time didn't work for some of the residents, we would adjust the time to accommodate them.

Top Row L-R: Joan and staff
Photo provided by Joan Davis

There was a change in staff again and we were moved around to different cottages. I was moved to State Cottage under Resident Manager, Mrs. Maleia Williams in January 2006. In February 2006, I was one of the two House Parents that was chosen to be candidates to go to Thomasville, North Carolina to train for Human Services Practitioner II's and it would last for nearly ten months. I remember we had to work our normal shifts, study, homework, training, and travel back and fourth to Thomasville. After all said and done, it was a great experience. I enjoyed the training, and applied it to my daily routines with the residents. As time went on, there were new Resident Managers whom came to work in the cottage where I worked; I was asked to work with them and to show them how the program worked in their training. While some would question a House Parent training a Resident Manager, well that is what happen and I enjoyed helping out when and where I was needed.

The Spiritual life at the Home was done many ways. Church was every Sunday; choir rehearsals, play practices and events took place at church on campus. All the residents who wanted to participate in the events or services would go to rehearsals, house parents would make sure they would stay in place. To me the church was and still is a sacred place of worship. When it comes to going to church, I feel it should be respected as the 'House of God' still. That being said, I always talked to my residents about behaviors while in the church and how they needed to act while there. In the cottages, we had a time set for devotions. When it came time for devotions, everyone would come regardless if they wanted to participated or not … they would have to come. Devotions were good and residents got to say how they felt; they could read scripture out of the Bible, devotional book, sing or just be there. There were groups that would come to the church on campus and do programs; sometimes they would invite the children to their churches for services. Also, at one time FWBCH had a day set aside for Bible Study. There were lots of residents that got baptized while they were living there.

I enjoyed the residents and the spiritual side of the campus, really everything about FWBCH. It was great when we had visitors to come and entertain or have events for the children. It was really special when the residents were fed by guest. They enjoyed the visit and food.

Thanksgiving was always celebrated a few days before because some of the residents would go on family visits during the holiday weekend. On Thanksgiving Day, everyone that was left on campus was taken out to eat Thanksgiving Dinner at the Golden Corral restaurant. That was fun, they got a chance to get off campus and eat something different too.

The best time of the year would be Christmas. Wow, Christmas was great, you would get to see the residents open their gifts, even though some wouldn't be that happy at first but they would be much happier later because gifts just kept on coming in and they would see how blessed they were. I would encourage them and let them know how blessed they were.

December was a month of love in action. We started early preparing for Christmas. You see, not everyone has joyful memories of Christmas. As early as October, church groups and businesses would start calling Ms. Dianne Riley and Ms. Cynthia Batten wanting to share with children during the Christmas holidays. Residents and staff were eager to decorate and begin with decorations going up Thanksgiving week. On the first Sunday in December, the church comes alive with the 'Hanging of the Green' program. Every year the Woodmen of the World presented the annual Christmas party for the residents, sharing good food, and gifts. Santa would stop by to deliver goody bags. These bags included goodies from several church groups and individuals, all our special Elves. As you can tell, we celebrated well. Many memories were made and lives were positively influenced by the generosity of so many good people.

I know that we were trained to not get close with the residents, but it was hard not to get attached to some. All during the day, at night, when off duty, you can't help from praying for the residents.

When I first went to work at the Home, I had one resident that was in elementary school. Every day she (L.F.) went to school, Brownie (Campus Dog) would go to the bus stop with her, and when it got about time for her (L.F.) bus to run, Brownie would go, lay down, wait for her (L.F.) to get off the bus. They had a bond of love for each other. I had a lot of siblings in my cottage and they had siblings in other cottages on campus. I remember two sisters, they cried a lot, I would encourage them, prayed with them, and let them know that things would get better for them and it did. They were able to go back home. I cared a lot for all my residents that I worked with and for others that were at the Home whom I didn't work with but saw most every day. I remember one year it snowed. Wow, what a big snow! My cottage went out in the snow and I enjoyed being with the residents. We built a snowman, snow angels, rolled in the snow, went sledding down the hills, and snow balls were flying. There are so many memories from my life at the Home. I remember when some of the residents would be protective over me; they wouldn't let other residents talk or hug me. Those were some of the funny things I remember. I remember one Saturday I took the girls to the movies; the movie was so funny until I laughed so hard until I passed out for a minute. Every time after that, the girls would make sure they kept an eye on me if the movie was funny. The residents cared about the staff that they knew was there for them. I feel grateful for being able to touch so many lives at the Home.

As the years passed, I learned more and more how to be the best that I could be to help make the residents lives to be better, help them educationally, made sure of safety first, and always made sure they had nutritional meals every day.

There were residents that came back to visit FWBCH and they would come visit me if I was on shift. They would always say to me … "thank you for being there for me" … or … "you were a good house parent." Some would tell me to continue to be the good person you are, and some would say they loved me. Wow, those made me feel blessed to see the impact that was made from my services and help to the children at FWBCH.

There is so much that can be said about my career working at FWBCH. My life has been touched by so many people there, and I have touched so many people there as well. I would like to make mention of President/CEO Gary Lee, not trying to leave out many others there, but he really has touched my life in many ways. Someone else I am especially appreciative of is Ms.

Mary Ward. She has been working with the Home for 19 or 20 years this year. She has always been an inspirational figure for the residents at the Home and for the staff. She cared for residents, staff and me even when she was not feeling good.

I have met so many people of all walks of life and I have learned so much from being a part of FWBCH. I tried to always be on time, not miss days out of work unless it was important, be respectful to everyone, and just enjoy life as God gives it to me. I am really happy that God lead me to FWBCH on that lovely day in August 1999. In 2014, I decided to retire from work. My last day of work was December 31, 2014 after 15 years, 4 months of working at a great place.

Friends of Children's Day 2014
Recognized for 15 years of service
Joan Davis with President/CEO Gary Lee
Photo provided by Free Will Baptist Children's Home

Nana

Doris Maxine Wallace Warren
(Written by Allison Kiger)
1934–44

DORCAS HOME
OWOSSO, MICHIGAN

Her name is Doris Maxine Wallace Warren. My husband calls her Grandma. My children call her Nana. All the various and sundry children and folk she has loved on through the years including her church family call her Grandma Doris. When I think about her, in my head I call her Superwoman. I asked Nana if she thought that her difficult beginnings gave her a love for all the littles and losts and lonelies around her to which she said she thought that might have something to do with it. I told Jerry (J. Andrews Smith, *Cousins*) I would attempt to capture Nana's humble beginnings at the Dorcas Home. What this has turned into is a gift to us, her family, and has given us insight into why she is such an amazing and expansive woman for whom there is no such thing as a person who is unlovable.

She was born August 9, 1929 to Lowell and Arolla Lulu Wallace. Lowell was a barber in Vernon, Michigan. Her older brother Eugene wanted a brother to call Max hence Nana's middle name Maxine. When Nana was about 4 years old, she and her siblings were taken by the state and all given away. Her not

148

even yet a year old baby brother Dick was given to their grandparents in nearby Perry, Michigan. Her older brother Eugene went to an uncle. Nana and her baby sister Beverly were sent to live at the Dorcas Home in Owosso, Michigan. After just a few weeks at the home, three year old sister Beverly was adopted by a childless couple in Owosso.

Both her parents were heavy drinkers. Nana says that her mom liked to "run around if you know what I mean." Nana remembers her mom talking about traveling around with men on motorcycles. Arolla moved to Lansing, Michigan after leaving her husband. Nana's dad was heartbroken over "the mess." He was unable to take care of their four children. He didn't live very far from Owosso and tried to visit Nana at the home whenever he could. He was very poor and didn't own a car so he would borrow one from the neighbors. If Lowell only came to see Nana once a year, it was on her birthday which was always during the county fair to take her. During her time living at the Dorcas Home, Nana was able to have something like a half dozen or so overnight visits with her father and his second wife Mabel. She never stayed with her mother.

Doris and her mom

Nana rarely saw her mother. She was "too busy running after men". On one occasion when Nana was about 8 years old or so, her mother came with a gift in hand. Nana, still being rather babyish and plump in her figure, was the recipient of a girdle. Her mother made her put it on, and any time after when she visited, she made sure that Nana was wearing it.

Established in 1892 by Mrs. Ellen Quinn and the Dorcas Society, a group of charitable ladies, the Dorcas Home was originally a place where the wives of working men could leave their children while downtown. It was so successful that the ladies decided to broaden their scope and, in 1901, it became a home for "orphaned children and those unfortunate by having indigent or neglectful parents". The children could be placed there by their parents, the state, or the courts. It seems they housed

Doris at Dorcus Home

149

Dorcus Home
Photo published by the Argus-Press, Owosso, Michigan, July 2, 1976

10–12 children at any given time. Sometimes more. Nana said they also had two locked rooms where they would "jail" juvenile delinquents referred by the courts.

Nana doesn't remember many details about her years at the Dorcas Home. The first and clearest statement she made years ago the first time I asked was "IT WAS NOT A NICE PLACE!" She was nicknamed Dorie at the home. She and her sister were the youngest when they arrived. She does not remember her actual arrival. She doesn't remember who took her. She does remember being very upset in the courtroom, and the judge talking to her about why she needed to be taken from her parents.

Nana said that the husband and his wife who ran the home weren't too hard on them unless someone made the husband angry. One time he got angry at a young guy and backhanded him. The boy fell out the upstairs window and hit the ground. Nana said that all the children made a huge bunch of noise. The police came. The husband told the police that the boy was running and fell through the window. The boy was taken to the hospital, but Nana said she doesn't think he got much but bruises and scrapes for all that. She remembers that quite a few children were shoved down the stairs, and that "of course" the husband blamed it on the children. The children were sometimes locked in a closet for 2–3 days if they misbehaved. They might not get anything to eat but were allowed water. That was terrible for Nana because she was terrified of the dark and felt so closed in and, I suspect, very alone.

Nana did say that every single time the wife went into the toilet, the husband would stand outside and call in to her in funny voices. He would say things like "whachu doin' hunny? I mith you hunny." She said she and the other children would hide around corners to listen and would crack up! To this day she is still laughing about that. Nana said she saw him years later long after she was married with children of her own. He was walking ahead of her on the street. She said wanted to run right up to him and "boot him in the bottom".

There was a wonderful German lady housekeeper who worked at the home. Nana said she does not remember doing any heavy cleaning or dishes nor does she remember any of the other children doing them. It seems the housekeeper took care of most of the housework. All of the children loved that housekeeper. They loved watching her "tatting" which is a kind of knotted lace made by hand with a small shuttle. Tatted lace is used for fancy trim work and such. This lady made such beautiful things that she sold for more income. She would let the little ones lean on her knee and watch that amazing process. I could see it in Nana's eyes when she talked about her…that wonderful German lady gave her some of that love that baby Doris needed in her life.

Once or twice a year the housekeeper was allowed to make the children homemade potato chips. Boy, Nana said, were they good, and they looked forward to eating them. Nana never remembers drinking milk. She said that they always had food even though there never seemed to be enough or to be very healthy. There was never enough meat. She said they ate a lot of hash which she still loves to this day. Other types of meals were pasta, soups, or stews; the types of meals that could make food stretch. It seems there was a garden plot to provide some vegetables for their meals. The children never helped in the garden. That was left to the adults at the home. Nana has had consistent troubles with brittle weak bones that are easily broken. I asked her and she thought maybe it had something to do with poor nutrition while growing up.

There was the neatest Candy Store that had every kind of candy. It was called "Joe's". Once or twice a year, Joe would give each of the children a nickel, and someone would walk them to the store so they could shop with their nickels. Nana said they would look for what seemed like hours at the rows of wonderful candies. They stayed as long as the adult in charge would let them. That store was still there after Nana got married.

There was a 'Butternut Tree' between the sidewalk and road at the home. Nana loved those butternuts! She tried very hard not to get caught eating them , because she would be put in the closet. Even with the threat of the closet, she just could not help herself. All these years Nana has tried to find another butternut tree with no luck. I have tried to find butternuts for Nana through the years. What I discovered, much to Nana's chagrin, is that a parasite of some kind has mostly killed ALL the butternut trees in North America including that tree outside what used to be the Dorcas Home.

They didn't have many toys at the Dorcas Home: balls and also 3 swings. There were so many games to play, Nana said, that they didn't need purchased things to make do. They all really liked swinging on the swings. Their favorite thing was to drop themselves back so that they were hanging by their knees and swing as high as they could. So much fun! Fun that was not allowed however. Nana only fell to the ground once, and of course she was face down. Her face got messed up quite a lot, and she was put in the closet for that one. And even now as a dignified lady of 86 who depends on her walker to keep her steady, one can glimpse the unabashed joy that she felt and feels as she describes what being on that swing meant to her as a little child… FREE she said to me… so FREE!

Nana said that they got one pair of shoes per year and tough luck if you outgrew them even if it was winter. She said the clothes were all mission barrel-type worn out hand-me-downs. There were no bells to call the children. The adults in charge handled waking the kids up or call to meals. There were no mirrors or any decor to speak of in the home. Nana doesn't remember holidays of any kind ever being celebrated at the home. She does not remember receiving gifts or decorating for holidays or getting a birthday cake. Nana said that it was so difficult not having a family that maybe she just blocked out any holiday celebrations.

The children were all sent to the Owosso city school. When Nana was about in 2nd grade, her teacher sent her out to prune the bushes. She had not done anything wrong. The teacher said they just needed pruning. Nana said she didn't know how, but the teacher insisted she "get out there and get it done and you'll learn." Nana tried her best but butchered the bushes. Her teacher was furious, and Nana got a good chewing out.

They were encouraged but not required to attend church. Nana did attend a church which was within walking distance of the home. She doesn't recall the denomination. When she was about 6 years old, she accepted Jesus as her Savior and was baptised. She said the adults at the home said they were glad she was baptised. She didn't understand what it all meant at the time but recalls that she felt a real peace after that. She continued to attend that church until she was put into the work program at 10 years old.

Nana was never in foster care. When she was about 9 years old, she went to stay with a family in Lansing for what now would probably be considered respite care. Nana called it a vacation. She doesn't remember much about the family, but she does remember that the lady of the house gave her a book to read while she was there. At 9 years old Nana started to read and devoured "Gone with the Wind" in two weeks!

At the age of 10, the home began to farm her out to folks. Sometimes it was an afterschool job. Usually Nana had to live with the family. She was careful to explain that this was not a foster family program. This was a work program. There was no hand holding. She was put with strangers. There was no living with the family. She remembers having a pallet on the floor in the kitchen of one family. She said that the hardest part of the work

Doris at Dorcus Home

program is that she went to school with the children of those families. She would be cooking and serving them breakfast one minute and then later sitting next to them in school. Some of the people were kind, but Nana remembers that most were not. They were looking for cheap labor to help with chores.

When she was 14 years old, Nana left the home on her own. She had been working for a family in the community. The husband's brother tried to rape her. She succeeded in getting away. I could tell that even these many years later it is a painful memory for her. She said she decided she was not going back. She said that she never talked to anybody about it. She just walked out. She was certain that they must have kept up with her whereabouts somehow. She could not imagine that they would just let a child walk away. However, she never talked to anybody from the home afterward.

Nana went on to graduate from high school while she was working to support herself the best that she could with no home to call her own. She married wonderful Virgil "Pops" Warren and had a long and happy marriage of 66 years until the day he died. She had two daughters of her own. She said that her girls and later her grandchildren knew that she grew up in the Dorcas Home, however she did not talk about her experiences with them much at all. Nana felt blessed to have her own family and worked hard so that they could

Doris: high school senior picture

153

have a good life. She was grateful to have them "with" her. They did not have a lot of money early on. When her girls were very small, Nana was gifted with 20 yards of lime green fabric. She said it was not the prettiest fabric. She sewed two little outfits complete with ruffled britches and bonnets that she created from a pattern that she made herself. She said they were so precious. She continued to sew the girls' clothes throughout their growing up years. She was worried that the girls would feel different or stick out from their classmates because their mom made their clothes. However, a teacher told Nana that everyone was amazed by the girls' clothes. After that she felt better about it.

A couple of years into her marriage with Pops, her little sister Beverly, who had been adopted after a very short stay with Nana at the Dorcas Home, called Nana. Beverly and her adoptive parents had moved out of state. She and Nana had lost track of one another. Beverly told Nana that she wanted to move back to Michigan. Nana and Pops let her move in with them for about a year. She helped with housework and taking care of the babies. Most important, Nana and Beverly were able to establish a strong relationship that lasted until Beverly lost her fight with cancer in their maturity. Nana and her brother Dick maintained a close relationship through their adulthood until Dick died from cancer not so many years ago. Dick had been a very successful businessman, and Nana worked as his secretary and bookkeeper for years. They were never really able to find Eugene in his adulthood nor did they ever really find out how his life turned out. Nana still wonders from time to time. She did maintain a relationship with her mom and stepdad when she was an adult although it was uneasy at best. She also continued a loving relationship with her father and stepmother until they both died.

According to "Children Under Institutional Care and in Foster Homes: 1933 Dependent and Neglected Children Under the Care of Public and Private Institutions or Agencies, Not Including Juvenile Delinquents" published by the U.S. Department of Commerce Bureau of the Census (the year that Nana was put in the Dorcas Home), 16 children were under care at the Dorcas Home as of January 1, 1933. They received 24 children throughout 1933. During the entire year, 19 children were discharged or transferred. Nana guessed that there were 10–12 children at the home at any given time during her years there. I researched on the internet, and from what I can see, no one knows for sure how many children the Dorcas Home housed in total throughout the years. I did not contact the state of Michigan directly, however in my research I found that many folks have tried to obtain records without success. No one seems to have any official documentation or the original records aside from a handful of census reports and a few newspaper articles. The county probate court took over the Dorcas Home in 1948. It continued in its same capacity as a state run facility. Eventually, the house was falling apart and was condemned as a fire hazard. It was considered too costly to get it up to par. The Dorcas Home was closed April 30, 1959. The day the last child walked down the steps and on to a new home.

It seems that this reminiscing has also given Nana some time to process and reflect. She says that in the end, she has rather mixed feelings about her experiences at the Dorcas Home. She says that she had a bed and food. She was not beaten. She thinks maybe it was not such a bad place after all. While there, she was introduced to the church, and it is where her relationship with God began. A relationship that has held her steady throughout her adult years. She was the church librarian and Sunday School teacher most of her adult life. She and her husband worked to support their church always and still. They would take young folks new in the church under their wing and help them get settled in life. They often hosted meals (Nana being an excellent cook) for any number of folks. At any given time, they would have groups of kids of various ages at their house for slumber parties after their own kids were grown. Nana also has her own personal mission that she established years ago. Each week still, Nana writes letters and cards to shut-ins and folks who are sick or having a difficult time. She takes the time to write words of encouragement and love. One cannot be in Nana's presence without kisses and hugs. So many folks, especially my husband and my children and I, have been loved by this woman. Nana has touched us, and we have grown.

Note: Allison Kiger is the writer of NANA. She is the wife of Sahn Kiger. Sahn and Scott Warren are grandsons of Doris. Michele Warren is the wife of Scott Warren.

Allison is so very happily married to her best friend Sahn (who is grandson to Nana). They have one grown son, Ty, who wings it on his

Back: L-R Allison Kiger, Michele Warren
Front: L-R Sahn Kiger, Doris (Wallace) Warren, Scott Warren

own and two teen daughters, Morrigan and Maeve. They homeschool the two youngest and are extremely grateful for that opportunity. Their favorite activity is escaping into the mountains of Western North Carolina as a family and tent camping as often as possible... that is until they bought a homestead high up in the Blue Ridge Mountains with Allison's parents. Now they receive their dose of fresh air every single day while tending chickens, gardening, or splitting wood. Allison attended North Carolina State University and received her BA in English Literature. She does have a particular passion for the written and spoken word whether in daily conversation or in conveying information or in the magic of creating.

Hope in the
Heart of West Africa

Rev. B. Kris Kramer
1998–Present

MAMPONG BABIES' HOME
MAMPONG, GHANA

I remember sitting down in the grass with two children either side of me. They gazed into my eyes as though they had never seen a white skinned bald man before. There was love in their countenance. They were deeply curious. One boy wanted to wear my glasses. The other boy wanted to wear my baseball hat. We would enjoy this moment of innocent discovery together until the word juice box was shouted from the front porch. Then something special happened. One of the little boys went and grabbed a juice box and brought it to me. He wanted me to have juice too.

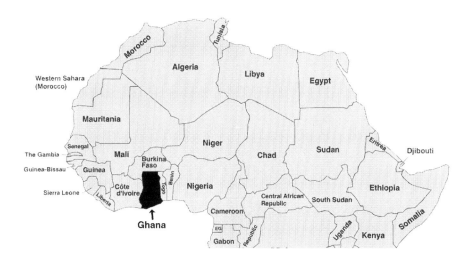

Such is the world of the Mampong Babies' Home. Children learn the concept of community and the practice of generosity from the beginning, and live with an interdependence which, for an outsider, is quite refreshing. The older children are often seen helping with the babies and there is a tenderness and love which pervades the compound. Of course later in the day I watched my two buddies get into a scrap about a toy which I had given one of them, sharing is always a challenge, but they quickly figured out how to make it work, which almost always involves sacrifice. As I left on a back road heading to Cape Coast, I found myself thinking about that little juice box, and the little hands that gave it to me. If those hands can take, bless, and share, then why can't mine? A question I still ponder today.

Mampong Babies' Home Campus

There are places of poverty around the globe and those affected most directly in those places are often children with no surviving parents. When 47 percent of the populations of sub-Saharan Africa live on approximately $1.90 per day, then there is hardly revenue left to feed and care for orphans. The end result of this lack of

resources is an undernourished
population. Recent studies suggest
that over 230 million people are
undernourished in sub saharan
Africa with a significantly increased
percentage amongst orphans. That
equates to 1 in 3 people in the
region being under nourished. It is
estimated that almost 590 million
people do not have electricity and
almost 740 million people lack
access to clean water. These realities
converge to create an environment
which makes childbirth a high risk

Inside Mampong Babies' Home

activity which in many cases leads to death. The presence and prevalence of
Malaria, Typhoid, Yellow Fever, and HIV compound life in this hostile place.
A baby born into this world, without supportive family or caregivers does not
stand a chance.

It is in the very heart of this reality that the Mampong Babies' Home lives
and seeks to embody hope in the heart of West Africa. Despite limited access
to electricity, there is work to expand solar power. There is a new well which
has only recently been dug and there is hope to provide running water to the
entire compound so that the water is safer and does not need be carried.

The Mampong Babies' Home is a bright light in the heart of West Africa.
It is a relatively young Orphanage/Babies Home having been founded in
1967 by a group of Anglican Nuns from the Sisters of the Holy Paraclete.
These sisters came to Ghana in the 1960's and quickly discovered infants from
mothers who died during or shortly after childbirth. The nuns were moved
by the reality that these children had no one to care for them. The discovered
children would be left alone for long periods of time. They felt lead to do
something and the result was the beginning of what is now the Mampong
Babies' Home.

The concept of the mission of this Baby Home has really not changed
in fifty years. The nuns are no longer there in the compound running the
mission, but there is a large team of folks who provide basic nutrition and 24
hour support to a population of children which has just exceeded 40 in 2017.

New Baby

These children have received love and support and in many cases introduction to their basic education. Staff clean and wash diapers without the luxury of running water, as well as cleaning and washing babies! There is limited time available to hold each of these babies and so in recent years teams of people have come to the MBH to help with the general duties, but more importantly to spend time holding the babies. It is not unusual during school holidays to see teams of university students with babies strapped to their backs in a traditional way, walking around the compound, holding bottles, and eliciting smiles and giggles.

Sometimes a mother will die and there isn't family to care for her child. The picture above was taken the day a baby arrived to Mampong Babies' Home. The new baby arrived from the North after the mother died the previous day, and staff immediately cared for this vulnerable infant.

In situations where both parents have either died or are destitute or mentally unable to care for children, the home seeks to support these children as they grow enabling those of age to attend primary school, and indeed creating a pathway to secondary education and beyond.

In cases where babies are abandoned at the home, every effort is made to locate the families and work with them for continued connection, support, and relocation. It is a difficult and demanding task in such a harsh environment.

Rev Kramer teaching at the elementary School

There are many babies who are born to fathers who are migrant laborers, whose wives die giving birth. Many feel unable to cope in the early months and years with a new baby and so the Mampong Babies' Home takes care of these children and endeavors to reunite them with their fathers and families in due course.

Frequently babies who arrive at the home sick and malnourished are restored to health and returned to birth families at an age when they are more robust, and able to feed and dress themselves (around the age of four). Their ability to help with simple chores makes them more likely to adapt to family lifestyles in harsh environments.

In 2013 the superintendent of the Mampong Babies' Home retired and an energetic 48 year old mother of three with a long history with the home was appointed as the new director. Her name was Maggie. She exuded love and her interaction with the children was as if each of these children were her own. In many ways they were and most of the children saw her as a mother figure. She worked tirelessly making the home a safe and clean place with food and

Superintendent Maggie Addai
Died March 24, 2017

resources. She travelled and tried to secure funds to ensure the future of the home, which meant finding ways to pay for needed expansion, new buildings, guest quarters, and upgrades such that there might be water sourced locally and one day available throughout the compound. She seemed so excited to have reached the milestone of the fifty year celebration week in April 2017. She had worked hard on all of the events and plans which culminated in one final party at the end of the week of events and worship services. Shortly after offering her kind thoughts and expressions of joy on this great occasion of 50 years of helping babies, Maggie's big heart would finally beat its last. She collapsed and was rushed to a local medical facility where she was pronounced dead at the age of 52.

These 40 children were faced with losing yet another mother. Friends, family, and

Rev. Kramer sharing Christmas with the older children

so many church people who had met her were left reeling at the thought that our fifty year joy could suddenly turn so dark and feel so bleak. As 2017 progresses there are people coming together to take Maggie's vision, which was a vision of a small group of Anglican Nuns in the 60's, and carry it forward with a new sense of purpose, and utilizing new technology and new methods of bring resources to these 40 children, giving the a chance at a good life.

In 1998 my path would cross with a missionary who was returning to the United Kingdom after a long stint serving in Ghana. He introduced me to this special place which rested at the heart of his work in Ghana, the Mampong Babies' Home. Over the subsequent 19 years my journey would cross the Atlantic many times, but each port of call and each place of ministry would bring new encounters with West Africans and repeated opportunities to send money to this Babies Home. In Nothern Virginia, in the shadow of George Washington's Mt Vernon estate, we planted a wonderful West African congregation, filled with hopeful Africans who found themselves away from much of their culture and in many cases, family. Upon leaving Northern Virginia to return to England, I made a promise to come to West Africa in the coming years and to continue my commitment to support the work of God there. I was truly blessed and inspired by these amazing pilgrims who I was able to journey with for a few short years.

My return to England and work at St. Edmund Hall, Oxford University as their Chaplain and Senior Welfare Officer would not cause me to forget this commitment which I had made the previous year, a commitment which was made after a church full of Africans clothed me and presented me with Kenti cloth and gifts.

Archbishop Daniel Yinka Sarfo

Our first major fundraising effort during my time at St. Edmund Hall was focused on the Mampong Babies' Home. It was a year of fundraising which seemed to capture the imaginations of the students culminating in the personal delivery, by their Chaplain, of the funds raised along with toys and goodies for the children including lots of Teddy Hall Teddy bears!

There was constant talk of moving this project and idea FORWARD, and one day this name became the moniker for taking this work forward to fruition.

I received an invitation to attend the installation and enthronement of the new Archbishop of Ghana, the Rt Rev Daniel Sarfo, someone whom I had first met and befriended in London many years before. I also discovered that my old colleague from London was back in Ghana and offered to personally escort me to the Mampong Babies Home to deliver funds and meet the superintendnent and other staff...and of course, the children. The minister of our church plant in Mt Vernon was now back in the suburbs of Accra, and so a visit to him would also be on the agenda as well as an invitation to visit and tour the Volta region staying with the Bishop of Ho, and preach in Cape Coast at the Seminary and to experience some of the amazing culture of this part of Africa as a guest of the Dean of the Seminary who is now the Bishop of Cape Coast.

Of course the heart of my pilgrimage was the time spent being a human jungle gym for 40 children who clambered to receive human touch and warm affection. Their buildings were simple, and there was no running water. Despite these limitations there were devoted carers looking after a large room full of small babies, and in fact a newborn arrived as I was sitting in the front room. Each child had a story of loss and poverty. Some of the children were orphaned and some had lost their mothers during childbirth. The Mampong Babies' Home offers hope and help to all of these children. It was amazing to finally see it in action. It helped me to see the faces of the children and to see the love in the eyes of those who care for them. I realized in that moment that support this work was worthwhile. I realized as I drove across the bumpy roads of Ghana that I would continue to move FORWARD....and do what I could to impact the lives of these children.

Presently we are seeking to do several things through the newly created charity FORWARD Now inc. to help with the Mampong Babies' Home. Our first project is raising money to expand the existing solar array and add a pump and filtration system to the newly installed well. We are hoping in 2018 to raise funds to complete the building of a guest house to house the visitors who come and participate in the baby holding program, a program which it is hoped can be expanded one this building with a shower and toilet is completed. The roof of this new building hopefully will provide power to the compound and to a new pump for the well. Finally, it is our hope to honor Maggie's memory by providing a bright and colorful playground in the middle of the compound, as a constant reminder of her love and joy. The playgrounds have already been sourced and the response has been remarkable! We now need funds to transport the equipment which has been donated and funds to pay local workers to reassemble the playground and safely install everything.

It is hoped that by the end of 2018, a pilgrimage program will be established which could enable the readers of this piece an opportunity to journey to Ghana and in fact go and stay in the Mampong Babies' Home. There is an expressed desire in these early days after Maggie left us to reimagine ways to build bridges between these children and the wider world. For those with a deep experience of knowing someone with a childhood in an orphanage, or someone who lived in an orphanage, this opportunity may become the greatest gift you could be given, as the potential for transformation is so rich and real for young children.

Rev. B. Kris Kramer

I am now living in Northern Florida and ForWARD now inc. is a registered 501c3 organization continuing to raise money to support the Mampong Babies Home. For those wishing to donate to the Home, please consider visiting **www.forwardnow.org** and making a secure tax deductible donation using the donate link on the web site.

Note
Rev. B. Kris Kramer was educated in a small Western North Carolina town, attended Mars Hill College (now University) and studied International Business with a minor in German language. He also played varsity Football and Tennis and was the president of the Campus Activity Board as well as a National Champion Bailey Mountain Clogger. After graduation Rev Kramer attended Duke University Divinity School where he studied theology and became an avid Duke Basketball fan. During a year away from graduate school Kramer lived in Taize monastery in France as well as traveling throughout Europe and exploring the geography and variety of humanity. This journey ended on the small island of Iona where he would meet and later marry his wife. After a further three years of postgraduate study at Oxford University, Kramer

was ordained and deacon and then priest in the Church of England. He then served parishes in Surrey, Central London, Southwestern Virginia and Northern Virginia before returning to England to serve as part time Chaplain and Senior Welfare officer at St. Edmund Hall, of Oxford University as well as serving as a part time Fellows Chaplain of Magdalen College, Oxford. Rev Kramer completed a Chaplaincy training program (Clinical Pastoral Education) in Jacksonville, Florida in 2016 and made a decision to devote his time to furthering the work of Forward inc. as well as supporting his wife who is in ministry in a 5000 member church and continuing to help raise his four children who are now 21, 19, 17, and 15.

3

Jerry Smith Papers

University Archives
Free Will Baptist Historical Collection

Moye Library
University of Mount Olive
Mount Olive, North Carolina

Photo Courtesy of University Public Relations/Marketing
University of Mount Olive

Gary Fenton Barefoot, MSLS, Curator

FWB Historical Collection/University Archives
Moye Library
University of Mount Olive
Mount Olive, North Carolina

Sometimes, some things must be written and preserved for posterity and Jerry Smith continues to do just that in the sequel to his book, *The Family*. It was from a revelation some thirty years ago when Jerry wanted to show his sons something about the history of orphanages in North Carolina while visiting the Museum of History in Raleigh, N.C., that he realized there was "no such information about any orphanage on display in the museum." Out of that visit, the idea of *The Family* was birthed.

As the Curator of the Free Will Baptist Historical Collection, I am keenly aware of the need to collect and preserve all aspects of a denomination's history. The Free Will Baptist Children's Home is a ministry of the Original Free Will Baptist Church. I have been involved in both the organization and development of what has become the best collection of historical materials on the Original Free Will Baptists to be found anywhere. However, it should be emphasized that George Stevenson, Jr. who was reared in the FWB Children's Home (formerly FWB Orphanage), Middlesex, N.C., was without question the most important person who helped establish the FWB Historical Collection in 1957. He was, even as a college student at the time, most knowledgeable about the history of Free Will Baptists and continued until his death in 2009 to help develop the Collection through his research, his writings, his gifts of materials, and his financial support.

With his professional background in social work, Jerry Smith, also an alumnus of the FWB Children's Home, has over the years written and published material on the social dynamics of those reared in substitute care facilities; examples being *I Have Hope* (1978), *The Family* (2010), and numerous articles in the Tazewell (VA) *Free Press* and other publications. As important as his written records are—"sometimes, some things **must** be written"—Jerry has given permission to the University of Mount Olive for his work along with other of his physical records to be preserved in the Jerry Smith Collections, FWB Historical Collection/University Archives, Moye Library, University of Mount Olive. He has also been instrumental in bringing together denominational and Home officials as well as the FWB Historical Collection Curator in an effort to stress the importance of cooperation in preserving the history of the Home. Because of his efforts, the Home now has, though in its infancy, a collection/museum of its own, housed in the Chapel on the campus. President/CEO Gary Lee, the Reverend Ray Wells, Jerry and I met on numerous occasions to plan and give direction for birth of the collection/museum on campus at the Home.*

The Free Will Baptist Historical Collection, however, because of its age and its more comprehensive nature, has among its holdings a wealth of information about the Orphanage/Children's Home, including minutes of the sponsoring body (Convention of Original Free Will Baptists), papers and records of former Orphanage/Home superintendents/boards, and pictorial and recorded materials as well. The Collection is also the repository for the official records of the Orphanage/Home itself, in microform and electronic formats. Although the history of the FWB Children's Home may not be represented in our state museum of history, it can be found well-documented and preserved at the Home and in the Free Will Baptist Historical Collection in the Moye Library, University of Mount Olive. Jerry has helped make this happen.

Moye Library, University of Mount Olive

Many of Jerry's newspaper publications are preserved at the University of Mount Olive. Here are few of his writings about children and staff from children's homes/orphanages in North Carolina and Tennessee.

Thank you, Jerry.

Gary Fenton Barefoot

---

* *See Appendix*

She's Heavenly,
But the Thunder?

Jerry Smith with his sister Nancy
1949–60

FREE WILL BAPTIST CHILDREN'S HOME
MIDDLESEX, NORTH CAROLINA

Published: November 6, 1996

Nancy and I are twins, and we were admitted to the orphanage in 1949. My sister Nancy is one of the great women of all times and no one is more caring and committed to all that is good.

The Bible tells us that two men walked on water—Jesus and Peter. Some may also know of a lizard living in Mexico and Central America commonly know as the Jesus Lizard that can walk on water as well. If anyone else can perform that feat, it would be my sister. She is my solid rock and I love her more than bees love honey.

Sometimes we take "annual weekends" together without our spouses. One recent weekend, we revisited our childhood, caught up on family news and simply visited. She lives in another state and we do not get to see each other often. It was a time of laughter and a few tears.

As mentioned earlier, Nancy and I are twins and we seem to have a closer relationship than other brothers and sisters. It is a special relationship that I cherish and value.

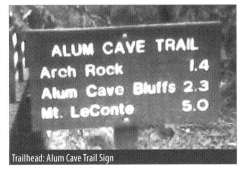
Trailhead: Alum Cave Trail Sign

On this particular weekend we spent the first night in Gatlinburg, Tennessee, the 24 hour/7day a week/365 days a year state fair of the Smoky Mountains. We spent our second night in a cabin on Mount Le Conte in the Great Smokies National Park. We had no running water or electricity, and we gratefully escaped the normal hustle and bustle of everyday life. We backpacked the five mile Alum Cave Trail up Mount Le Conte to an altitude of 6,500 feet. The trail was virtually straight up, and it took us more than four hours.

The day was gorgeous with fall colors and clear skies, though we saw very little wildlife except a few chipmunks, squirrels, and birds. We spent our time walking with the sounds of nature. We stopped for lunch at an overlook, and as we dined on pork and beans, crackers, and lemonade, we gazed contentedly over miles of God's beautiful creation.

I looked at Nancy and told her I was glad she was my sister. She responded in kind, commenting she too was glad to have me as her brother. It was a unique and spiritual time together.

Cabin #10

We arrived at our lodgings for the night, Cabin #10, and there met a few other guests and the reception crew, who soon went about preparing a lovely meal for us all, replete with wine. After dinner, we all climbed to an overlook called "Cliff Top" to watch the sunset. Nancy had her camera, and we enjoyed what was probably the most beautiful sunset I've witnessed. The colors were magnificent with radiant shades of orange and red against a backdrop of a clear blue sky.

On returning to our cabin in the dim of darkness, we lit the oil lamp and talked about the day's activities, and that sensational, wonderful sunset. In a short while Nancy said she getting tired but wanted to continue our conversation, so she climbed into her lower bunk while I stayed put nursing my wine. I realized again our importance to each other and the neatness of our relationship.

My sister grew quiet as I talked of the beauty of the mountains, of family, children, and past experiences. Soon I began to hear small sounds from her in the lower bunk. First I thought she was saying something, but then I realized I was hearing the rumblings of deep sleep.

Then without warning, the quietness of the cabin was engulfed with the sound of my sister snoring! Never before had I heard a woman snore, and now the woman who might one day walk on water was—unbelievably—snoring! Well, she got louder and louder. I tapped on her bed and it did quiet her down, but a short while later she started up again. I tapped her bed again, but she kept snuffling away. Finally on one of my taps, she woke up and asked if I had hit her bed.

"Who, me?" I replied. I did not have the heart to tell her she was snoring louder than any man I had ever heard.

I then climbed up into my upper bunk and proceeded to experience a night I've never forgotten. For hours, I was kicking the bed post and making sounds in efforts to stop the onslaught of sounds. I even threw a hiking boot across the room! The next morning I crawled down sleepily from my bunk. As we had coffee and breakfast, Nancy remarked that she had had a fitful night and didn't get much sleep, but that every time she woke up, all was quiet in our cabin. Then she said I slept the quietest of any man she knew. I smiled as I set my coffee cup down. I responded that that night was one I'd never forget, and that I had never heard sounds like the ones that came out of her mouth. She smiled saying, "Was it that bad?" Kidding with Nancy, I told her I would leave Mt. Le Conte with a new name for her, "Thunder Jaws," and that she may have tarnished my image of women forever.

Nancy smiled again, knowing she will always be my special sister and that I would always love her better than bees love honey!

Rising Above the Past

Walter Rufus Whitt
1945–52

HOLSTON UNITED METHODIST HOME FOR CHILDREN
GREENEVILLE, TENNESSEE
Published: November 17, 1999

With a gleam on his face, Rufus discussed his craft and the various types of wood he uses. Walnut is his favorite, although oak, cherry, maple, pecan and persimmon are often used in many of the furniture pieces he constructs.

Rufus is an accomplished furniture maker, specializing in styles of the 1860–70s. He takes pride in his reproductions. You can usually find Rufus at his shop, Time Past Antiques in Morristown, Tennessee. Visiting his shop, you'll see his work displayed and you'll often find Rufus talking with someone about furniture. If he doesn't have it, he'll make it for them. He's proud of 100,000 feet of wood he has stored up from years of cutting. Rufus has kept records of the dates all the different woods were harvested.

At age 7, Rufus Whitt, his three brothers, and a sister were admitted to the Holston Orphanage in Greeneville, Tennessee. They were placed there by the Salvation Army. He recalls his first day at the orphanage: *"I cried all day and night. I missed my mother. The second day I cried all night. It hurt that I had to leave my mother, two brothers and three sisters."*

Rufus was at the orphanage from 1945–1952, and saw his mother once during that time. One of his brothers left the orphanage and joined the Marine Corps; another brother was sent to a reform school, while his youngest brother and sister stayed in the orphanage until they completed high school.

Holston Orphanage founded in 1895

Rufus's father was a miner, and died in a mine explosion. He recalled hearing the whistle blowing, signalling an accident. "My uncle was a deputy sheriff," said Rufus. *"He came and told mother that our father and other miners had been killed in the mine at Boissevain, Virginia. We lived nearby in the Burnard town community. All of the 15 miners had separate funerals. I remember tiptoeing up to the casket and looking at y father. He did not have any shoes on. After the funeral he was buried in the Tipton Cemetery. This accident changed my life forever."*

Rufus Whitt as a child

The Whitt family lived in the company house where Rufus was born. His father was paid for work with "script," which was a voucher to purchase food and supplies from the company store. After his father's death, there was not enough income for his mother to care for the ten children, ranging in ages from 5 to 15. She took odd jobs to keep the family together. Rufus recalled not having food in the house, and how he stole a bag of turnip greens from a neighbor. It was served for breakfast. For dinner that night they had boiled cornbread and sugar. He admitted taking apples from a tree for food. The mining company did nothing to help them. Unable to find means to support the family, Rufus mother moved the family from Boissevain to Kingsport, Tennessee. There the family lived in the basement of his mother's sister house for two years. Unable to provide the support needed for her children, Rufus mother agreed that the five youngest children be placed in the orphanage.

As Rufus and I talked, I inquired if he had visited the place where his family lived when the mine exploded? I vividly remember his facial expression changing as he began to talk: *"Later in life, I went back to Boissevain and saw the houses lived in by those that ran the mine. I was angry and wanted to burn them down. The house where we lived was no longer there, but the old company store is still standing. Today when I return, I start getting depressed going to Tazewell, Virginia from Hungry Mountain State Park. As I start going over the mountain and down the hillside to Tazewell County, the more depressed I'd get and the more I wanted to leave. I don't know why I go back, and have only returned six times since mother moved the family."*

Rufus gives his father, mother, family, and the orphanage (now called Holston United Methodist Home for Children) credit for his values and his success. He is unwavering with his feelings that life would not be what it is today if he had not gone to Holston Orphanage. *"They gave me a chance,"* he said. *"While there, for unknown reasons to me, I was passed from the sixth to the eight grade. I graduated from high school and attended college for several years before enlisting in the army, where I stayed for seven years. I have six children and they all graduated from the University of Tennessee. I am so very proud of them."*

Today Rufus is an accomplished furniture builder. He was recently elected President of the Alumni Association at Holston United Methodist Home for Children. Like so many people with a difficult and often painful childhood, Rufus found a way to rise above the past to become who he is today.

As I was gathering my notes and preparing to leave, Rufus turned to me and begin reminiscing about a conversation he'd had with his father. He said,

Holston Orphanage Cemetery

"Jerry, my father was sick in the bed and I stood at his bedside and he said to me, 'Rufus, I want you to make good in this life. I know you can do it.'"

Rufus made good in his life. His father, the coal miner from Boissevain, Virgina, must be very proud of him.

Note: Walter Rufus Whitt died September 20, 2010. His cremation remains are buried in Holston Orphanage Cemetery on the campus of Holston United Methodist Home for Children, Greeneville, Tennessee. The first child from the home to be buried in the cemetery was in 1900.

Additional thoughts from Rufus's Daughter, Kimberly

Note: While visiting the campus of Holston United Methodist Home for Children, Greeneville, Tennessee on March 15, 2017, Kimberly Lindsay met Jerry Smith for the first time. After talking with Jerry, she ask him to visit the Orphanage Cemetery with her to visit her father's grave. Before going to the cemetery, he gave Kimberly the article he had written about her father on November 17, 1999. Later she read it and this was the first time she had read the story about her father. Jerry told Kimberly the writing would be in his book Cousins, *which was soon to be published. She asked to include her story about her father Walter Rufus Whitt with the article published in 1999. This is Kimberly's story.*

◇◇◇◇◇◇◇◇◇◇◇◇◇◇◇◇◇◇◇◇◇◇◇◇◇◇◇◇◇◇◇◇◇◇◇◇◇◇

My Dad, Walter Rufus Whitt, who was orphaned at age 7, enjoyed being a family man. He had six children, three girls and three boys. He was very proud of all of us. He had a beautiful wife as well. My parents were a handsome couple. They looked better than Ken and Barbie. Maybe they looked even better than George Clooney and his wife, Amal.

Kimberly's parents Joan and Rufus

My dad kept us busy and would not allow us to be lazy. We had our own chores to do and had to look after one another. The daughters had feminine chores—cooking, house-keeping, and baby-sitting. The sons had masculine chores—yard work and lots of it. I remember the boys had to keep the yard mowed, keep the woods close to the back yard mowed, and they had to rake the leaves. We had lots of trees in our yard.

We were expected to do well in school, and all of us graduated from the University of Tennessee, Knoxville, Tennessee, as a result. Education was very important to my dad, and both my sons, my dad's grandsons, attended the University of Tennessee in Knoxville, Tennessee.

His grandson, Jonathan H. Lindsay, will graduate from University of Tennessee in August 2017 with a Ph.D in Biochemistry and Cellular and Molecular Biology, with an expertise in Neuroscience. Jonathan has received a job offer and will be a Neuroscience researcher at Virginia Commonwealth University in Richmond, Virginia beginning fall 2017. I know my dad is very proud of Jonathan.

Kimberly on her wedding day with her father

The month my dad knew he was dying, we talked on the phone; and he asked me to do several things for him, and one thing he wanted me to do was make sure Jonathan finished his education. He also asked me to take care of my son Tate who had become seriously ill.

At that time, we did not know Jonathan would go this far! Before my dad passed in 2010, Jonathan graduated Magna Cum Laude with a Bachelor of Science degree majoring in Biological Sciences, minoring in Biochemistry and Cellular and Molecular Biology. He then received a full assistantship to study his Ph.D in Biochemistry and Cellular and Molecular Biology. Jonathan decided within a few years of his Graduate Studies that Neuroscience would become his expertise.

Now, my dad's grandson is Jonathan H Lindsay, Ph.D in Biochemistry and Cellular and Molecular Biology whose expertise is Neuroscience. My father has a neuroscientist in the family!

My dad enjoyed holidays, especially Christmas. When I was very young, he had to wake us up for Christmas morning festivities. As I grew older, I remember one Christmas, my dad dressed as Santa. There was a Christmas party going on in the home, and when the front door opened and there stood a stranger with a white beard in a red suite with a crazy matching red hat boasting a big, "HO! HO! HO!" I was frozen! I thought the whole thing was madness, and I ran to the furthest corner in the furthest closet in the house. I was going to hide in the closet until the tall man with the white beard and crazy red suit and matching red hat, left.

However, my dad comes after me, pulling me from the closet while I'm screaming and crying the entire time. I wasn't going with him! And, he wasn't taking me with him! I was terrified! Finally, My dad took off the white beard and red hat to show me he was the Santa. That took a lot to calm me down. Needless, he never played Santa in front of me again. It wasn't worth watching his daughter have a nervous breakdown over.

My dad had the energy of an energized bunny. He always had a project going on. And, as soon as that project was finished, he had another project planned. However, he finished all his projects. I don't know if my dad knew he was setting an example or not, but like my dad, I have new projects and I finish them all. I like that I learned that from him.

There were two huge projects he planned, and thank god I did not have to participate. My parents bought the adjoining property to our yard, and the land had to be cleared. Guess who got to clear the land and level it? My brothers!! I loved being a girl in my family. All I had to was cook dinner for eight family members in an air-conditioned home. I was a pampered girl from early on.

After the land was leveled, there was a brick wall to be built from one end of the property to the other. And, guess who had to help with that project? My brothers!! I am grateful I did not have to be outside and sweat in that heat!

However, once that wall was built and the land leveled, dad's next project was to grow the father of all gardens. And guess who got to help can all that garden-grown food? Me!

I could not believe I was canning food that could be bought in a store. It was like a lesson from an Extension agent's office. I honestly believe I sweated more in that hot kitchen canning those vegetables than my brothers did while they were working outside in the heat of the sun building that brick wall. However, my dad and I talked a lot about food that summer. He made homemade sauerkraut that I simply loved! I guess I ate all of it. He taught me how to use a canner. We canned okra and tomatoes together. I thought that was a crazy combination of vegetables, but, I liked it. And, I learned to like succotash! And, only God knows how many beans I broke.

My father loved to teach. I must have been his favorite subject. Or, maybe it was my age. Any how, my dad taught me how to cook.

Another one of his crazy projects was The Chickens. Dad worked the midnight shift at Southern Railroad at the Bulls Gaps switchyard.

It was a nice spring morning when I woke up. The kitchen windows were open, and I heard chickens clucking! So, I looked out the window and saw a trap of live chickens. I asked mom what was going on She had no answer. When I came home from school, all the chickens were gone. There was no evidence of them anywhere. No feather, nothing. My dad had disposed of the waste.

I knew they had to be somewhere, so I set out to look for them. I suspected they were in the freezer. When I opened the freezer, there were the chickens with no feet and no heads, all neatly packed side-by-side in plastic bags in the freezer. I was stunned! I knew I would not be eating those chickens.

I felt guilty for having those feelings, because I knew how hard my dad worked to preserve the food for us, but for the life of me, I could not eat a dead chicken I knew was alive before it was dead.

Walter Rufus Whitt, U.S. Army

I remember when we lived in Clarksville, Tennessee and dad was in the Army, stationed at Fort Campbell, Kentucky. He dug a hole in the back yard. I don't know the reasons for this, but as I ran from the front of the house to the back, there my dad was standing in a hole in the back yard. It was like a cavern. I really thought my dad had lost his mind, but I believe the ground caved-in and for some reason, my dad had to jump down in the cavern and stand on the boulder in the hole. I will admit, sometimes, my dad's behavior scared me. But, my dad was an adventurous sort and did whatever he felt like doing. This project involved filling in that hole with dirt.

In the 1980's, he began his wood working projects. My dad was a cabinet maker, and he made lots of furniture, he made special pieces for all of his six children. I loved how he dated and signed each piece. Deep inside my soul, that told me my dad did not want to be forgotten. I asked my son, Tate, what he remembered most about my dad? Tate said, "Every Christmas he would take us to his workshop and show us the furniture he was making." My father loved to talk. Everyone was an audience.

I have to say, he was a wonderful grandfather as well. He begged me to call him whenever I went into labor so he could be there when his grandchildren were born. He was as gentle with my children as he was with me when I was little. When my oldest son, Tate, broke his arm at preschool, my dad shows up later that evening to visit Tate to see how he was. I have a picture of the three of them—Dad, Tate and Jonathan. Tate had a big smile on his face that grandpa had come to see him.

I remember once falling on the gravel and bloodied my knee. I ran indoors, and my dad took me to the bathroom and sat me down on the edge of the bathtub. For some crazy reason, I start sliding backwards into the bathtub and cried more. I look up for my dad's help. He turns to see what's happening, and begins to smile and starts to laugh. That's how he was with me. If I was upset, he would first smile, then laugh and say something to reassure me I was going to be okay.

My dad was a tall man. Sometimes he scared me, but I knew I could trust him because he had a kindness and a gentleness about him that made him trustworthy and not a tall man to be afraid of.

Dad loved current events. In 1972, I saw Mark Spitz win 7 gold medals in swimming and from 1969 to 1972, I saw all the Apollo

L-R: Shannon, Paul, Missy, Kimberly, Mark, Greg

landings, and I even watched President Nixon resign!

It never failed that whenever my dad yelled, "Kim, come down here and see this! This is history!" I dropped whatever I was doing, and I ran to the TV to watch the event. Incidentally, I think the swimming events made a lasting impression on me.

I married a champion swimmer. Both our sons were champion swimmers. And, one of them achieved All-American status in swimming! And, I never miss the Summer Olympics swimming events because my dad encouraged me to watch them.

Whenever I speak about my dad, I say he is the strongest man I have ever known. He also had an innate ability to solve problems. Somehow, he instinctively knew what to do.

He gave his six kids a lot of freedom, only calling on us whenever he needed our help or our chores needed tending. Both our parents were strict. We may have sassed our mother, but we did not cross our father.

The kids in the neighborhood had a chant about my dad, "Ole' man, Whitt, thinks he's tough." You better believe he was tough. And, you did what he said or he "knocked you into the middle of next week!" He had the mouth of a sailor, "Don't give me that shit off the wall!" Remember, he was a military man. He never talked to me like that, only my brothers.

I loved my dad for many things, but mostly because he faced his fears when he was a young boy. He faced his forever changed life with sadness, loneliness, depression, fearfulness, but grew into a fearless man. He was a homeless child, and I'm sure scared to death, but he faced his challenges and owned up to his dad to make something of himself.

My dad and mother gave us six kids a nice home with nice furnishings and food to eat. We lived in nice neighborhoods, had nice clothes, had nice friends, had a nice education, and grew into nice adults.

I was 8 months pregnant with my first child when my dad told me he was so poor as a child that he had to steal turnips for food for breakfast. He laughed it off as if it was normal. That night, I went home and cried because my dad went hungry as a child and I knew my children, his grand-children, would never go hungry.

Before I end, my dad was a mysterious man. There is so much about him and his family I do not know. I don't know his parents; I don't know his 10 brothers and sisters. I didn't know he had that many siblings until I read an article about him recently. So, in a way, I feel like an orphan discovering they have a family.

My father was a very independent man. I liked that in him. I liked that he instinctively knew what to do in any situation. I liked that he solved the problem instead of dumping the situation on someone else. One thing my dad was not, was lazy.

I am that way also. I innately know how to solve problems. My ex-husband is an architect. He once complimented me by telling me I was the smartest person he knew. I was stunned by that comment. He continued, "You can figure anything out. Those engineers, contractors etc., can't solve anything!" I am convinced that I inherited my dad's DNA to innately figure it out.

My father lived up to his father's challenge: "I want you to make good in this life. I know you can do it." I asked my son, Tate, to read the article, 'Rising above the Past' by Jerry Smith. Tate said to me, "Rufus did make good in life."

I know my father and the grandfather I never knew are proud they have a grandchild and great-grandchild with a Ph.D in Biochemistry and Cellular and Molecular Biology who will challenge neuroscience research and discover information that will improve the lives of everyone.

I have a great father. He is tall, well-groomed, smart, and athletic. He taught me many things. I have always been very proud of my dad. And, I am glad I did not let him down and saw to it that Jonathan completed his education. And, incidentally, I took very good care of Tate, and he is now much, much better.

My dad set the standard of excellence for me.

Kimberly Whitt Lindsay

A Special Santa

Captain Elvin Stone
1946–47

KENNEDY BAPTIST CHILDREN'S HOME
KINSTON, NORTH CAROLINA

Published: December 13, 2000

At no time of the year is a fat man so adored, so sought after, so talked about and so talked to as during the Christmas season. This is the fat man's time of the year. Dressed in red with his snow white beard, the fat man listens to children and brings delighted smiles when he laughs. The season is not over till the fat man sings—Happy Christmas to all, and to all a good night.

Elvin Stone is a jolly ol' man. He has twinkles in his eyes, cheeks like roses, and dimples how gleeful. He does not ride a sleigh pulled by eight male reindeers, but he can be seen at the end of the parade riding a sleigh on a trailer bed pulled by a John Deere tractor. He drives a pickup truck.

Yes, he is the fat man, dressed in red with a snow-white beard and waving to the satisfaction of all.

It all started about 25 years ago when I asked him if he would be Santa for foster children and children with disabilities. Since then, he has dressed up in his red suit as many as thirty times some Decembers. Once Elvin was the town's Santa, but due to high demands has had to cut back on his activities.

183

Captain Elvin Stone

Elvin was a captain in the Wilson Fire Department, and was also the fire prevention supervisor. He was in and out of foster homes to inspect for fire hazards and to teach fire prevention. Social workers noticed him going beyond his duty; it was more than just a job to him. Elvin took special interest in foster homes and the children. He had empathy for the kids and a special relationship with them. When I looked into his background, I found that he had two sisters who were put into foster care, and he himself had been placed for a time at the Kennedy Baptist Children's Home in Kinston, North Carolina.

Everyone loved Elvin. Social workers adored him and when he was around there was always happiness, laughter, and the spirit of Christmas. It didn't hurt that he had a twinkle in his eyes, dimples, and an infectious laught. Elvin is very sensitive and caring, and just a genuinely nice guy. I was pleased when he agreed to be Santa for the children under care of the Wilson County Department of Social Services, Wilson North Carolina. I knew he was the right man for the job as he bellowed out Ho! Ho! Ho! as he entered the room carrying gifts for the foster children. He would talk to each child sitting on his lap. I looked at the social workers and they looked at me, and we knew we had us a Santa for the children—perhaps for many years.

After Christmas one year, while having coffee and eating chocolate cookies with Elvin, I asked if he thought of any special children he'd met over the years during the Christmas season. Without hesitation he shared memories of certain incidents with some special children:

- "The little boy that wet in my lap. I never acknowledged it and only he and I know it happened;
- A child, age three, that had Spina Bifida lay on a board beside me while I talked with other children;
- The feeling of blind children touching my face;
- The single mom with a Down's syndrome child;
- The two sisters ages seven and fifteen in an orphanage. The younger sister told me that her sister was having a hard time, but she was making the best of it. She told me the only thing she wanted for Christmas was happiness;

- A boy, age four, who never smiled and could not speak. Social workers put him in my lap and he started smiling and smiled for a long time. He was so happy with Santa that he was brought back twice more to sit on my lap. He had a beam on his face the last time he left me. That night he died. Later his parents told me how happy Santa had made him the last day of his life. That really touched me;
- On the humorous side, when I asked one three-year-old boy what he wanted for Christmas, he looked at my sack of gifts and asked to see the monster.

I asked Elvin why he liked being Santa. He said it's the time of the year when people are really outgoing, like they should be all year. Maybe it was from his time in the orphanage, or maybe it was because of his sisters being in foster care, but he always had a tremendous spirit of happiness and caring about people. Elvin feels Christmas is the one time of the year he can be more free to outwardly express this care. He really took his role as Santa seriously. He told me, "It's the genuine reindeer bells from Alaska and the Ho! Ho! Ho! that does the trick and sets me apart from all those 'fake' Santa's."

The most lovable Santa I've ever met.

Backpacking in Great Smoky Mountains National Park

Note: Elvin Stone was admitted to Kennedy Home at age 6. He was Santa for the town of Kenly, North Carolina Christmas parade for more than twenty years.

Blackie of the North Woods

Elder Cummings
1876–1963

FREE WILL BAPTIST CHILDREN'S HOME
MIDDLESEX, NORTH CAROLINA

Published: November 21, 2001

Walking through the Marsh Swamp Church Cemetery in Wilson County, North Carolina, near my childhood home, I came across his tombstone. I was enthrall and wrapped up with childhood memories of him. Much remains a mystery, and I wanted to know more.

Why was he called Blackie? Where did he come from?

Discovering his past would not be easy. After all, anyone that knew of him would not be a 'spring chicken.'

ELDER MOSES
LAFLAVER CUMMINGS
TRAVELING EVANGELIST
& HOME MISSIONARY
JUNE 2, 1876
DEC. 26, 1963

KNOWN AS "BLACKIE
OF THE NORTH WOODS"

Marsh Swamp Church Cemetery
Free Will Baptist Church, Rock Ridge Community

"Yes, I remember Mr. Cummings. When he was placed in the rest home, I was assigned to clean out his closet. He had black and white striped prison clothes," said Martin Morris (1952–59), age 59. *"He was pretty intelligent."*

"When they called on him to bless our food at dinner, he always prayed a long prayer," remembered Winifred Winstead (1944–52), age 67.

"I remember when I was about age 10 seeing him preaching under a pecan tree. He wore a round, black-felt hat, black suit, white shirt, black shoes, and a black bow tie," recalled Jacob Lane (1946–59), age 61.

Sudie Mixon (1948–59), age 83, recalled, *"Mr. Cummings walked with dignity. He did not have good hearing. When he died, a group of concern citizens pooled their money to bury him."*

Mary Mitchell (1945–50 and 53–88), age 74, remembered, *"He died in a rest home, but lived at the orphanage a short time before his health deteriorated. He kept his clothes in his car and dirty clothes were cleaned at the dry cleaners. He told me once that he deserted his wife and two sons. He did not blame his sons for having nothing to do with him. Mr. Cummings made his living preaching. He would stand on street corners, wearing black and white stripe prison clothes as he preached the gospel and sold his book for 50 cents."*

Mary gave me her copy of his, 32-page paperback book titled *Avenues Leading to Crime*, copyright 1947.

Blackie's mother, a schoolteacher, moved from America to Canada in 1848. His father was a blacksmith. Their first child was a "brown-eyed, black-haired" girl named Unita. Four years after her birth, during a blizzard, her father—late for dinner for the first time, "staggered into their once happy home all covered with snow and blood. On his way home that night, the faithful husband and father had met up with the tempter in the form of a friend, who persuaded the curly-headed smithy to

Blackie

stop into a public-house and have a social drink, which awoke within him a terrible appetite inherited from his ancestors."

Unita's father continued his drinking binge for many months. "The faithful wife and mother never ceased to pray for her erring husband; and to her surprise, one night he returned home sober, and knelt by the side of his wife and girl and gave God his heart. He commenced life over again by establishing the family alter in the home, and learned to love and serve God better as the days passed by."

The family moved to rural northern Canada, where they lived in a log cabin and Unita's father became a blacksmith for farmers and lumberjacks. "God gave them the desire of their hearts, a beautiful baby boy, with jet-black hair and big brown eyes. The lumber-jacks named him Blackie."

During Christmas 1878, while talking of their children's future, the parents had a premonition. "As they gaze into the fire, a vision seems to rise out of the flames. The father saw his boy grown up to manhood with the terrible appetite for drink leading him captive, and he shudders as he thought of how near that awful appetite came to wrecking his own life. The mother sees her Gypsy ancestors, with their wagons and tents and their roving, restless spirit, and she shudders at the thought of her boy inheriting the wanderlust. The desire of the parent's hearts is that he may grow up to be a preacher of righteousness."

In 1881, Blackie's mother died from the "Great White Plague." Near death, with tears in her eyes, she asked for Blackie. She handed him her Bible saying:

"Take it, my darling, and when you can read you will find a message in its back pages from a dying mother to her only boy. You will also find within its pages a chart from your mother's God that, if followed, will lead you to where she is going soon."

"After those few words, Unita lifted little Blackie up so that he could kiss his mother's thin pale cheeks. She smiled as he backed out of the room holding the little Bible in one hand and waving the other at the bestest mother he had ever knew."

Blackie's father remarried. In the winter of 1889, an epidemic called "la grippe, very similar to the flu" swept across Canada. His father was dying, and Blackie, age 13, hooked up the faithful old horse to the sleigh and drove many miles to the city for the family doctor. It was a cold night and he stopped at a hotel to get warm. "He went to the sitting room, just off of the barroom.

Lumberjacks spied Blackie all covered with snow shivering and ordered the bartender to fix him several hot toddies. Not realizing it might make him intoxicated, they wrapped blankets and furs around him, put him in the sleigh and the horse took him back home through a blinding blizzard."

He return home intoxicated. His father, "tears trickling down his thin pale cheeks thought of the vision he had seen leap out of the flames. The shock of seeing his only boy intoxicated proved fatal, and a few days later he died." Several days after his death, the step-mother auctioned off all the family's belongings, including the blacksmith shop and cabin. "After the sale, the step-mother returned to her people, and Unita, 17, went to work in the city. Blackie just drifted from one job to another."

Blackie had not seen his sister for three years when he found out she was in the hospital. He visited her there, and she told him of the man who had wronged her and then left her when she was about to become a mother. He vowed he would kill the man who had dared to treat his orphan sister in such a way. He located his sister's betrayer working in a Railroad yard.

"Shortly after midnight, Blackie managed to get within a few feet of the man without being seen. Unconscious of any danger, the man was waiting with a lantern in his hand for a fast-approaching train. The engineer saw the switchman's lantern go under the wheels and stopped the engine. A little later, the crew found a hunting knife sticking in a pole with a note, 'Unita is avenged.'"

Afterwards, Blackie committed robberies in Canada, Ohio, and Florida. He was arrested, found guilty and sentenced to the convict mines of Florida. On his release, he turned to drinking and petty crimes.

In 1901, Blackie met a beautiful, brown-eyed, black-haired Canadian girl and married her. They were happy and prosperous, and God gave them two beautiful black-eyed boys.

Blackie again turned to alcohol and left his family. In 1913, while lying near the San Francisco Bay, he considered suicide. "His soul took advantage of his drink-crazed mind. Blackie could see his faithful wife with her eyes swollen from weeping over her erring husband. He could see his little boys as they cried themselves to sleep because daddy didn't come home." He thought, "Now it was time for him to end the miserable life that had caused so much sorrow and so many heart-aches. No one loved him now."

Blackie decided to end his life in the chilly waters of the San Francisco Bay. But on his way, he spotted a Salvation Army Band and followed them to church. As the band played, Blackie knelt at the altar and gave God his heart. That night, September 13, 1913, he preached his first sermon. He "didn't know how to offer up a flowery prayer, he prayed the little prayer he had learned at his mother's knees, in the north woods: Now I lay me down to sleep, I pray the Lord my soul to keep; And if I should die before I wake, I pray the Lord my soul to take."

Children at the Free Will Baptist Orphange, Middlesex, North Carolina called him Mr. Cummings. He never worked at the orphanage, nor was he an alumnus of the home. No one can tell you when he first arrived or when he left. He ate meals with the staff and children in the dining hall and he slept in the boys' building. If any of the boys wanted to chat, he'd take time to talk with them. He preached at the home from time to time, but no one remembers him preaching in church. Always, 'Preacher Cummings' preached under a tree or out of the back of his jeep, usually parked in the flower garden. Sometimes, he held up chains from his prison years. Occasionally, he would dress in his black and white prison garbs and talk about the penalty for sin. He was always "old" in our eyes.

I knew Mr. Cummings. He was courteous and kind to us boys. We all liked him.

Note: Many quotes were sourced from Cummings' 1947 publication, Avenues Leading to Crime and Blackie of the North Woods.

Thanksgiving Dinner Isn't Just a Meal

Charles Ray Hinson
1944–58

FREE WILL BAPTIST CHILDREN'S HOME
MIDDLESEX, NORTH CAROLINA

Published: November 26, 2003

Thanksgiving Day 1949 began like all days at the orphanage. The dining hall outdoor bell rang at 6 a.m., followed shortly by Petey, our matron, coming through our bedrooms making sure we 40 boys were getting up. Petey switched on the lights while bellowing, "Rise and shine or you will be mine." We knew not to be in bed when he made his second round.

By the time we heard the bell ring the second time at 6:30, our beds were made, clothes on, bathroom visited, and we were in the hall anticipating the second ring. Our dining hall was in another building.

We walked together and lined up outside the dining hall to enter as a group—youngest to oldest boy. Once inside, we all stood behind our chairs until after the morning prayer, then in unison we sat down. There were 40 boys on one side of the room and 40 girls on the other side of the room. Thirty minutes later, after eating our eggs, grits, bacon, toast, and milk, each

Dining Hall at the Free Will Baptist Orphanage

table left the dining hall in unison. The chickens and hogs were fed, coal boilers stoked, and other chores completed before we returned to our building. On school days, we completed these chores before we boarded the bus for school.

On Thanksgiving Day, however, we knew there was no school and there was a certain excitement in the air as we left the dining hall. We knew we would be visiting with family off campus for the weekend.

This was my first Thanksgiving at the orphanage. My twin sister and I had been admitted earlier that year, in August 1949. We were seven years old. My first memories of Charles Ray are from that Thanksgiving. He was age nine and had been at the children's home for five years. I remember following him as he explored the long outdoor table near the church. As food was being removed from baskets and placed on the long buffet table, Charles Ray introduced me to the art of food surveying. With his five years experience, he had learned not to get in line with everyone at one end of the table, but to work his way to the center when it was time to eat. He had surmised that guest and older children were taller and tended to fill their plates with choice foods, leaving fewer selections for younger children. Charles Ray programmed my conscious that day: "Thanksgiving dinner isn't just a meal: It's an attitude."

As the lengthy Free Will Baptist blessing ended, "Now Lord, bless these children and this food, Amen," I quickly followed Charles Ray as he bypassed the line to the middle of the table. Everyone else was busy looking after themselves and before they realized what had happen our plates were overly filled with wonderful food, though not turkey. We waited until the line passed the table, then we went back for turkey. My conscious is still programmed to know that there is always extra turkey.

I can still remember that Thanksgiving dinner and the teachings of Charles Ray. Because he and I jumped the line that day, my plate was full of brown sugar, marshmallow and pecan topping that I lifted from a sweet potato soufflé, leaving just the sweet potatoes for older children and guests! Charles Ray's nickname was Wiley, due to the untambed way he carried himself.

That nickname followed him throughout life when he was in the presence of someone from the orphanage. Truth be known, I believe most of us still enjoy being called by our nicknames, and Charles Ray certainly never raised an objection to being called Wiley.

After nearly 14 years on campus, Charles left the orphanage in 1958 without finishing high school. Like most of us, he shouldered a lot of anger through the years. His mother had been killed and he did not know his father. On his birth certificate, no father is listed. Charles Ray had no family to care for him, and having lived as an institutional child, he felt alone.

I lost contact with Wiley until I received a phone call from former Superintendent S.A. Smith from the orphanage. He told me that Wiley had been in prison and was later paroled. I saw Wiley several times throughout the years at the annual children's home homecoming. Once I stopped in Atlanta and had lunch with him.

S.A. Smith

In July 1992, Charles accepted an invitation to speak to the alumni at our homecoming. In the audience was his wife and many of the men and women that were at the home when he was there. He began, "I had some good and some bad years here, but this was home. A man killed my mother in 1944. I held her death against the world and this home. It kept me in self-pity. I felt the world owed me a living and would not listen to anyone. When I left here, I did not know how to love, how to give love, or how to receive love.

"For 30 years I tracked the man that killed my mother. When I found where he was living, I went to his house and knocked on the door. He was crippled and using his cane when he came to the door. I introduced myself and ask him why he killed my mother. He had no answer and looked like he was seeing a ghost. I had imagined what I was going to do to him, but at that moment I felt like a fool looking at him. He had lived with the killing for 30 years and would the rest of his life. I now am sorry for the visit.

"Today, I am grateful that I can tell you I can give love and receive love. I am married to a wonderful woman who means it when she says, 'I love you.'

"God has helped me rise above my troubles. I am grateful for my years here. I got punished because I needed it. I wanted to be at the center of attention, even if I was being whipped. I felt like I was the black sheep of all the children.

We can let hardships go with us through life or we can work with them, or we can let them drag us down. I beat myself up for years.

"Becoming a member of Alcoholic Anonymous made me realize where I came from and where I belong, and how to live life on life's terms. I let my pride and selfishness drag me down before coming to grip with life. We are put her for a purpose and that is to serve God. I start each day with the Serenity Prayer."

Tears were flowing as Wiley finished speaking that day. It was a healing experience for all.

Last summer I learned that Wiley had died from emphysema. The last few years he had attended homecoming with an oxygen tank at his side, but he always had a smile on his face.

This Thanksgiving there will be an empty chair and a place setting at our table for my orphan brother Wiley.

I miss him.

The Old Bell

Free Will Baptist Children's Home
Bell 1920–Present

FREE WILL BAPTIST CHILDREN'S HOME
MIDDLESEX, NORTH CAROLINA

Published: September 14, 2005

I suppose to many people it is just an old iron bell. On the campus of the Free Will Baptist Children's Home in eastern North Carolina, the bell is a mainstay on campus, and has been around about as long as the children's home itself, dating back to 1920. Through the years the old bell has withstood hurricanes, torrential rains, cold weather, muggy hot summers and mischievous children.

Years ago it was relocated from ground level to its current place in the sky; ten feet above land to prevent naughty, impish orphans' easy access. I must admit it always brought a smile to hear the old bell clang once or twice at an unscheduled time, even when tolled by others.

At homecoming this summer I heard the bell ring again. As if Maslow himself had conditioned me, I knew barbeque and fried chicken were waiting. The old bell always rang twice for each meal… thirty minutes before to quit our chores and clean up, and again when it was time to gather for our meal. I also was conditioned by the bell to attend all church services on Sunday morning, Sunday night and Wednesday night. So when I hear a bell clang, I know it's time to eat or pray.

Sitting on a bench outside the chapel waiting for lunch, I found myself trying to figure out the number of times I'd heard the old bell ring. My guess is that over a span of 11 years I must have heard the ding-donging more than 45,000 thousand times; six ringings each day for meals, four ringings on Sundays for church and twice on Wednesdays for church. Today, there is never a time when I hear a bell ring that I don't revert back to yesteryears.

Since 1920, nearly 2,000 children have spent part or all of their childhood at the Freewill Baptist home. Every summer, the children's home invites alumni to enjoy homecoming where they can reminisce, attend church and share a meal together. The weekend usually begins on Saturday evening with an off-campus barbeque. Then on Sunday morning we attend church, and often hear from a guest speaker, usually an alumnus, and a short memorial service for those alumni that have passed. This year twelve of us went to be with our Lord. After church we ate lunch and had afternoon fellowship.

Throughout the day, there is story telling, laughter and just wandering around campus. You'll usually witness small groups together laughing at shared memories. And no matter how many of these homecoming events you've attended, you'll always hear a new story among the ones told every year. This year I heard two new stories, one told by Margie.

In the 1950s, all the nearly one hundred children and staff ate together in one central dining hall… girls on one side of the room, boys on the other side. Meals were served before everyone arrived at the dinning hall. During the meal, if a particular table needed something, say extra biscuits, younger girls would be assigned to "wait" on the tables. You would just raise your hand and one of the girls would come to your table. Margie was one of these young wait girls.

"One morning at breakfast, Evelyn Jean (EJ) and I got to playing in the kitchen instead of waiting on tables. I bet her that she would not go out to wait on her tables if I tied her apron strings around the two of us. All of a sudden a hand went at one of her tables and out she went, with me in tow. Did we get in trouble! The dietician got so angry with us and could not get up out of her chair fast enough. She came into the kitchen, gave us a 'brow beating' and

then a severe punishment: we had to stay "tied together by apron strings" the entire Saturday morning. I had to follow E.J. around like a puppy dog and that wasn't fun. She was older and much stronger. My face is still red!"

Another story was shared by Steward, a former superintendant.

"It was always great fun to have to chase runaways. One night I get a call from the director of Campus Life saying a couple of teenage girls were on the run and wanted to know if I wanted to ride along to pick them up. I said sure and off we went. Before we went far he turned off the main road on to a small county road. I asked, 'Why are we turning here?' Looking at me the director said, 'I don't chase them anymore, I just go pick them up, you'll see.' As the county road neared a wooded area near the railroad track, he pulled up almost to the track and stopped. Grinning, he turned the motor off and we just sit there in the dark, silently. Before long the two girls rounded the bend in the railroad tracks and were quite surprised when we stepped out of the car and invited them to ride back to the home. They got into the car grousing as kids who get caught do. He looked over smiled, saying, 'It works every time; I just come here and wait for them.'"

One story that surfaces every year is about the baptism. Each time I hear it, I think it grows a little more.

The story takes place in the early 1950s. We were always having revivals; young preachers wanting to save us orphan from the sins of the world. On this particular Sunday night sitting in church it was hot, windows were all up, no air condition. Some of the kids were waving fans to feel a breeze. It was one of those sermons that made us mischievous guys and gals review our life, to decide if a meteorite dropped out of the sky if we would be looking down from heaven or up from hell. Many of us were sweating when the alter call came from fire and brimstone preacher Cummings; piano music played softly the old great hymnal "Amazing Grace". "If you died tonight, will you be ready? Have you confessed your sins?" the preacher asked.

In the chapel, boys were seated on one side of the church and girls the other. As the alter call continued, sobbing kids started walking to the alter. Eula Mae got up to go. Willis seating at the back of the church with Rabon, nicknamed "Rabbit," nudged Rabon with his elbow. Willis pronounced the letter "r" as a "w".

"Wabbit, Wabbit, Eula Mae is getting up," said Willis. "She's going to be saved." Eula Mae continued down the aisle. "Wabbit, Wabbit, there goes Eula Mae. She's going to be saved," repeated Willis.

Rabon just sat there thinking of his sins, but with a little smirk from Willis's comments. As the preacher knelt with Eula Mae at the alter, Willis leaned over to Rabon whispering, "Wabbit, our girlfriend is now saved." Sure enough, after the altar call that night, Eula Mae would not date Rabon or Willis again, although they kept asking her.

Nearly two weeks later on a Sunday afternoon, everyone turned out for the baptism of those who got saved that night and other kids saved earlier in the week. All the girls were dressed in white, boys had on dark pants and white shirts. It was an old fashion baptism with everyone singing the old gospel hymnal, "We shall gather at the river." The fire and brimstone preacher was shoulder deep in our pond, leading the singing, as the girls where led into waist-deep water, boys stood behind on the bank waiting their turn. The crowd looked on as Eula Mae waded out to deeper water.

Even standing on the pond banks, Rabon and Willis still had hopes that Eula Mae would change her mind and continue courtships with them. As the preacher placed one hand behind Eula Mae's shoulder, using the other to squeeze her nostrils, he started lower Eula Mae into the water.

Willis sadly looking at Rabon, his head says no with movement, "Wabbit, Wabbit there she goes, there she goes. There goes our honey Wabbit, there goes our honey."

As homecoming ended, I left the home late Sunday afternoon and stopped by the old bell. I got out of my car—I just had to do it again—Clangggggg! Clangggggg! A huge smile spread across my face.

Ah, the memories that bell brings back!

The Color of Love

Gene Cheek
1963-69

BOYS HOME
LAKE WACCAMAW, NORTH CAROLINA

Published: November 15, 2006

After reading his book, *The Color of Love*, I decided to try to find author
Gene Cheek. Two friends, Elvin and Carol, had given his book to
me. "We enjoyed this book and can't wait for you to read it. We were
reminded of you when we read it," they said.

Searching the web, I found to my surprise that Gene lived nearby, in my
part of the Blue Ridge mountains. His email address was listed on his website,
and I emailed him. A short time later I got a reply. We talked and scheduled
coffee a few days later.

It was a rainy day and I was a few minutes late arriving to the Dripolator
Coffeehouse in Black Mountain, North Carolina. As I entered the coffee shop,
the waitress waved for me to come over where Gene was sitting. Extending
my hand, I said, "Hi, I'm Jerry." He smiled and as I was seated, the waitress
ask if she could bring us anything. I nodded yes and asked for a cup of coffee.
Gene already was working on the cup sitting on the table.

Like all adult institutional children, we started mentally assessing each
other—a survival trait learned from childhood. I knew from reading Gene's

199

book that we had similar experiences. With his question, "Why were you in the orphanage?", I shared more than usual about my life to someone I had never met. As I talked, he became more at ease and we moved from being total strangers to bonding. We talked and laughed for close to two hours while reliving our pasts.

"Your book reflects many of my feelings, and you did a good job describing how one feels with our childhoods," I said to Gene. This paragraph of laying down the past fairly well reflects where I am today:

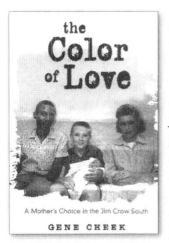

the
Color
of **Love**

A Mother's Choice in the Jim Crow South

GENE CHEEK

"I am often asked by those who know me if I can now lay this down and move on with my life. It would be nice if I could answer yes, but once again that would be a lie. The truth lies somewhere else. While writing this book, I did gain understanding, and with it came forgiveness, but I have not forgotten. The facts are that this will remain a part of my life, as long as there is life. I'm not sure complete healing is attainable. I don't think I will ever forget, and I'm not sure that I should."

As Gene and I talked, we got into childhood holidays. Thanksgiving, Christmas, and Easter were some of my most exciting times at the orphanage. They offered the chance to be a part of the rest of the world, when family would visited, and opportunities arose to return home to visit relatives and friends. The holiday many of us enjoyed most was Thanksgiving. I asked Gene for his thoughts.

"Thanksgiving was my favorite. Probably the most memorable isn't because of good memories. I was taken from mom on the 18 of November 1963, and then spent a few days in a detention center before going to a foster home. I remember sitting around that great big table the foster people had with all those other foster kids, all smaller than me, thinking I must have died and gone to hell. I couldn't eat. I walked out of the house and walked down to the baseball field and spent the day sitting on the outfield fence crying. Why that one sticks out far more than any other Thanksgiving I had as a child, all those good ones I had before all that stuff took place I don't know. But every year at Thanksgiving, especially now that I have my own family, I think about that one back in 1963.

I also think about the kids in this country who at one time or another had a Thanksgiving with family, but are now in the company of strangers."

Several days before Thanksgiving 1963, Gene, age 12, was removed from his mom by a court order. His life was uprooted because of racial intolerance. While racial intolerance was the catalyst behind Gene's placement in foster care, his father's failure to be a dad and husband was the underlying reason for the dysfunction of Gene's family. Gene's father was an alcoholic and used his income for that and gambling. In his book, Gene describes one of the many occasions when his father would come home drunk:

"When I got out of bed Sunday morning, I found Dad sleeping on the couch still in his work clothes. He'd fallen off the wagon all right, and he smelled like he'd landed in a vat of Ten High bourbon. As I walked toward the bathroom, Mama came out of her bedroom. She motioned for me to follow her to the kitchen and whispered, 'Don't say nothing to your father if he wakes up. He was drunk when he got home, and he's going to be in one of those moods.' I was crestfallen. 'One of those moods' meant the so-call new improved Dad had become his old soused self. The sober spell had lasted longer than its predecessors, but it ended the same way all those others had with a headlong sprint back into the bottle. We dressed for church and left him asleep. We walked the half mile to Urban Street Baptist Church."

They had to move several times because Gene's father lost jobs from his use of alcohol. At one point, Gene's mother couldn't take it anymore and left his father, taking Gene with her. His mother and father tried to get back together again and again, but alcohol destroyed each attempt. At the very young age of ten, Gene became the "man of the house" when his father left for the last time. His mother got a mill job, and with family support they pulled together for their livelihood and happiness.

One day, near age 11, on returning home from playing football, Gene heard his mom crying over the phone. After hanging up the phone Gene pressed her for reasons of her sadness. Finally, his mother said, (from his book):

"'You know about boyfriends and girlfriends, huh?' she asked, stalling. 'It's when the boy gives the girl Valentine cards and chocolate and flowers and other junk, and they hold hands and go to movies, stuff like that.'
She laughed.

'Is he nice to you?'

'He's a wonderful man,' she said, blinking back her tears. The nicest and kindest man I've ever known. He thinks we should stop seeing each other. He's worried that you won't approve, and he doesn't want to hurt you.'

'If he's nice and you like him, then why does he think I won't approve?'

She looked down at her hands folded in her lap. I'd never seen her so sad or anxious. She cleared her throat and said. 'Because he is a colored man.'

'Do you love him?' I asked her.

She smiled. 'Yes honey, I do love him.'

'Does he love you?'

'Yes.'

'If you love this man and he loves you, then the color of his skin doesn't matter,' I said to mom."

Gene's mother met Cornelius Tucker (Tuck) at the mill where were both employed. Gene became fond of him. "I had no doubt he'd make a wonderful stepfather. I admired and respected him. He was a decent man with a wonderful sense of humor. He was a proud man who walked with dignity and held his head high. Despite living in a Jim Crow world, he bowed to no man. He was a Mason, a 'Keeper of the Seal,' a high honor, and wore his ring with pride. He volunteered and worked at his church, where he was a senior usher. He was a well-respected member of his community who could be counted on to lend a hand."

In June 1962, Gene's brother Randy was born from the relationship—a relationship not sanction by the laws of North Carolina at that time. Blacks and whites could not wed. Randy's father's family and his mother's family became outraged over the relationship and this newborn child. They took legal action and the courts ruled in their favor against Gene, his mother, Randy, and Tuck.

Speaking to Gene's mother (Sallie), the judge said, "You can keep Gene if you give up your illegitimate child with the Negro man. If you choose to keep the illegitimate child, then I have no choice but to recommend that Gene, for his own protection, be taken away from you and placed in foster care. The choice is yours."

Gene shared his thoughts at that moment: "I was stunned by the judge's words. What kind of monster was he? I could not let my mama make this choice. It would destroy her as if the judge himself had plunged a knife into her heart. In an instant I knew what I had to do. I leaned over to her and whispered into *her ear, 'Mama, if they take Randy, we'll never see him again. He's just a baby. Let them take me away. I'm twelve years old. I know how to find my way home. Before she could protest, I stood up and yelled at the judge, 'Take me, not my brother!'"*

Over his mother's protest, the judge ordered immediate custody of Gene. He was removed from the courtroom while resisting and struggling with court officials. This was November 1963, shortly before Thanksgiving. Gene spent the remainder of his childhood at the Boys Home in Lake Waccamaw, North Carolina.

The Color of Love is the story of a boy's grief from living with an alcoholic father, and how he survived the decision handed down by a racially intolerant court. Eventually laws were changed allowing interracial marriages, and his mother and Tuck were married. Unfortunately, Gene's placement at the Boys Home weakened family bonds and he lost important years living apart from his brothers, Tuck, his mother, and other family members. I encourage everyone to read Gene's book. It can be purchased at Lyons Press or Amazon.com.

On leaving the coffee house that rainy morning, I asked Gene if he would sign my copy of his book. His note read: *It's not where you've been! It's where you're going! Gene*

Note: Gene shared that his story, The Color of Love, *may be made into a movie in the future. The photo of Gene is current and from his website.*

Ambassadors Did a Magnificent Job

Photo courtesy of Holston United Methodist Home for Children

HOLSTON UNITED METHODIST HOME
GREENEVILLE, TENNESSEE

Published: September 9, 2009

The sky was overcast that August day. I almost picked up my umbrella, but realizing I was just a short distance from the outdoor Hull Pavilion, decided against it. I was headed to the campus of the Holston United Methodist Home for Children in Greeneville, Tennessee, to attend the Houses of Hope Consecration and Dedication. Two new residences had been constructed for boys and youth at the children's home.

Elizabeth Reeves was teaching college at Martha Washington College, Abingdon, Virginia, when she married Dr. Ephraim Wiley. He later became President of Emory and Henry College. After his death, Elizabeth founded this children's home as an orphanage in 1895. The home has been a Christian respite for orphans, homeless, disabled, and troubled kids ever since. The name "orphanage" was changed to "home" in 1947.

Holston (UM) Home has family service centers in Wise and Bristol, Virginia, and in Tennessee, there are family service centers in Johnson City, Greeneville,

204

Knoxville, and Chattanooga. Today it continues to provide services to children and is the pride of the United Methodist Congregations in Tennessee and southwest Virginia. From special education, early childhood education, in-home care, foster care, day care, and adoption to residential treatment programs, the home is a Christian and professional child care presence in the lives of so many, and is often the only set of hands caring for a child. Thousands of children have passed through Holston (UM) Home on their journey to adulthood.

I mingled among the crowds and visited several friends as we waited for the invocation to start. I settled into a chair up near the front, and noticed a group of boys standing with their hands crossed in front. One boy had his hands in his pockets. They were to the left of the speaker podium; all were wearing ties and in a line facing the audience. Some smiled to one another, others stood earnestly; all were orderly, wanting to do right for the occasion.

While other guests were getting into their seats, I could not take my eyes off those boys. They brought back memories when I took part in the celebration of a feed mill opened by Purina in the late 1950's. Ten or more of us boys at the orphanage were transported 20 miles to Parker's Bar-B-Q in Wilson, North Carolina, and were told to serve barbeque to the large crowd attending the opening. We were dressed in white and red checkered shirts for the noon serving of pig, slaw, cornbread, potatoes, and sweet tea. I remember seeing the queen of country, Grand Ole Opry Country Music Comedian Minnie Pearl, wearing her straw hat with the $1.98 price tag hanging off it. Everyone wanted her attention and a signed program. I have never forgotten the event, and I've hung on to the Purina shirt given to us afterwards. We were special orphans that day.

Similarly, on this day at Holston, I was thinking those boys up front must have a part in the day's celebration and it was going to be a lifetime memory for them as well. Sure enough, President/CEO Art Masker of Holston later announced the boys were "Ambassadors and Tour Guides" for the two new residences for boys.

Thumbing through the bulletin, I noticed the names of all those who helped raise nearly five million dollars to make the two residences possible. As with most new facilities, buildings and parts of buildings are named to honor people for their contribution—either for the project or for past services. I was particularly impressed, even found myself a little teary-eyed, to read two names of those that had lived in institutional care. Wow! I thought to myself…This says quantities of what Holston Home for Children is about. I know of no other children's home that has named any of their structures after a child of the home; even the home of my childhood bears no orphan names.

One of the common areas in one residence was named for Ginger Bewley —"The Ginger Bewley Common." Ginger was a resident of Holston Home for over 30 years of her life. She suffered from physical and mental disabilities. Ginger died on January 7, 2009 at the age of 62. Some of the honorary pallbearers at her funeral were caregivers at Holston Home, and Rev. Charles Hutchins from the home assisted in officiating her funeral.

There were two new residences for boys, and one was named for adoptee Rodney Atkins—the "Rodney Atkins Home for Youth." He was born "Jimmy" in Knoxville, but was immediately given up for adoption by his birth mother and went to Holston Home for Children. When he was first placed at Holston, Jimmy was given the last name Holston. He was a frail infant, and seemingly always sick. Jimmy experienced two failed adoptions before a permanent home was secured for him through a third adoption.

Allan and Margaret Atkins, who reside in Cookeville, Tennessee, adopted Jimmy after their infant son, Jeffrey, died shortly after birth. There was eight months difference in Jimmy and Jeffrey's age. Jimmy Holston became Rodney Atkins after the adoption. Rodney was adopted all three times within six weeks of his birth on Friday, March 28, 1969. For those of you that wonder if this Rodney is Rodney Atkins, country music star, you're correct. On his website, he comments about his adoption placement with his parents: *From what I understand, I became more sick than I had ever been during that time… It just never crossed their mind to take me back.*

Reverend Charles Hutchins took part in all three of Rodney's adoptions and was the Associate Executive Director of Holston Home for Children at the time of Rodney's placement there. Today, Rev. Hutchins and Rodney have a friendship. While being interviewed at the ceremony, Rodney referenced Rev. Hutchins as *"the fellow that handed me to my mom and dad."* Rev. Hutchins does not look at the first two adoptions as failed adoptions, rather as a process to

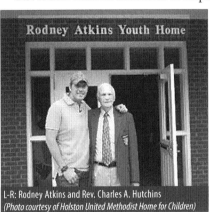

L-R: Rodney Atkins and Rev. Charles A. Hutchins
(Photo courtesy of Holston United Methodist Home for Children)

find the right fit for a child and his parents. Today, Holston Home sometimes alludes to Atkins as "Our poster boy for Hope." Rodney has not forgotten his roots. Like other orphans, he champions' resources for the home and finds time for the youth in care.

As the service was winding down that warm afternoon, I kept checking on the boys waiting to be "Ambassadors and Tour Guides." You would have had to be a child in institutional care to understand their dressing for such an event. I could tell those boys were taken to shop for clothes about the same time and at the same place, and might even have had their ties tied by the same person, or got their tie-tying lesson from the same teacher. Yep, some things just never change in an institution. Ah..., I thought, (smiling to myself) I bet those boys even had "humorous" conversation about their pants, shirts and shoes all looking alike. Their ties, however, were different shades of color and design, and they were attractive.

As alluded to earlier, I still remember those white and red checker shirts we wore to serve barbeque, and I remember our smiles at our attire. I'm betting these Holston boys will remember their clothes, too. And I'm betting they got to keep their dress slacks, white shirts, black dress shoes, and ties like the orphans of the past that served barbeque. It's the way of the institution.

Now what these boys did get from their services that we did not get for serving barbeque back in the 50's, was a personalized thank you card from the CEO with their picture included. While I think Holston (UM) Home has wonderful staff, I have even greater admiration for their CEO, Art Masker. He did not forget those boys among all the other responsibilities that consumed him that day. They were special to him... and now they know it.

The "Consecration and Dedication" was a lovely day; the Ambassadors did a magnificent job and everyone was proud as they should be of the new residence for youth. Elizabeth Wiley's 114-year vision continues to provide a caring and professional Christian ministry.

My Big Brother

Dr. W. Burkette Raper
1936–45

FREE WILL BAPTIST CHILDREN'S HOME
MIDDLESEX, NORTH CAROLINA

Published: September 14, 2011

Sitting in the bleachers at the Mount Olive College Kornegay Arena, I looked down at all those celebrating the life of Dr. W. Burkette Raper, He died at age 83. My thoughts went back and forth to times he and I spent together.

Burkette's casket rested center stage between his "biological family" and those presiding over the religious service and celebration of his life. Hundreds filled the seats on the basketball court to pay their final respects and participate in his funeral. Overflow moved to the bleachers.

The longest serving governor of North Carolina, The Honorable James B. Hunt, Jr., sat near his casket. Nearby sat the presidents of three colleges.

Burkette was one of my "big" brothers—not by "blood," but by our being placed in the same orphanage. We formed strong family ties from that childhood experience. He was the giant of my big brothers.

When I arrived on campus in the fall of 1949, Burkette had already left and was enrolled at the Duke University Divinity School. He would drive back to the orphanage on Sundays to pastor the chapel on campus. After church, he'd gather the young boys on campus for a game of "orphan football." It was during one of these games that we met. Burkette never forgot our "orphan home" through the years and was always there for homecoming and other campus events.

In 1954, Burkette became President of Mount Olive College, Mount Olive, North Carolina. At age 26, he was the youngest college president in the United States. Forty years later, he retired as the longest-tenured college president in the country.

Several weeks before his death on August 1, 2011, I talked with Burkette. I asked him how he was doing, he replied, in a joyous and optimistic spirit, "Jerry, I've got the best God, the best doctors, and the best family… I'm going to be okay whatever happens."

Last year, Burkette and I talked frequently about the publication of my book, *The Family*, a history of the Free Will Baptist Orphanage (now called Children's Home). Burkette wrote in the book:

"My eight years at the Free Will Baptist Orphanage—now Children's Home— are epitomized by two days: the day I entered and the day I left.

"The Day I Entered: "It was a hot July afternoon when I, my brother James Earl, and my sister Mary Lou arrived at the orphanage. I was age eight, James Earl had turned five the day before, and Mary Lou had just reached age three. As the car carrying my mother and my uncle, who had brought us, disappeared down the hill and out of sight, I suddenly had the loneliest feeling I ever remember.

"It was not that I was alone—the large front porch of the old three-story building, which was the central focus of the campus at that time, was filled with dozens of children. Actually, there were one hundred children at the Orphanage at that time, but they were all strangers to me, my brother and sister. Mary Lou began to cry, and then we experienced our first act of kindness. Miss Velva Daughtry, a matron who was later to greatly influence my life, reached down her strong arms, lifted Mary Lou and said to James Earl and me, 'Come with me.' I see her yet as she carried us to the basement of the building where the dining hall was located and gave each of us a  *"Graham Cracker."*

James Earl and Burkette

"Back on the front porch, one of the 'big boys,' as I would later learn the boys of his age were called, named Ivy Linton, sat me on his knee and in a friendly voice said, "You are my buddy. If any of these boys bother you, you come to see me." Although I never had to go to him for rescue, I have never forgotten those bright blue eyes under that large straw hat.

"Then a group of boys, slightly older than I—whom I would later come to know as the 'middle size boys'—came over to where I was and said, 'Come, let us show you around.' They took me to the dairy barn where I saw the most cows I had ever seen. 'You are in with these,' the boys said. The tour continued to the barn where the mules were housed, to the chicken houses and to the hog fence. At each stop, I was told 'You are in with these.' Finally, I asked the meaning of being 'in with,' and the boys explained: 'That means that these—the cows, mules, chickens, hogs and farm land—are as much yours as anybody's. They are ours—they belong to us.'

"The Day I left: The day was Saturday, July 1, 1944. World War II was reaching its climax. Three weeks before had been 'D' day—the allies had opened a second front against the Germans by landing on the bloody beaches of Normandy in France. In the Pacific, U.S. Marines were paying a heavy price in casualties as they fought on a chain of islands, moving ever closer to Japan for the anticipated invasion of the mainland. Of the eight boys from the Orphanage who had entered Middlesex High School in the fall of 1940, I was the only one who had remained to graduate. The others had left for jobs in the war effort or were already enlisted in the armed forces.

"I was sixteen years old. With everything I owned packed in one suitcase; with $50 in money I had earned from farm work or received from high school graduation presents; and a loan of $300 from the Anna Phillips Educational Loan Fund. I ate my last breakfast as a resident of the orphanage and said goodbye to the children who had gathered in front of the three-story girl's dormitory—the site that had welcomed me eight years earlier when I arrived.

"Mr. Evans (Superintendent) walked with me the short distance to the Nash automobile, on which he would carry me to Duke University. The schedule called for me to be in an assembly of new students at 11:00 a.m. We stopped at Belk's in Durham where I spent one-fourth of my $50 to purchase the bed sheets, towels and other items I would need for my dorm room.

"During the hour I was in the assembly hearing the dean of freshmen welcome us and provide the information we would need for enrollment the next week, Mr. Evans waited. Then he went with me to the rooming office where I was issued a key to my room. Back to the car to get my suitcase, Mr. Evans accompanied me to my room. Very kindly, he wished me well and invited me to let him know if he could be of further help. Then he left. Seeing that one of the beds had been made up, it was evident that my roommate had already arrived, but he was not there and I was yet to meet him. I knew no one on campus, except Dr. Jordan, and only one person in Durham—a member of Edgemont Free Will Baptist Church who had done some plumbing work at the orphanage. "Day two had ended—I had left the orphanage.

"Once again, I faced an unknown future, just as when I arrived at the orphanage eight years earlier. Only this time, I was in a much larger world, and I alone was responsible for my finances and welfare. I had never written a check, I had never seen the ocean or the mountains. I had never been out of North Carolina—in fact, I had never traveled farther west than Durham.

"From a small rural high school with a graduating class of twenty-seven, I was now on a campus of several thousand students, most of whom were enrolled in the Naval Reserve Officers Training Corp (NROTC), preparing to become Commissioned Officers in the U.S. Navy. With World War II at a crucial point, the academic pace was accelerated and rigorous.

"But for me, the course was set. The day I left the orphanage, another boy was waiting to move into what had been my room. I did not have the choice of retreating—there was no place else to go. Not until I graduated in 1947 at the age of nineteen, would I remove my clothes and books from my dormitory. Duke University was now my home."

Late one Sunday night, this past spring, Burkette called and thank me for writing *The Family*.

"It's the truth", he said, "Now our history has been told."

After the funeral, and while waiting for the family to arrive at the cemetery, I thought to myself how through the years Burkette had married many of us from the orphanage, buried many of us from the orphanage, and baptized many of us. He baptized me. To so many of us, he was bigger than life.

As the funeral ended and his family had left his graveside, I quietly went to the casket and gently touched it. I bowed my head and thanked God for my big brother… my big orphan brother.

Believed To Have Died

Joe Andrew Hartsfield
1959–69

FREE WILL BAPTIST CHILDREN'S HOME
MIDDLESEX, NORTH CAROLINA

Published: April 10, 2013

I was the only senior boy on campus in August 1959. Andrew, age 10, was admitted to the Children's Home, Middlesex, North Carolina on Saturday, August 22 and none of us older boys gave any attention to it. In my years at the home (1949–60), I'd experienced 101 admittances and Andrew was number 93. I was told there were 100 children on campus when I arrived in August 1949, so this suggests I shared my childhood with at least 201 other kids, and every one of my "orphan" brothers and sisters still remain my family till this day.

It was the following Monday after his admittance that I first noticed Andrew. It was during breakfast. Andrew was sitting with other boys his age at a table near me, and as I was enjoying my pancakes, eggs, bacon and milk, you could hear his voice raise with, "Pass the turp!, pass the turp!, pass the turp!" The other boys at his table were smiling as another boy was pouring syrup on his pancakes. From that day onward, Andrew was known by nickname "Turp". Gosh, can children be cruel at times… yet Turp would always grin when we called him by his nickname. I learned later he was tongue-tied. He had difficulty enunciating "s" and "l" and he stuttered through the years at the home.

Andrew was the youngest sibling of four. He was admitted to the home in '59, but his older siblings (a brother age 19, brother age 16, and sister age 14) were not. I have no knowledge about the siblings' care. Andrew's father died in 1951 at the age of 34 from a gun shot wound to the head, and his mother died in 1958 at the age of 37 from arteriosclerotic heart disease. The family was from eastern North Carolina.

Those who were with Andrew at the home from '59–'69 attest to his always having a smile. Everyone liked him. He took kidding about his lisp with a smile, never showing anger towards anyone. Phil, '53–'68, was at the home most of Andrew's years and had this comment: "The best I can remember, Andrew had a slight stutter and sometimes we picked on him. Also, he sometimes said things without thinking about what he was saying. I remember one time Moose (nickname), '55–'64, was in the shower and Andrew asked him if he had any finger clips on him. *(In the shower with nail clippers?)* Another time he was trying to ask for some string and said st... st... st... stwine. Andrew was in the Boy Scouts with us. I remember as a teenager he had mail-ordered a drawing course advertised in a magazine."

Yvonne, '55–'69, shared this memory of Andrew: "I have a picture of he and I dancing at one of our proms *(See them dancing in picture)*. Andrew was a nice guy. The thing I remember most about him was that he was our bus driver, and he was very considerate about waiting for us girls. Sometimes he would be almost around the corner coming up to the sign leaving the home and someone would say 'here comes Yvonne [or some other girl]' and he would wait. He also allowed us to fix our hair and makeup on the bus ride to school due to our morning chores not allowing us time to finish our attire before the bus came."

1968 Dancing with Senior Yvonne Rouse

In a letter dated December 4, 1961, from the Superintendant of the home written to a church looking to sponsor a child for Christmas, is a list of requests from Turp, age 12, which included a hatchet, scout knife, waterproof sleeping bag, lantern, and a Bible.

Other boys talked about Andrew's drawings and how good his portraits were. Some of the boys laughed about how Andrew became popular from taking his drawing lessons by mail. The company sent Andrew a drawing manual and the administration was excited about Andrew's interest in art. What the administration never did was review the manuals. In the book there were numerous illustrations, and some of the pictures of women, well... the pictures revealed much to the teenage boys. Andrew chose whom he wanted to share the pictures with, and which of the older boys got a sneak peak of the forbidden pictures. Andrew was smiling with the popularity this brought him.

Everyone witnessed Andrew's work ethic. He never complained. Beginning his sophomore year in high school, Andrew became the home's school bus driver and drove two loads of children each morning to school for three years. He also worked out in the community helping farmer's harvest their tobacco. He was very thrifty with the money he earned, and by the time Andrew was a high school senior, he was allowed to purchase a car. This made him perhaps the first child to own a car while still living on campus. It was a 1962 white, four-door Chevy II Nova. Andrew kept it exceptionally clean. Ted ('56–'69) laughs about a time with Andrew and the car: "We were both seniors and went out for the high school football team. We could leave the hot tobacco fields and go to football practice before school started. On one occasion, Andrew drove his car to the theater and we looked at a movie while skipping football practice. No one found out!"

Andrew's grades would go up and down through the years, but he always studied and worked hard on his school assignments. He was a 9th grade marshall, played basketball, received a Citizenship Award, and was in FFA. His 10th and 11th grade years were not as good, but in his senior year he played football, was on the Annual Staff, and was a member of the Bus Driver Club. His was strong in art, but weak in reading. He had an 87 average in his senior year.

It is reported the home found medical help for Andrew's speech problems early in his high school years. His frenulum was removed or clipped. This is the tissue that anchors the tongue to the floor of his mouth and it impeded his enunciation of words. The procedure was helpful.

In 1969, Andrew graduated from high school and served as the home's Alumni Association President from '69–'71. He was 20 years old, and the youngest and only child to become president of the association immediately after high school graduation in the 50-plus year history of the association. He enrolled in college and became a licensed pilot and flying instructor. The dedication to his studies and work ethic displayed at the home carried over into his adulthood. He was a member of the National Guard for seven years, active five years in the grape industry, hauled tobacco to warehouses for farmers, and did other odd jobs for income, including flying. He loved to water ski and camp.

On Saturday, February 18, 1978, three planes left Jacksonville, N.C. en route to Daytona Beach, Florida. They planned to attend the Darlington 500 being run on Sunday, February 19. Andrew piloted one of the planes, a

1969 Seniors: Ted Worthington, Joe Andrew Hartsfield, Steve Mitchell

single-engine Piper Cherokee, and carried three passengers. The other two larger planes were Cessna Cardinals. The Piper Cherokee crashed. One of the newspapers reporting the crash was *The Wilson Daily Times*, Wilson, N.C.:

> *A plane piloted by Joe Andrew Hartsfield of Bailey, N.C. is believed to have crashed during a heavy rainstorm in the marshes of Cumberland Island south of Jekyll Island, Georgia. A spokesman for FAA said Hartsfield radioed about 3:42 p.m. that he had two minutes of fuel left, but that he was trying to reach Jekyll Island. Two minutes later, the control center lost radio contact. A battery powered radio locator beacon on the plane sent signals for 90 seconds before it fell silent.*

Other reports stated Andrew made three attempts to land at Jekyll Island, but could not due to light rain and fog. He tried another airport at Brunswick, Georgia but could not make it. Air, land, and sea searches were called off days later. His body was never recovered.

On February 16, 1978, a memorial service for Andrew (Turp) was held at the White Oak Hill Free Will Baptist Church near his home. He left behind his wife Lib, and two sons, Joseph and Travis. And too, he left behind over 150 of us "orphans" who had lived and enjoyed him at the home. Today, his headstone reads: "Believed To Have Died".

I've struggled for years to write this column, but feel this moment that this is the time for this story to be told and for you to know the struggles of Turp and his final journey.

JOE ANDREW HARTSFIELD
APR. 4, 1949
BELIVED TO HAVE DIED
FEB. 18, 1978

Think of Art

Art Masker
1973–2013

HOLSTON UNITED METHODIST HOME FOR CHILDREN
GREENEVILLE, TENNESSEE

Published: October 9, 2013

The Speaker of the House of Tennessee and a local representative introduced the proclamation that September 26, 2013 would be declared "Arthur S. Masker Day." On the same day in Greeneville, Tennessee, Mayor W.T. Daniels issued a similar proclamation there, and Arthur was presented with an Award of Merit, signed by Governor Bill Haslam.

After serving Holston United Methodist Home for Children (HHC) for 40 years, Art Masker retired. He had worked there since 1973, and his last 14 years were spent as President/Chief Executive Officer. During his tenure at HHC, thousands of children were served; since 2009 alone, 3,300 children from Tennessee and 401 from Virginia have been helped.

His retirement gala was held on the campus of HHC. Family, friends, board members, former staff and children traveled to the campus to be part of the celebration. Accolades were abundant, tears trickled at times, and laughter was plentiful. Art is not one to seek recognition, and at times he seemed unsure of how to respond to the recognitions being heaped by those who loved and respected him. One of the Art's biggest surprises was seeing eight former girls and their housemother in attendance at the party.

Art with former girls and housemother

"I was totally caught off guard and it was the best surprise of the day. I had been communicating with one of the girls (Kim, L-R third woman in photo) who organized Holsten Home's Facebook page (Holston Home children all grown up). She connected with the other girls. One of the biggest rewards in this job is seeing some of these children grow up, get married, and be good parents and good citizens— then come 'home' to say 'thanks'," said Masker.

I caught up with Kim ('77–'82) following the afternoon program, and she told the story of her marriage on the campus at HHC.
"Later in my life, I met the man of my dreams. Richard asked me to marry him. I had no clue when or where I wanted our bond to be consummated. He said how about the children's home? I contacted Art for the first time in 16 years. I heard his voice and I knew I was going home for my marriage. Art contacted the chaplin who was at the home when I was there, the Reverend Ken Verran, and he came back and married us. We, too, contacted my house parents from the home, Mary and Roy Allen ('75–'85), Mom Mary and Dad Roy Allen. Dad Allen gave me to my husband. Art walked me up and handed me off to Dad Allen. It was a great and most happy day for me and the beginning of my wonderful life."

Kim and Roy now live in Vinson, Virginia.

Other girls attending Art's retirement celebration: Ivy ('77–'79), Tina ('81 –'84), Lisa Diane ('76 –'84), Vivian ('77 –'84), Jeanette ('77 –'83), Deanna, Wendy ('76 –'88), and housemother Mary Allen ('75 –'85). Two of the alumni live in Virginia and others in Tennessee.

Art grew up in Pleasantville, New York. He remembers it this way.

"We grew up in the house that originally belonged to my maternal GM. It was the only house we lived in all those years. The town, I guess you could say, had a lot of well-to-do people; we scraped by but it was a nice home. I

describe my parents (affectionately) as Archie and Edith - dad never cared too much about what other people thought and he was rarely in church. He was era big man and at times an intimidating man. His parents divorced when he was three and he and his mother moved in on the farm with his maternal GPs. Dad dropped out of school after an elementary education. He was pretty much a self-made man but didn't learn much about 'relationships'. Mother always cared too much about what other people thought, was in church every time the doors opened, served as church treasurer for so many years.

"I worked hard growing up to raise the money I needed for Scout activities—shoveling snow, mowing yards, delivering newspapers, etc. I grew up in the church in a youth group (was a leader), Scouts and singing in the choir. I played the violin from elementary school through 9th grade when I let peer pressure get the best of me (one of my lifetime regrets—of course we didn't know anything about the 'fiddle' then)."

Art earned his Boy Scout Eagle and God and Country award in his youth. He's held nearly all leadership positions in scouting, and last year was awarded his 50-year pin from the Boy Scouts of America. In 1995, Art was awarded the Silver Beaver Award for distinguished volunteer service, and the Pioneer Award for Distinguished Service to Boyhood. He has completed Woodbadge training and served as a crew leader at Philmont Scout Ranch, Cimaron, New Mexico.

He and his wife of 45 years, Marty, have three daughters. They met at Maryville College, Maryville, Tennessee, where they were both students. They married June 22, 1968. Mary, a school teacher, has been a rock by his side throughout the years, and he has stood by her.

During the early years of their marriage, they had to face Art's federal charges for refusing the draft during the Vietnam War.

"I was immersed in Quaker thinking while I worked at Friendsville Academy (FA) (Headmaster/Principal). That's when I declared myself a conscientious objector and refused (something I tried to achieve through normal routes with the Selective Services). I returned to Friendsville and was assigned there. When I resigned my position at FA, I had to find a place approved for Selective Service. I found Holston United Methodist Home in a listing of such approved organizations, and sent a letter and resume, outlining that I was seeking a selective service approved employment. Then Executive Director Richard Roe called me, invited me for an interview, and offered me a job

after that first interview. I completed my Selective Service requirement while working at HUMH and was later pardoned by President Gerald Ford."

At Art's retirement, he was greeted by a former employee of the Home, Dr. Keith Bailey, now employed by the University of Tennessee (Art and Keith worked together for 21 years). Dr. Bailey handed Art a letter, within which read:

"I honor you and have great respect for your services to the children in your care, to their families, and to the staff who served under your leadership. Not only do I respect the work that you have done at Holston Home, I respect your decision as a conscientious objector that led you there. You are a man of integrity."

Art heard from a parade of people during his retirement celebration:

- Bill Bryant, Network Administrator, made available the photo for this column. He worked with Art for 15 years. His note on Art: "A real person, a real leader and a real servant! He is the most consistent and genuine person I have ever known."

- Kathy Meyers, Administrative Assistant to Art for over 19 years, told this story of his humor and tomfoolery. Everyone on campus knew Kathy's mouse phobia. One night she sat on her kitchen table waiting for her family to return home while a mouse played under the table.

"The next morning, I conveyed my story to my co-workers; they were all sympathetic, but thought it was quite humorous since I'm such an in-control person. The very next morning (two whole nights from the incident), I walked into my office and over to my desk. I removed the cover from my typewriter; and there was a dead mouse in the carriage of the typewriter! I'm such an expert on mice, I knew immediately that it was fake—but the fact that someone did that to me was simply shocking. I asked everyone from the maintenance guys to the receptionist to the ladies in the kitchen—no one knew who did the dirty deed. My husband asked me if I thought Art could have done it; I immediately replied, no way... Art would NEVER do anything like that—not to me. The next morning, Art walked into my office with his head down, and sheepishly said that he had a confession to make: he had done the dirty deed of planting the fake mouse. I know this is hard to believe, but I was actually speechless. When I caught my breath, I pointed my finger in Art's face and told him in no

uncertain terms, that he should never do that again. If he did, I and all my knowledge would be out the door. He profusely apologized (even brought me coffee), and then suggested that I seek counseling for my phobia." Vice-President and Human Resources and Staff Development Director, Kathlene Hoard has known Art for over 30 years. She told the audience: "If you want an example of someone who dreams and works hard to achieve that dream, think of Art. If you want an example of someone who is stubborn and persistent against all odds and fiercely loyal, think of Art. If you want an example of someone who loves Holston Home with his whole being, think of Art. If you want an example of someone who has followed John Wesley's rule: 'Do all the good you can, by all the means you can, in all the ways you can, in all the places you can, at all the times you can, to all the people you can, as long as you ever can,' think of Art. And if you want an example of someone who has made a difference in the lives of children and families and will continue to make a difference in the lives of children and families, think of Art Masker."

I have known Art since the late 1990s and while he did not share the experience of spending part or all of his childhood in a children's home, he comes as close as any child care professional I've known who understands the footprints of our sandals. Through the years he has remarked to me, "You understand better than us." Today, I would say to Art, after 40 years trying to understand us… you do get it. Thanks.

The Winds Have Welcomed You

Cynthia Batten
2001–2015

FREE WILL BAPTIST CHILDREN'S HOME
MIDDLESEX, NORTH CAROLINA

Published: December 11, 2013

'Ride in a hot air balloon' was written in 54-year-old Cynthia Batten's bucket list. This Christmas, a celebratory cork hangs on Cynthia's Christmas tree. It's from the champagne bottle opened by the pilot on October 15, 2013, as he and his crew toasted her successful hot air balloon flight. As he uncorked the bottle, he recited "the balloonist prayer:"

"The Winds have welcomed you with softness. The Sun has blessed you with his warm hands. You have flown so high and so well that God has joined you in your laughter and set you gently back again into the loving arms of Mother Earth."

At age 40, Cynthia was diagnosed with Multiple Sclerosis (MS). She was experiencing severe headaches at the base of her neck and shoulders and later had a facial stroke. Doctors first suspected Bells Palsy, but after testing concluded it was MS. Cynthia was open to sharing her MS progression over the years: *"Since being diagnosed with MS, I have experienced several different things. I tire very easily; I have difficulty sleeping; I have no sense of balance, and have lost some of my coordination. I have difficulty climbing steps. I fall frequently. I take a shot every day; the injection is supposed to keep my MS in remission and it has worked well so far. MS moves in different stages. It is worse on males than females. Your brain is thought to shrink as the disease progresses. Your muscles become weaker and weaker as time goes on. Your vision worsens, and usually patients become wheelchair bound or bed ridden."*

Three years ago, October 31, 2010, Cynthia's father passed away at age 75. He was 6'4" and had worked in a rock quarry all his life. In his last days he was bent over at the waist and could not hold himself up from his three year battle with Polymyositis, a rare inflammatory disease that leads to muscle weakness. He attended church every Sunday of his life up until three weeks before his death. Cynthia admits to being a tomboy and daddy's girl. His death had a profound impact on her.

It was after her father's death she added a hot air balloon ride to her bucket list, which she started after being diagnosed with MS. *"When I was diagnosed with MS,"* reflected Cynthia, *"it made me realize just how short our time here on this earth really is. There are so many beautiful and wonderful things close by that I thought were 'out of reach'. I just started to feel like there were things that I could do that would give me a sense of accomplishment.*

Freddie and Cynthia

Simple things like snorkeling (done that), parasailing (done that), climbing jockey's ridge (done that), outer banks in North Carolina (done that), white water rafting (done that), snow skiing (done that), and [after watching her Dad slowly deteriorate before her eyes] later adding on top of my list riding a hot air balloon (thankfully...now I have done that)."

So it was in October, the month of her father's death, that Cynthia and her husband Freddy experienced the high of their life by flying in a hot air balloon. *"After we launched and were in the air, the rays of sun were very prominent coming through the clouds... It was like what Freddie and I likened unto 'the glory of God' radiating throughout the earth. My husband has since remarked on the peacefulness he felt and the glory of God that was shining through the clouds."*

Cynthia recalled the morning of the flight (in Asheville, North Carolina). *"We got up early so we could leave on time. We met in the lodge kitchen area and heated up our ham and biscuits from the day before. We loaded the truck and headed off to the Asheville Chamber of Commerce, where we were suppose to meet a shuttle. We got there in no time, and pretty soon there were other couples arriving. We met several couples who had been scheduled and tried to fly on more than one occasion, but their flights were cancelled due to wind and weather. One couple was there from Tennessee—they were still cautious that even though we were getting ready to board the shuttle...we still might not fly, since they had experienced so many cancellations. The shuttle arrived promptly at 6:45 and we loaded up. There were 14 of us. I was concerned about how big the basket would be. We drove out of town and turned into a subdivision. As we wound around the subdivision we ended up alongside a field. We could see the balloons lying on the ground... not one balloon, but two. There were several men standing around the balloons, with a couple of vans parked near by. We walked through the field and waited for further instructions as the balloons were inflated. They were tethered to the ground. Our pilot, Addison, arrived; he had a clipboard in hand with names on it. When we originally booked our flights we had to give the weight of everyone flying. He divided the groups up according to weight. The basket had a center compartment, where the controls were and then on each side there were two sections. The outer part of the basket looked like wicker, but was made of some type of heavy plastic material. The inside of the section was lined with some type of black material and there was a type of padding around the top edge. The bottom was not solid, kind-a felt like woven something... but seemed sturdy enough. The basket was tall, coming up about 4 feet and there were slots in the side (staggered in height) for you to put your foot in to climb in. In our basket were my husband and me, the couple we traveled with on the other side, and then there were two older ladies, one thin and the other a little heavy with some handicap. The helpers came over and instructed us to 'put your foot in the slot and pull yourself up so your behind is sitting on the edge of the basket'. Then you could swing your legs around and slide down into the basket'. I was a little afraid I might have trouble getting in, but 'it was a piece of cake'. I climbed right on in and my husband came right in behind me. We watched the others climb in our basket (the lady with the handicapped had a little trouble getting in, and the crew had to hoist her in. We had been instructed to wear hats, since the fire that helps inflate the balloon sometimes gets warm to the top of your head. Our pilot Addison greeted us and then talked via radio to someone and we were ready to fly. He let the pilot (a lady) of the second balloon go up first. Their balloon lifted straight up off the ground and because there was no wind it seemed to hover directly above us, which kept us from taking off. After just a few minutes our pilot was able to see the other balloon, so the tethers were loosened and we started to rise."*

As the balloon ascended, Cynthia observed, *"It was very still and you could only tell you were rising because the ground was getting further away. We drifted up above the trees and it was a wonder feeling of "wow". I had worried it would be cold, but the heat from the burner and lack of wind made it a very pleasant ride. Addison told us we were on a mountain that was already 2,000 feet above sea level and that we would ascent another 2,000 or so feet. He told us where he thought we would be landing, but that really would be just guess work. We drifted across the interstate highway and the vehicles looked like matchbox cars and trucks below. I couldn't help but wonder how any people were looking out their car windows to see the balloons, or if it was just a common occurrence in that area. As we drifted along, maybe 30 minutes or more, we could see not only the balloon that launched with us, but we could see four more balloons. It was an absolutely perfect day to be flying....Addison, our pilot, said more than 50% of his flights had to be rescheduled due to weather....*

"I felt like I was on top of the world... knowing we scheduled only once and we got a picture perfect day. We were blessed. While flying it was indescribably peaceful. There was very little conversation... just the look of awe on everyone's face. When the pilot started talking via radio to the "chasers" I did get a little concerned when he had to change his estimated landing about three times. But like he said... this balloon doesn't have a steering wheel... or breaks. I found out the true meaning of 'Going with the Flow'. The entire flight lasted about 38 minutes from the time we launched until we landed. It was just beautiful being 'free' and unencumbered... floating through the air. You could see the landscape for miles, and other balloons floating along the horizon."

Prior to descending from the flight, the pilot radioed the "chasers" of the balloon's location. As the balloon was coming down in a pasture, he asks the passengers to stay in the basket until the "chasers" had control of the balloon.

As the balloon descended slowly in the pasture, the "chasers" began running towards the balloon. The pilot released the tether lines and the "chasers" hurried to grab them as the balloon landed on unlevel ground. *"They literally pulled us to a more level spot in the pasture. Some of the "chasers" stood on the edge of the basket while the others pulled on the tethers as the balloon started to deflate. We couldn't get out because if the weight was displaced while the balloon was still inflated it would rise up into the air again. One the balloon was stable, we had to hoist our behind up on the basket and then swing our legs around and jump to the ground... not much of a drop. My husband got out of our side first and then helped me out."*

Cynthia still has a few items on her bucket list: trips to London, Hawaii, and Australia; she would like to own a small antique or craft shop, as well as a peach orchard (she has two peach trees now); she wants to spend a few days high in the mountains in a log cabin with a huge fireplace... overlooking mountains; and she wants a '65 red Mustang.

Note: Cynthia Batten attended Nash Community College. She worked closely with the Alumni Association during her employment with the Free Will Baptist Children's Home, Middlesex, North Carolina. Cynthia was an Administrative Assistant II and her work assignment was in Development. She was appreciated and respected by alumni.

Batten Family: L-R Freddy, Cynthia, Chris and Carter

Our Mother Teresa

Sudie Mixon
1948–59

FREE WILL BAPTIST CHILDREN'S HOME
WILSON, NORTH CAROLINA

Published: September 14, 2016

Sudie Mixon was the Class Poet of her 1934 high school graduating class. At age sixteen she enrolled in Campbell Junior College. After completing one year of college, she married Horace. He was nineteen and She seventeen. Horace was one year out of an orphanage where he'd spent eleven years of his childhood.

I first met Sudie on August 28, 1949. She was 31 that year, and I was in the second grade. She cooked a birthday cake for me that December, and one for my twin sister Nancy. Until that year, Nancy and I had always shared a birthday cake. It was important to Ms. Sudie that we each have our own cakes. I've never forgotten those cakes. Nor have I forgotten the next ten years of cakes she prepared for me. She also cooked birthday cakes for the other 100 children on campus each year. It was important to Ms. Sudie that each child at the orphanage receive a cake on their birthday. Ms. Sudie was the orphanage dietitian.

Her husband Horace was the farm manager at the home. We boys helped with growing our beef cattle, milking cows, gathering eggs, growing tobacco, corn, and soy beans, and planting our gardens. Our proteins came from milk, beef, pork and eggs. We harvested the crops from the farm and cared for the livestock. Horace was responsible for the farm and oversaw our work there.

Horace had spent time as a child (1923–34) at the same orphanage of his employment. When Sudie and Horace arrived on campus in 1948, their two children, Peggy and Charles, were with them. Peggy and Charles were friends with

1949 Nancy & Jerry Smith

all of us at the home, and we all attended the same public school. In 1955, Peggy graduated Valedictorian of her high school class. The previous year, 1954, Lillie Faye Watson (1946–54) graduated Valedictorian at the same high school. Children from the orphanage walked with pride knowing for two straight years in high school one of them from campus had top honors in the graduating classes. In 1962, yet another resident of the orphanage, Margie Herring (1952–62), was Valedictorian of her class. Ms. Sudie's son Charles played on the orphanage baseball team and the high school team with many other boys from the home.

Sudie's husband Horace enjoyed playing pranks on her. Tommy Lancaster (1955–65) smiled as recalled this story of how Horace castrated pigs on the farm and placed all the testicles in a bucket. He then gave Tommy the bucket and told him to take the "mountain oysters" to Sudie for her to cook. Seeing the contents of the bucket, Sudie smiled and sent the bucket and contents back to Horace. Tommy also remembered Sudie cooking him pies from blackberries he collected on the farm a day

Mixon Family – Back Row L-R: Horace, Sudie; Front Row L-R: Peggy, Charles

227

earlier. He recalls sharing the pie with his fellow orphan brothers at his table during meal time.

Phil Mercer (1953–68) said to me recently that a friend told him he had not had a birthday party since he was in the 3rd grade. While he did not say anything to his friend, he felt sad for him. Phil recalled Ms. Sudie always asked what was his favorite kind of cake was, and at dinner on the day of his birthday all the 100+ children and staff sang happy birthday to him. Afterwards, a cake with candles burning was carried to his table. He would cut a piece for all at the table, and afterwards would send a piece to a staff member or another child. He had two biological sisters at the home with him, Ona and Sandra, and they had cake too. Sandra died while at the orphanage.

Kathy Hines (1957–66) remembers Ms. Sudie's birthday cakes fondly. She remembers how Sudie transformed an ordinary birthday into something very special. It was a time none of the children receiving cakes had a biological parent attending their birthdays. This gift was only made possible by Sudie's genuine care to make a another mother's child's birth a memorable day for the child.

Margie Herring (1952–62) referred to Sudie as "Ma Sudie". Margie said Sudie taught her how to cook. While Sudie's birthday cakes were special for Margie, her best memory was of Sudie going to a high school function with her. At Middlesex High School, there was a mother-daughter banquet. Sudie was Margie's stand-in for a mother at the event. They enjoyed the event together and Sudie remembered that into her last days.

While Ray Worthington (1956–63) remembers his birthday cakes from Sudie warmheartedly, his fondest reminiscence is when he and Leroy Miller (1952–60) ran away from the orphanage. Along the way they spotted a car stopping to give them a ride. When they got to the car, they saw Sudie and Horace inside, smiling kindly. They offered to take them to a nearby town where they could catch a ride back with the children from the orphanage who were there shopping for school supplies. Ray was grounded for a month after he returned to the orphanage, but he always appreciated the fair treatment he received from Sudie and Horace.

Sudie and Horace left the home after eleven years. She became Food Service Director at the Eastern N.C. School for the Deaf. Horace died July 5, 1982. I was honored to be one of his pallbearers. In 1999, floods from Hurricane

Floyd destroyed Sudie's home and car. She lived in an apartment until 2006 when she moved into senior assisted living care.

JoEtta Worthington (1954–62) visited Sudie at her assistant living residence. At that time, Sudie had lost her glasses and hearing aids and everyone was searching for them. Sudie still was talking about the birthday cakes. She remembered JoEtta's favorite was pineapple. It was JoEtta's last visit with her.

Sudie's Birthday Cake

1 pound of butter, softened
2 cups of sugar
8 large eggs
4 cups of flour
2 teaspoons of vanilla

Cream butter and sugar until light and fluffy. Add eggs and continue to beat. Gradually add flour and vanilla and mix thoroughly. Bake in tube pan at 325° about 1 hour and 15 minutes.

On the most important days of my youth, Ms. Sudie always saw that a cake was cooked for me. I have tried to honor her for being there for me. For most of my adult life, I've sent Ms. Sudie a Mother's Day card. I saw to it that she received my card and love for doing what a mother would do for a child—cook a birthday cake.

Ms. Sudie had a way of treating each child as special. I had rabbit boxes and caught many rabbits and squirrels in my youth. I remember checking my rabbit box immediately after breakfast, then returning to the dormitory and placing the live rabbit in a barrel before catching the bus for school. Returning from school in the afternoon, I'd immediately get the rabbit and dressed it for eating. I'd placed it in the refrigerator at the dining hall where Ms. Sudie would make sure it was fried and given to me that night for dinner. I could choose to share if I wished, and almost always did with the other boys. I'd also send a piece to my twin sister Nancy sitting with the girls across the dining room.

On another occasion I remember going to the woods and picking blackberries one summer. It was a Saturday afternoon. On returning I inquired from Ms. Mixon if I could go to the dining room and eat the berries with my

Army Medic Jerry Smith

sister. She made sure I had a can of Carnation milk and sugar to mix with the berries. It was a special gathering for Nancy and me.

In 1965, after two and half years stationed in Germany with the U.S. Army, I ended my tour of duty. Before I left Europe I had to send my personal possessions to a permanent address in the states. I did not have a permanent place to send my stuff, so Ms. Sudie allowed me to mail them to her address.

On August 8, 2016, at age 98, Ms. Sudie died. Today, she rests next to her beloved Horace.

For many girls and boys, Sudie was our saint, our Mother Teresa. Her kindness and love are wired into our subconscious... in our hearts and souls. She will forever be with us as we continue on our life path.

Sudie McLeod Mixon, 98, died August 8, 2016. She was truly my Mother Teresa. My love for her will always be in my heart.

The Valedictorian

Margie Herring Sullivan
1952–62

FREE WILL BAPTIST CHILDREN'S HOME
WILSON, NORTH CAROLINA

Published: March 8, 2017

She was valedictorian of her 1962 high school class, a member of the Beta and 4-H clubs, and a member of the basketball team for all four years, co-captaining in her senior year. There were 46 students in the class, five of whom were from the orphanage of Margie's home. She learned of her honor the day before graduation, and wrote her speech overnight so she could deliver it at graduation. When the time arrived, she could not bring herself to do it and sat silently. Margie was shy and lacked self-confidence, and ultimately refused to deliver her speech to the class and those in attendance.

Margie's orphanage home was my home, too. With 100 other children on campus, we accepted each other as brothers or sisters—through sometimes we became boyfriend and girlfriend. When that didn't pan out, we went back to being brother and sister again. This was true of Margie and me. Our boyfriend/girlfriend relationship ended my senior year in high school when I left the

231

Margie and Jerry in 1960

orphanage. She stayed for two more years. Throughout it all, we've had an unbreakable bond and a strong brother/sister relationship that's lasted for more than fifty years. Our spouses have understood and accepted our closeness. Margie and her husband have spent nights in our home in the mountains of North Carolina.

Our transformation friendship goes back to June 1952 when Margie was admitted to the Free Will Baptist Children's Home, the orphanage of my youth. She and her two siblings had only the clothes on their back when they arrived. Margie was a skinny little girl who was very bashful and scared. Her clothes were later thrown away. She came to campus without other clothes, toys or a baby doll. In fact, Margie never owned a baby doll in her youth.

This was my second eulogy and by far the most difficult and most enjoyable. It was a celebration of Margie Herring Sullivan's life. She passed on February 17, 2017, at the University of North Carolina Medical Center, Chapel Hill, North Carolina. She was 72. The church seated 300 people and was nearly full when the celebrations began. Fifty of the front row seats in one section of the church were reserved for alumnus and family from the Children's Home. Another section up front was reserved for her biological family and in-laws.

Margie's husband Michael asked me to give the eulogy, and to make sure there was humor in my words. I honored his wish.

Even with her shyness, Margie was very mischievous little girl. It might coincide with her arrival at the Home, when the big girls held her hands under water until she told them her deepest secrets. She admitted to them she wet the bed at nights.

On another occasion she was caught spying on the older girls dating in the first floor parlor of the three floor brick building where all the girls were housed. In the fifth grade she was given "U's" (unsatisfactory) on conduct for numerous grading periods... although her other grades were good. Her "U's" usually came from throwing rocks during break or talking during class.

At the orphanage her mischievousness was different. The dietician would scold her for cooking scrambled eggs too hard for the 100 plus being fed. She would laugh about it in later years saying the eggs were so hard you could play ball and jacks with them. On one occasion Margie was waiting on tables during breakfast during the summer months. One of the older girls dared her to tie

L-R: My sister Nancy and Margie

themselves together with their apron strings. Margie got behind the older girl and was fastened facing the girl's back. A hand went up from one of the tables to fill an empty bowl and I remember we all laughed seeing this skinny little girl being dragged by the older girl going to the table. The dietician didn't laugh. Their punishment was to stay tied together until lunch time that day.

Dancing and playing with dice or cards was not permitted on campus. The belief was that those activities would send you straight to hell. Dice were removed from games like Monopoly and a thump wheel was used; wherever the hand stopped after turning told you the number of moves to make.

The girls rode a different school bus than the boys. Returning from school in the afternoons and before doing their choirs, the girls would turn on the television for few minutes to watch dancing on Dick Clark and American Bandstand. Afterwards they'd go to their rooms, closed the door, turn on the radio and dance together listening to music of the '50s and '60s. If there was an odd girl, she would dance with one of the bed posts.

With her high grades in high school, Margie was awarded a scholarship to Atlantic Christian College, but she turned it down to attend Mount Olive Jr. College. The president of the college was a former child at the Free Will Baptist Home, Dr. Burkette Raper. After she graduated from college, she worked with the Walt Disney Company in Florida, then with an insurance company, and her final employment was with a law firm.

In May 2009, Margie, age 65, received a liver transplant. It was from a 27-year-old man. Her blue eyes sparkled as she told me it made her feel younger and stronger. It gave her seven more years of life. She'd smile when I kidded with her about her voice changing. When she would call I would insist "he" was not Margie and to put her on the line to talk with me. I still remember her laughter.

We've shared many laughs during her time receiving medical treatments at the hospital of my alma mater, University of North Carolina—Chapel Hill. Margie was a Duke fan. On one stopover to visit her in the hospital, I informed the nurse that Margie was a "Dooky." Several days later UNC and Duke played each other... I need to say UNC won. Prior to the game, doctors and nurses came to see her and asked if she really was going to pull for Duke while being treated at the UNC Medical Center. After leaving the hospital she called and we laughed about it. I told Margie the "Tar Heel" hospital was a good place to leave for the other side when the day came. It is a straight line to heaven, I suggested. We both laughed.

In her adult years, Margie found two brothers and a sister who had not been sent to the orphanage with her. I remember saying to her she was dreaming; she really didn't have other siblings. She gave me this beautiful smile and she knew I was kidding with her. I met these siblings at Margie's funeral.

During my eulogy to Margie, I looked at the biological family and said to them... Margie really does have other kin-folk. Everyone laughed. I then asked all those in reserved seats from the Children's Home to stand. There was laughter as I introduced Margie's "orphan" family to her other family sitting in reserve seats too.

My eulogy concluded with my reading an excerpt from the postscript of Margie's memoir, published in my book *The Family* (2010, Lulu Press and Amazon.com, by J. Andrews Smith):

"As I reflect back over my years at the Home, I realize and appreciate what God did for me when he removed me from a very poor life style and placed me in a safe environment. Where would I have gone—would I have received the training, education and religious upbringing that I received by being an orphan? I tremble, and yes, I sometimes cry, when I think about what kind of life I might have had. I believe I would have suffered tremendously and would have died at a young age. I am thankful I was placed in the orphanage at the age of seven because it gave me a better opportunity to mature above everyone's expectations. The psychologist in 1952 was right: 'In a more normal environment where she is loved and accepted and where some effort is made to understand her and to satisfy her needs she should be able to

*make a good adjustment, whether this is in an orphanage or a foster home.'
The orphanage/children's home provided that environment for me.*

*"Life is what we make of it and we are given choices. Life is too short to let
unhappiness and unforgiveness get in your way. Choose to move on and replace
the hurt with happiness. Think about it—being an orphan was not all bad; if
we had not become residents of the orphanage, we probably would not be as
successful as we are today and our morals would have been less desirable. Forgive
those who hurt you in the past—they cannot hurt you anymore, but they will if
you constantly dwell on the hurt and pain they caused you. We all had lots of
baggage and different personalities when we were admitted to the orphanage, but
I believe we all had similar circumstances that brought us together as a family.*

*"The orphanage/children's home provided us with a warm building and nice
beds to sleep in; we had good food; we wore nice clothes; the girls were taught
how to cook, iron, clean house, and preserve food for future use; the boys
were taught housekeeping, yard maintenance, and farm work; we were given
a chance to attend school; we were given money to spend, though maybe not
as much as we wanted; most importantly, we were taught about God and the
importance of doing what is right. I can tell you, without any hesitation, that
I would never have had life as rich as I had at the orphanage had I stayed in
the poor environment from which I came. Yes, I grew up without a mother,
a father, and most of my siblings and the love of my blood family, but look
at the family members I came to love, respect, and appreciate by being an
orphan. I will cherish my children's home memories forever, the good and
bad. I am proud and thankful to be a part of 'the family'."*

As I stood near Margie's grave for the final services, before the interment,
a group of singers stood near her casket and sang the great spiritual 'Amazing
Grace'. During the performance I experienced a metaphysical moment. I felt a
gentle warmth on the back of my right shoulder, seemingly from being pressed.
I turned my head and there wasn't anyone near me, but I felt an inward peace
from the warmth. In my mind's eye, it must have been my friend Margie.
Leaving the cemetery that day, I told my wife Susan about the moment.

The valedictorian and I have a special relationship that will continue to the
other side. She'll always be my friend and my sister, and my heart is wounded
with her passing.

Note: Photo at the beginning of the piece is Margie's high school senior picture.

4

New Stories for *The Family*

The following section contains three stories that should have been included in *The Family*, first published in 2010 by author J. Andrews Smith. Narratives for these stories weren't available at the time of publication. *The Family* tells the history of the Free Will Baptist Children's Home in Middlesex, North Carolina through memoirs by the children, staff, and staff's children who lived at the home for some duration over the 1920 to 2010 timeframe. It is important that these stories be published as they are historically significant. My thanks to the authors for sharing them now.

J. Andrews Smith

Serving Children
Was Their Calling

L-R: Edward, Charles, Edith with Kay in arms, Clifton, Lima and Richard, 1953

Edith Hedgepeth, Houseparent

FREE WILL BAPTIST CHILDREN'S HOME
MIDDLESEX, NORTH CAROLINA
1950–53

The Hedgepeth family moved to the Freewill Baptist Orphanage, Middlesex, North Carolina (as it was called then) sometime around Christmas and the first of the year, in 1950. We wanted to settle in our new home so Charles and Edward, our sons, could start to school after the holidays. Our daughter, Lima Keyes, was too young to attend school.

Walter M. Croom
Superintendent, 1949–51

Some may wonder why we left Greene County where we grew up, to go to Middlesex, North Carolina. The current Superintendent Walter Croom was a child at the orphanage 1930–39. He had been the Agricultural teacher at Maury High School, where Charles and Edward attended school. He and his wife attended our home church, Ormondsville Free Will Baptist. This is where we met and became friends. The Superintendent visited in our home and ate several meals with us.

In the fall of 1950, the Superintendent came to see us, and offered Clifton, my husband and me a job at the orphanage. It would be Clifton's job to farm the tobacco fields; while other times, he would work at the home. Both of us were to serve as relief house parents for the regular house parents, during their weekends and vacation time off. After moving to the orphanage, the current Superintendent and his wife never acknowledged our friendship, and we were ignored, which hurt us quite a bit at the time. The hiring had been by word of mouth, so many of the promises were not kept.

After being at the home for several weeks, we realized the economy was really bad, and some of the promises could not be kept. The young superintendent and his wife were a fine young couple whose lives had changed under the stress of all the responsibilities that came with being the superintendent. Times were hard, and very little money was coming in our household. It was more than they could cope with, for he had taken on a job he wasn't trained to do.

In the spring of 1951, the superintendent told my husband, Clifton, that he could not put oil burners in the tobacco barns as he had promised to do. He would have to cut fire wood for them. We knew the board had approved the burners, so it took only one trip to Micro, North Carolina to see Board Member R.N. Hinnant to solve this problem. The oil burners were installed before the tobacco went to the barn. We were disappointed in the superintendent, but we had become acquainted with most of the children and really loved them.

Mother and Daughter Banquet

There were a lot of fun times with them. One occasion that has brought me laughter over the years was my first Mother and Daughter banquet. Hilda Harrell (1938–53) invited me to the banquet to be her mother. When the night finally came, Hilda had on a pale green dress and a corsage of yellow roses. She was so pretty. All the girls were beautiful. The funny part was that this was the first time the girls had worn heels. You should have seen them walking. I can still remember how they walked for the first hour or two; they were stepping high like they walking on air. By the time the banquet was over, they had adjusted to the heels and were walking normal.

Jerry's Duck, Big Boy

Another memory that my family had enjoyed over the years is about "Big Boy," Jerry Smith's duck (1949–60). In the spring of 1951, when I went to gather my eggs one afternoon, I was surprised to find a big egg in the corner of my hen house. The next day there was another big egg, so during the day, I began to watch my hen house. What I saw really shocked everyone. Big Boy, Jerry's duck, had turned into Big Girl. My children had never seen a duck

1949 Brenda Mitchell, baby doll, Jerry, and Big Boy

egg before, so they wanted to taste one. We had plenty of hen eggs, so they decided that duck eggs were not as good as hen eggs. Big Girl continued to lay her eggs in my hen house. She sat on those eggs and I think she hatched some baby ducks. I can't remember her coming over the hill to lay again. She laid her eggs around campus so Jerry would have to search for them.

Laboring in the Tobacco Fields

When planting time came, what a surprise we had. We were used to sandy soil that was easy to cultivate; now we had red clay with plenty of rocks. We had become friends with Mr. and Mrs. Earl Deans on the adjoining farm. They gave us a few tips on how to cultivate the soil.

Finally the tobacco was planted and when harvest time came, the older boys and girls helped us put the tobacco in the barn. One very religious boy, Charles Page (1940–54) helped us. He worked in the field with my husband to prime the tobacco leaves. Charles didn't work as fast as the other boys and when you checked to see why he was behind, he was found on his knees praying. We couldn't decide if he was praying or killing time, so the other boys would help him finish his row of tobacco.

The last time I went to a homecoming, I went with Carrold (1946–53) and Hilda Harrell Little (1938–53) before they passed away.

I saw about 25 young men and women that were children, when I was there. One was a very distinguished young man and his wife. This was Charles Page who came up to me and said, "Mrs. Hedgepeth, I want to tell you the truth about my praying in the tobacco fields. I was praying that God would send a hail storm and destroy the tobacco." Thank God, his prayers were not answered. My family had some good laughs when I came home and told the story. At the time, I think Charles was a serving as a pastor somewhere in South Carolina.

The Birth of Richard, our Explorer

On August 22, 1951, we became proud parents of another son. I had promised the boys at the home, they could name the baby. After two weeks, they couldn't agree on a name, so we named him Richard Wilson. The next day, they came up with the name of Irvin Thomas; a very pretty name, but one day too late.

Richard was a favorite of all the children and when he began to walk, he would run away and go to the campus. Richard said he didn't run away, he was only exploring. When he was about 5 months old, he disappeared one evening and couldn't be found. We had searched everywhere. The men were about to go to the pond to look for Richard when someone found him in the kitchen being fed by the kitchen girls. This was one of many times that he was "exploring", as he now calls it.

One Sunday morning, the older children went to Sunday school and Church. Suddenly, we missed Richard, our two year old. We began to look for Richard and it's hard to believe what he had done, but we have pictures to prove it. Richard had put on my straw hat and a pair of my shoes. He walked all the way to the Church in my shoes. When he walked in the Church wearing my straw hat and my shoes, you can imagine what happened then; he broke up Church. A young preacher, Hansley who lived on campus was preaching that day. He said he dismissed the children because everyone was laughing at Richard and there was no way to calm them down. Over the years, Richard has been teased about breaking up Church.

A Man of Action

There was a change of superintendents in the spring of 1951. Stephen and Bertha Smith came to the orphanage and immediately everything changed for the better. My husband had worked on the Albemarle Cottage for a month before the change of superintendents. Mr. Smith told him there was no money to pay the bills, so write that month's work off as a gift to the orphanage, but in the future he would be paid. At the time, it was hard on us. We had a family to feed but God always provided for us.

My husband was called the 'Colonel' by the children because they respected and loved him. He had their best interest at heart, but he let them be children. When he saw girls and boys doing anything that was dangerous, he took action. He sometimes threw a rock to get their attention. If this didn't work, he could be firm but he did not report the children for being children. Driving to the ball games at night was especially hard. Horace Mixon would drive behind and shine his lights in the bus to see what the children were doing. He was afraid the boys and girls would hold hands or put their arms around each other.

Mr. Smith was a man of action; if he wanted something done, it must be done immediately. A good example, Larry Powell (1945–52) did something late one evening. The punishment he received was far greater than the crime. Because of his brother, Billy (1938–49), who was in prison; Mr. Smith said he must leave the orphanage that night. He told the Colonel to take him to Charlotte, North Carolina to his aunt and uncle's home. He would not agree to wait until the next morning. The Colonel took Carrold Little, an older boy and they drove all night taking that child to an aunt and uncle who didn't want him. My husband said that broke his heart leaving a young teenager with people who didn't welcome him in their home.

Stephen and Bertha Smith
1951–55 and 1956–58

We visited my sister in Charlotte, North Carolina a year or two later and went by to see Larry but no one was home. I have wondered what happened to Larry. I always thought Mr. Smith could have handled this situation in a different way.

Another example of "doing it now" was an afternoon in the early fall when Mr. Smith, now known as Pa Smith told the Colonel he wanted him to go up to Asheville, North Carolina to pick up canned goods and apples the churches had collected. He told my husband to leave then, spend the night and come back the next day. The Colonel came home and changed clothes and told me where he was going. He decided to take our boys Charles and Edward with him. He went by the school and picked up the boys. It was a warm fall day so they didn't take a coat. That night, in the mountains, it became very cold and the boys wished they had one. It was an exciting trip for them. The boys talked about the trip for months. Living at the orphanage did not allow for as much family time as we had before we went there.

Most of the time, I agreed with Pa Smith. Some of the boys at the orphanage and our sons, Charles and Edward did something he didn't approve of so he punished all the boys. We as parents were not consulted at all. Pa said if I didn't like the punishment, to keep my boys at home; that when they were on campus, the rules applied to all. Our boys decided they had rather play on the campus and take Pa Smith's punishment.

Pa Smith was a man of action. The orphanage began to prosper and it began to feel like we were living in another place. Ma and Pa Smith had no children of their own so they adopted all of the children. They worked hard to see that the children had a better place to live. Most of the children grew up to be responsible adults with a college education.

She Was a Mother to All Children

In the fall of 1951, the house mother left the Old Boy's building about two months before the new Albemarle building was finished. The Colonel and I were asked to move in with the boys.

What a change for us. We had three boys and one little girl. The reality of what we had taken on hit me a few days after moving in. Our son Charles and another little boy had a disagreement; both boys were crying and I heard the little boy say to Charles, "You have a mother to run to but I don't have anyone." What a sad situation, to have no one to talk to. I loved my children but this taught me to love all the children and be a mother to all of them.

There were both good and bad experiences and also some funny times. One of the younger boys got into Charles Harrell's (1938–51) candy. Charles was an older boy who had permission to sell candy to the other boys. This young boy didn't have money to buy a piece of candy, so he took it. I planned to spank him so I took him in our bed room to let him know we couldn't steal and to give him a spanking with my hand. To my surprise, our little dog, an Eskimo Spitz named Snowball had other ideas. He tried to bite me and in his way, he said no one was going to spank his friends. He defended all the children and if we had to punish a child, Snowball had to be placed in another room. This continued until the day he died. He loved all the children.

Richard Little (1951–56) age 7 had pneumonia; he was a very sick little boy. Dr. Powell came twice a day for a few days to look after him. I had to give him medicine around the clock. I slept very little while he was sick. Over the years I could not understand why his mother, Mrs. Lottie Little, who was also a house mother to the younger girls, didn't come to our building to check on her baby boy. After reading what Alice (1946-55), his sister, wrote in the book called "The Family," I realized the rules were so rigid at the home that she had to have permission to visit her sick baby. Alice wrote that it was hard on her to wave at her brother now that her mother was in charge of the smaller girls; she had to wave to her since she was an older girl. She could not go to her mother for comfort. She had to get permission to visit her. I am so glad to think that maybe the rigid rules are a thing of the past.

Christmas at Pope's Air Force Base

The Christmas in 1951 was a year that the children of the home and my family will never forget. There were 1,400 children from orphanages across North Carolina that were transported by train to Pope's Air Force Base in Fayetteville, North Carolina. The Air Force had a party and gave each child a gift. A turkey dinner was served with the most delicious dressing I had ever tasted. I asked one of the cooks how to make the dressing. He told me, and until this day about sixty years later, I get compliments when I fix my dressing. That day was warm and sunny and everyone enjoyed the train ride.

Family Time at the Orphanage

Life at the orphanage was hard on a family. When you went in the dining hall, all of us had to sit in three different places. My husband and I had to sit with the adults, Charles and Edward had to sit on one side with the boys, and Lima had to sit on the other side of the dining room with the girls.

We had every fourth weekend off so we back to our home. The children planned the menus. They wanted their favorite meals cooked with plenty of hot chocolate. We loved all the children but having family time became very special to us.

I learned many lessons on how to get along with other people while working in the home. I have learned not to get upset if my dinner plans are completely changed by my large family. The lesson I learned at the orphanage was to be flexible.

Cooking with the Preschool Children

After the Albemarle Cottage was completed, the boys moved into their new home. It was so different from the old boy's building. Every boy was so proud of his new room. Pa Smith had hired his staff so I wasn't needed anymore

Old Boys Building

Albemarle Cottage

at the home. My husband, the Colonel continued to work in the laundry room with Granny Sanderson and he also did other odd jobs. Pa Smith often asked me to look after the preschool boys so the matrons could have a break. I would take them to my house and let the little boys help me cook. They loved to take the biscuit dough and make little men using raisins for eyes and buttons. They enjoyed eating biscuits out of the oven with a cup of hot chocolate. This was a treat for the little boys for no one at the home had time to work with them.

Our Special Treat At the Ice Capades

Our children worked hard that summer putting tobacco in the barn, so we promised them a treat. In late August, my husband had a fiend in Middlesex that was selling tickets to the Ice Capades in Raleigh, North Carolina. He was able to buy front row seats for us. What a treat for all of us! My husband and I had never seen an ice show before. Charles, Edward, and Lima were so fascinated with the skaters that they never asked for anything to eat or drink that evening. They kept their eyes glued on the skaters. It was a night our family will never forget. We couldn't afford many treats for our children. There was a little place close to the children's home that made the best hot dogs and milkshakes you ever tasted, so we took them there every few weeks for a special treat.

My Worst Scare

In the early Fall, I was grading tobacco at the little stone house at the end of the farm next to the Dean's property. I was in a room with only one door with no one nearby except Richard, our eighteen months old baby. I looked up and there stood a convict in the door. I have never been so frightened in my whole life. I screamed so loud that it frightened the convict. He ran and brought back the supervisor who was in charge of the road work. This man was a trustee and he had permission to try and sell his leather wallets. They apologized for frightening me so badly, but to this day, that was the worst scare I have ever had. That was the last day I worked alone so far from anyone.

Lima and her Bicycle

Lima received a bicycle for Christmas in 1951. She didn't try to ride it, but pushed it to the children's home often so her little friends could ride. Around Thanksgiving, my husband told Lima if she didn't learn to ride the bicycle by Christmas, he was going to give it away. When Lima told her friends that the bicycle was going to be given away if she didn't learn to ride, all of the little girls worked hard to teach Lima how to ride. They pushed her around campus until she could ride by herself.

Lima Keyes Hedgepeth

They didn't want to lose their bicycle they had been riding and the enjoyment they got for almost a year. I really think my husband planned to give the bicycle to Lima's friends so it could stay at the children's home instead of being pushed each day from one home to another.

Our Special Angel

On April 18, 1953, we became proud parents of a little 6 lb. baby girl, who we named Deborah Kay. We soon noticed that something wasn't normal with the baby. She slept all of the time and a little noise would make her go into a coma and we couldn't wake her. We took her to our pediatrician in Wilson, North Carolina. He said he had been working with my gynecologist, and they decided it was best not to say anything to us as parents because they didn't think the baby would live to leave the hospital. She was a mongoloid with a malformed heart. To keep her alive, we had to be very careful of the noise and also feed her special foods so each mouthful would count.

Mary and Clarence Mitchell were now house parents for the boys. Mary became a living angel for me. She would keep Kay when I needed to do any work on the farm. We were still planting the tobacco for the children's home. As lively as the boys were, when Kay entered the building, you could hear the boys say to each other, "Be quiet, Kay is in the building." I cannot say "Thank You" enough for Mary Mitchell. This was really hard on our family. We couldn't go home for family reunions, birthdays, or any special events. Because of Mary's kindness, we were able to ride to Maury, North Carolina one Sunday afternoon for short visit to see my parents. That was the only visit I was able to make that year.

Our Life After Leaving the Children's Home

We decided after tobacco barning, it was time for us to leave the children's home. We had three dry summers, so we didn't make a good crop either year. My husband, the Colonel was not making enough money working part time to support us.

In late November of 1953, we leased a big farm near Walstonburg, North Carolina and moved there. We kept in touch with the children's home and when Kay passed away on February 10, 1954, we called Pa Smith and he planned the funeral for us. Three older girls sang some special songs with Miss Bonnie farmer playing the piano for them. Eight little girls from the children's home were flower girls and Pa Smith preached the funeral. I still have a dried orchid from the wreath of flowers given by the children's home.

The trio of girls that sang at Kay's funeral was Thelma Bradshaw (1944–54), Doris Tyson (1943–54) and Faye Watson (1946–54). The Floral bearers were Daisy Pope (1952–63), Nancy Pope (1952–61), Evelyn Herring (1952–63), Margie Herring (1952–62), Cora Lee Jones (1949–61), Louise Morris (1952–59), Nancy Smith (1949–60) and Faye Hardee (1952–63).

Leaving the children's home didn't keep us from loving the children. We visited Mary and Clarence Mitchell, but as we became involved with the activities of our church and 4-H, the visits became fewer each year.

Carrold Little adopted us the first day we went to the orphanage to clean the house and yard, so we could move in. When he was working at the dairy barn, Carrold could smell biscuits and sweet potatoes baking. Many times he slipped in the back door of our home to eat.

We didn't approve of the ways the children were punished but it broke our hearts to see Carrold abused by the farm manager. They didn't like each other and Carrold talked too much. Carrold fell off a tobacco barn and broke his back. Before it could heal, he was made to throw corn in the barn after it was harvested. This caused Carrold to have back troubles all of his life.

L-R: Charles, Lima, Edith, Richard and Edward, 2012

Carrold married Hilda Harrel from the home and they were our adopted children all of their lives. Through this couple and their family, we kept up with the news of the children's home. Bobby Herring (1952–59) spent a few Christmas' with us so he came by to visit when he was passing through Kinston. He came by to see me the last year he lived. William (1943–54) and Louise Lane (1943–54) dropped in to see us for many years. Their visits could be any hour, day or night. The most unusual one was at 12:15 am one night.

My husband passed away on August 24, 1995. I was able to visit the children's home with Carrold and Hilda Little twice for the homecomings in July. The first time I visited, I was able to see about twenty-five alumni from the early fifties. It was so good to talk to each one and learn of their accomplishments. My husband and I loved all the children and we were proud of each and every one.

Precious Memories

When *The Family* (written by Jerry Smith [1949–60]) was published, I read through it twice because I felt like I had gone to a family reunion. It brought back so many memories. There was a lot of excitement all the time, good and bad, happy and unhappy times. The years we spent at the children's home were never boring. I have tried to write the most interesting events that took place the three years at the children's home. The one lesson I learned is that family is so important and always work to keep them together.

In *The Family*, Jerry wrote about his memory of hitting my son Charles on the head with a rock. "I've always regretted hitting Charles," he wrote. Charles later read the book and what Jerry said. He wrote Jerry a letter.

December 5, 2012
Dear Jerry,
Merry Christmas!
I have read you book, The Family, *and I can identify with a large portion of it because I remember many of the people whom we knew when we lived at the home from '51–'53. I could visualize most of the places as they were described.*

I barely remember the rock throwing incident which you described. Anyway, I forgive you. The rock incident which I do remember most is when I threw a rock to skip it across the pond and it hit a girl above the eye.

I am semi-retired and working three days a week. Elia Mae and I have five biological children and two adopted children from ages 19 to 46. We have been blessed with fourteen grandchildren.

I enjoyed your interesting book about the lives of the children at the orphanage. We saw Carold and Hilda Little through the years when we visited in North Carolina. They kept an ongoing relationship with Mama.

Sincerely,
Charles Ray Hedgepeth
Middletown, New York

Note: Edith Hedgepeth was 91 when she penned her story for this book. In June 2017, Edith turned 96. She still drives her car. Her current North Carolina driving licenses expires 2021, the year she turns 100. Her son Edward, a heart transplant recipient, had his surgery in 1991 at Duke University Hospital, Durham, North Carolina.

Mr. Drake

J. Enid Drake, Coach

Middlesex High School
Middlesex, North Carolina

1954–65

In 1954, all the children at the Free Will Baptist Orphanage attended public school, both elementary and high school at the same site in Middlesex, North Carolina, located two miles from the orphanage. The number of children varied from year to year, but there were 80–90 students attending when Coach Drake began teaching and coaching. Children rode the bus to school each day and the driver of the bus was one of the older boys at the home. He made two trips to school each morning. The first bus carried all the boys; second trip was for all the girls.

In the early years, children received their first seven years of education at the orphanage and last four at Middlesex High School. There were only eleven years of school required in North Carolina until 1946.

In 1952, two years prior to Enid's coming to Middlesex High School, an orphanage alumnus, Ralph Pate (1933–43), sponsored construction of a regulation size baseball field on the orphanage campus. Prior to the field, there was always sandlot baseball played, but once the field was built, interest in playing teams from the community and even in other counties gave athletes a chance to compete and

Little Family at the Orphanage

measure their skills with outside teams. They soon realized they could not only complete, but were better skilled at playing the game of baseball than many of the teams they played.

During the summer, the boys did farm work during the week, including harvesting tobacco. They worked in the fields from 8:00–11:30 a.m. when the iron bell would ring and call them to lunch. After they ate, they were back at work by 1:30 p.m. Instead of resting during their lunch break, many chose to practice baseball before returning to the tobacco field. On Saturdays, boys went to the fields by 8:00 a.m. and worked until lunch, then afterwards it was time to prepare for the afternoon baseball game.

Foul lines had to be limed and the field prepared for the game. Sometimes there wasn't any lime to mark the first or third base lines, so flour was used to make the foul lines. Everyone turned out for games on Saturday... this was old-time baseball. Baseball bats were made of wood—some homemade by one of the house parents. In the sixties, one of the alumni, Jerry Smith (1949–60) was in the U.S. Army stationed in Germany. There he saw some uniforms being discarded, so he requested the army to send them to the orphanage. These were the first uniforms worn by the boys. Because of their love for the game and an opportunity to compete and develop skills, many of the boys went on to play baseball in high school and college.

The Watermelon Game

In the early years, they played sandlot with any team that would play them, including church teams, semi-pro teams, and prison teams. The orphanage did not allow the boys to play "outside" teams on Sundays, so then they chose up sides and played each other.

Nashville Prison played the orphanage several times a summer. Many of the inmates were gifted athletes and were very friendly to the orphanage team members. Usually the game was close until the later innings, when you could expect a few hits by the inmates to go over the left field fence into the cow pasture.

One game often talked about by some of the orphanage athletes is what eventually became known as the "watermelon game." It started out as a game with a church team from Nahunta. After lunch on Saturday, the boys loaded up on an old blue bus with the words "Free Will Baptist Orphans Home" painted on the side. During the game, the orphanage team fell behind by several runs. Petey, house parent and bus driver, was sitting in the stands and was challenged to a load of watermelons if the orphanage team could come back and beat the Nahunta team. He went over and talked with the players; it was the beginning of the sixth inning, and the score was Nahunta 6, Orphanage 2. He pointed to the man wearing the overalls and told the boys about the bet, and they got all fired up.

The orphanage team scored one run in the sixth, two in the seventh, one in the eighth, and one in the ninth; final score: Orphanage 7, Nahunta 6. True to his word, the farmer led the bus to his watermelon field. On their way back to the orphanage, the bus was filled with watermelons. After dinner that night, they cut a lot of watermelons.

Basketball

Basketball at the orphanage was played on an outside dirt court. Often, water had to be removed after a hard rain in order for the boys to play. A cloth fertilizer bag or another cloth-type bag served as the net. There never was a time when a boy couldn't find a pick-up game on the outside dirt court. In the 1950s, there were times when Coach Drake would remove the old nets from the school gym at the end of the school year and give them to one of the boys to take back for the dirt court goal. While the nets usually did not last until school started back in the fall, it was an instant incentive for the boys to get together for a game. There was no outside dirt basketball court at the orphanage for the girls until the late 1960s.

Taught a Work Ethic

Girls at the orphanage had chores, even on school days. Rising at 5:00 a.m., some were in the kitchen cooking for a 6:00 a.m. breakfast and cleaning up afterwards before getting ready to catch the bus for school at 7:30 a.m. Chores changed every three months, and girls were systematically rotated to all the chores: cooking, house cleaning, folding and ironing, waiting on tables during meals, canning in the summer months, and sewing. The girls who played on the basketball team or a cheerleading squad still had to do their chores. Those who played basketball would go to practice immediately after school and return to the orphanage for dinner, chores, study hall at 7:00 p.m., and showers were before bedtime at 9:00 p.m.

Boys at the orphanage had similar routines except their chores were: feeding hogs, cows, chickens and turkeys, planting and harvesting crops, stoking boilers, cutting grass, washing clothes, and house cleaning—the least favorite chore. They managed to attend basketball practice beginning at 7:00 p.m. and stay after school for baseball practices and the games. Chores had to be done with all of these school activities.

Although the orphanage encouraged boys and girls to play sports, they did expect their athletes to keep all their school grades at "C" or higher and to never have a "D" for conduct. Study hall was mandated unless you had a "B" average.

Mr. Drake clearly understood the orphanage work schedule for his athletes, and those students taking Drivers Education in the summer months. Steve Mitchell tells this story about taking Drivers Education under Mr. Drake's teaching:

Steve Mitchell

"One thing about Mr. Drake that really impressed me as a teenager was the extra effort he put forth to make sure that our Drivers Education training fit our schedules. He always carried a clipboard around with him. He would ask us where we would be working—what field, what times we had our mid-morning and mid-afternoon breaks, etc. He would record everything and show up wherever we told him we would be.

"He would drive down any path to get to us and blow the horn on the Driver's Ed car to let us know that he was waiting there at the end of those long tobacco rows. You could set your clock by him—he was always on time. He would let us get in (mud, tobacco gum and all) and do our time. He always made sure that he got us back as soon as our driving time was done.

"Everyone had to take a final driving test which included parallel parking, making turns using the proper hand signals—all the usual requirements on

a car with a 3-speed transmission. Mr. Drake put an extra twist in my test. I was bragging that my driving was as smooth as a gravy sandwich. He made me drive to a long, steep hill and stop as we started up the hill. He took the open bottle of Pepsi-Cola he had been sipping on and set it on the floorboard at his feet. Then he told me to put the car in first gear and take off without spilling his Pepsi. I think his exact words were, 'Let's see what you're made of.' I never was really sure whether he was actually holding the drink with his feet so it wouldn't spill or whether I really was as good as I thought. Either way, I felt a lot of extra pressure that day. I realized that Mr. Drake could come up with a test for anything."

Best Athlete

Mr. Drake, or Coach Drake, smiled when he thought of the talented pool of athletes and students coming from the orphanage. During his first coaching year (1954–55), he coached a sophomore from the orphanage that he considered the best athlete he ever had while at Middlesex.

In 1940, at age three, Chester Eugene "Rod" Page (1940–57) and his six-year old brother were placed in the orphanage after both their parents died. Rod played both basketball and baseball. Coach Drake remembered, "His physical maturity was just a step ahead of the rest of the guys in school. He could put the ball in the hole and was very good in both sports."

On Coach Drake's first championship team in 1957, Rod was co-captain and a member of the All-Tournament team. During his senior year in 1957, Coach Drake took Rod to Chowan Junior College to see the basketball coach. He was given a basketball scholarship and played both years at Chowan. When Rod graduated from high school, he left the orphanage after having been there for 17 years. He graduated in the spring and signed a professional

Coach Drake's 1957 Middlesex Boys' Tournament Champions
L-R: Co-Captains #6 Rod Page and #8 Jackie Davis

baseball contract with the Baltimore Orioles. During the summer after high school was out, Coach Drake coached a rookie league team for the Orioles in Kingsport, Tennessee, and Rod played for him on that league.

Top Guard

Coach Drake remembered another orphanage student, Patricia "Pat" Lane (1946–59). Pat was placed in the orphanage along with her four brothers.

Coach Drake receives hugs after winning Nash County Tournament
L-R: Sandra Bunn and Pat Lane.

She was co-captain and a member of the Nash County All-Tournament team and on Middlesex's 1958 Conference and Tournament Championship team. Coach Drake acknowledges Pat was the best female guard he had ever coached. Enid receives hugs after winning Nash County tournament.

Middlesex School Records

Coach Drake couldn't help but think of one student in particular—this student stood out above them all in basketball.

Ray Worthington

In spite of his early tragedies, Ray Worthington (1956–63) turned out to be an inspiring player. Ray's father was a farmer and his mother stayed at home. After the death of his grandfather, his grandmother lived with the family.

In 1951, his father was infected with tuberculosis, and shortly afterwards his mother was diagnosed with breast cancer. His father realized the gravity of their situation and after talking it out, the family decided that if both Ray's parents died the children would be placed in the orphanage. Ray's mother died in December 1952 and his father in November 1953. His grandmother became the children's primary caregiver after their parents' deaths.

In December 1954, his sister Ann (1955–65) was sent to the orphanage and in June 1955, Ray and his younger brother Ted (1956–59) were also sent there. Ray's older brother John stayed with his grandmother.

All of this could have made Ray bitter, but he was a fighter and that is shown by his incredible performance in the 1962–63 basketball season. Senior Ray Worthington set the highest single-year school scoring record with 529 points. His scoring average was 20.2 points per game and his shooting accuracy was 42 percent of field goals attempted. Most of his shots were long distance and opposing coaches assigned their strongest defensive players to guard him.

In an interview at the end of the season, Coach Drake told a reporter: "Ray can shoot with anyone from the outside, either set shots or jump shots. He is a good ball handler. He has real good hands that are as quick as anyone's. He can play college ball, I know."

Ray set another school record during his senior year. On Friday, January 4, 1963, he scored 43 points against Wendell High School and didn't even play the last four minutes. The final score was 77–60. Ray's single game scoring is still a school record.

Coach Drake took Ray to Louisburg, Chowan, and Campbell Colleges to introduce him to their coaches. Campbell College gave him a basketball scholarship.

Extended Family to Many

It was a rare occasion for Coach Drake to discipline an athlete from the orphanage. Children from the orphanage lived a fairly regimented life and learned early to follow rules: be responsible, be timely, be reverent, respect adults, work as a team, and live through difficult times. Most of these same rules were important to participate and play team sports under Drake's coaching philosophy. Incoming freshmen athletes from the orphanage learned about Coach Drake from upper classmen before they even entered high school. They knew what to expect and were seasoned by the orphanage athletes to follow his rules. Coach Drake followed the belief that it's not whether you win or lose, it's how you play the game, and those orphanage athletes were some of his best players.

Today, orphanage athletes will tell you that "Mr. Drake" was a great motivator; he was dedicated to their skill development, he prepared them, and he expected them to execute—no excuses. They have a fondness for him, see him as a bigger-than-life coach, and will tell you that "Mr. Drake" connected them with something that excited them. This has been a benefit for them all their lives. Mr. Drake taught them to dream and believe in themselves. For many, Mr. Drake was their strongest male role model.

Final Thoughts

Mr. Drake resigned from Middlesex High School in 1965. He took a moment to gather his thoughts before leaving. As he sat and thought about the years, a glimmer came to his eye as he concentrated on that special group of students—those from the orphanage. He remembered how the athletes worked extra hard at practices and played hard in games, and how they were a continuous stream of competitive skilled athletes for his Middlesex program. With a shine in his eyes, he realized he had been blessed with many good athletes from the Middlesex community, but he knew his number of wins would have been fewer at Middlesex without those athletes from the orphanage.

After leaving Middlesex High School, Mr. Drake coach Louisburg Jr. College from 1965–2006. He won 1,022 basketball games in his coaching career: 694 wins at Louisburg Jr. College, and 328 at Middlesex High School. On March 19, 2001, Coach Drake was inducted into the National Junior College Athletic Association Hall of Fame and is the top ten 'Winningest' Coach in the NJCAA. On September 28, 2007, he was inducted into the Louisburg, Jr. College Hall of Fame. Many of us from the orphanage believe he will one day be inducted into the North Carolina Sports Hall of Fame.

In 2009, Jerry Smith (1949–60) wrote Coach Drake's life story in his book *Road to Hutchinson*. The writing of this chapter is influenced by contents of the book. Jerry played basketball and baseball for Coach Drake when he was at Middlesex High School. Jerry was a four year starter on the high school baseball team. Enid was an influence on Jerry throughout his childhood and early adulthood, and Jerry continues to have respect and a dear fondness for him today.

Mr. Drake may be—most likely is—the most respected man by the majority of children who were in the orphanage from 1954 to 1965. He made a difference in the lives of so many children.

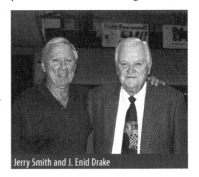
Jerry Smith and J. Enid Drake

God Was Working
In My Life

Gary Lee, President/CEO

Free Will Baptist Children's Home
Middlesex, North Carolina

1994–Present

What is the perfect family? Does it consist of two parents and one or more children with a father who works outside the home and a mother who stays home to care for the children and household? Is the perfect family one that is peaceful and calm, with no conflicts or tension? Is the family's success measured by the number of cars they have or where they go on vacation?

As a boy growing up in eastern North Carolina, I knew most of my family members but never considered them to be perfect. In fact, like most families, there were issues and secrets never talked about. My parents had four children before they reached the age of 30. Because my grandparents were farmers, I was introduced to work at an early age. Toiling in the tobacco field during the summer was how I earned money for school clothes. My family always struggled financially, and it was obvious to others that we were poor. I didn't realize how bad it was until I was older and wiser. I am thankful now for the aid of a social welfare system, which most likely kept us together. Once a month we would get lots of groceries with our allotted food stamps. I am grateful we always had a roof over our heads and food to eat.

My parents suffered from the stress of raising a family, their relationship with each other, and substance abuse issues. These factors contributed to an inability to meet other responsibilities. For example, their standard for school was simply to do what was minimally required to pass your grade.

I was described as the small, shy boy... one who never excelled in academics, athletics, or popularity. While in my early teens I left my parents and siblings and began living with other relatives. It was one of the best things that ever happened to me, although I didn't realize it at the time. My new home was filled with lots of attention, love, and respect. I began attending church, meeting new people, and experiencing new things. I excelled in my studies for the first time since early elementary. My self-esteem and confidence slowly improved.

Sometimes I wonder why I wanted to make a better life for myself. I hated the tobacco fields. I thought I would be successful if I furthered my education. Certainly the modeling of the couple who took me in, and my decision to accept Christ and become a Christian, brought about positive changes in my life. But never at any time did I blame my parents for the less-than-ideal environment in which I was reared.

I worked at the home for years before I ever shared the story of my personal upbringing. I understand now that God was working in my life long before I realized it. Perhaps he was preparing me to fulfill His plan for my life—to serve children, families, and hurting people.

During my years of working at the Free Will Baptist Children's Home, I have learned that no family is perfect. This ministry has become so much more than just a place to call home or a place to live... It is a refuge and place for healing. Even though children today do not stay here as long as they did in the early years, the Children's Home is no less of a home for children. In fact, this place has become more important than ever because the circumstances that bring them here are so devastating.

Each of us must find peace within our lives no matter what problems we have encountered, whether from our childhood, other adults, our children, family, or friends. For me it began with learning to forgive. I believe my parents did the best they could at the time, and I wish they had made better decisions. I will always respect my parents. All in all, I thank God because if it had not been for my past experiences, I would not be the person I am today.

Is my life perfect? Far from it, but I choose to live with love, understanding, and agreeing to disagree sometimes. Did I have the perfect family? Yes, because God gave me exactly what I needed to become who I am today.

Note: Gary Lee has worked for Free Will Baptist Children's Home for 23 years. Since 2008, he has served as President/CEO. The first children were admitted May 23, 1920.

Appendix

Free Will Baptist Children's Home
Alumni Historical Collection

Housed in Memorial Chapel
Free Will Baptist Children's Home
Middlesex, North Carolina

Chapel

Sanctuary

One of the original front doors to the chapel

Historical Collection Display Case: Includes dishes from different eras, metal water pitcher children used, ball from top of Home's past water tank and ball from top of past flag pole.

Historical Collection Display Case: Includes three Valedictorians and Elder Cummings (Blackie)

Historical Collection Display Case: Includes physical belongings of Dr. Josephine D. Newell, M.D. (Home physician 1951–69), water bucket for baseball team, homemade wooden bat and photo of team.

Historical Collection Display Case: Includes boys' shoe shinning kit, sling shots, barber clippers, camera

Historical Collection Display Case: Includes first aid box for blue activity bus pictured on cover of book The Family, Register of Inmates book

Afterword

Dr. Donna S. Thigpen, Ed.D.

Cousins are similar to but more distant than our siblings. When I look back on my time at the Free Will Baptist Children's Home, Middlesex, North Carolina, I think I am a cousin. I was at the home but not in it. Let me explain.

I was adopted by Rev and Mrs. S. A. Smith. They were better known to the children as Ma and Pa Smith. The Reverend Stephen Smith was Superintendent of the home for two different periods (1951–55 and 1956–58). The first time he and Ma Smith were working at the home I was not with them. They left the home after a few years and returned to Beulaville, North Carolina, Ma Smith's hometown. That was when my life changed dramatically.

Both of my parents were only 18 years old when I was born. To help make ends meet they rented a small apartment in the back of my father's much older sisters home and her husband. They were living there when I was born. My Aunt Bertha and Uncle Stephen had no children. From the moment I was born they doted on me. From infancy on I spent much of my time with my Aunt and Uncle. When I was with them all my needs were met and most of my wants. I could be a child.

My parents had a very tempestuous marriage. When I was with them my life was chaos. We moved frequently as my father changed jobs. Sometimes my two younger brothers and I lived with our parents, sometimes with our grandmother and with Aunts and Uncles on both sides of our family. I always stayed with my beloved Aunt Bertha and Uncle Stephen. During the periods of time I was with my parents I was the responsible older sister. I baby sat my brothers, cooked dinner for them, changed diapers, bathed and put them to bed. All this before I was 12 years old.

I was part of a large extended family, Aunts, Uncles, and Cousins. This family cared for me and my brothers in a family foster care system, no government, church, or agency were involved. As time passed Ma and Pa Smith adopted me. My life was wonderful compared to life with my parents. My home was a Christian home, very loving, calm and supportive. No longer did I worry about enough food or struggle with the responsibility of caring for two young brothers.

At the beginning of my freshman year in high school, Pa Smith was again called by the church to serve as Superintendent of the Home. He and Ma Smith moved back and I went with them. What a strange environment for me. I instantly had a hundred or so cousins. I had many of the same rules as the children in the home. As I became acclimated to the home, I loved having cousins my own age. Some of these cousins were Jerry Smith and his twin sister Nancy. We played together and went to school together. One little secret I'll share is that I had a crush on Jerry but he had eyes for someone else. I remember my days at the home with great fondness. I took with me from years there many of the principles I live by today. These include a strengthening of my faith, the value of sharing, cooperation and most of all love. After two and a half years we left the children's home and returned to Beulaville.

Changing school in my junior year was hard. I missed my cousins and my life at the children's home, but God gave me a gift that made my transition very easy. In my senior year I fell in love with my wonderful husband of fifty three years, Sloan Thigpen. We are blessed with two children and five grandchildren.

Over the years I had wondered where my cousins were and how they were doing. Years later I learned that Jerry had written a book about people living in the home titled *The Family*. In a search for a copy of the book I found the contact information for Jerry and after 50 plus years we reconnected. I enjoy the book and was thrilled when he asked me to write an afterthought for his new book. As I learned about his life's work I realized there were parallels in his work and mine.

Jerry and I both worked to better the lives of children; he as a social worker and me as a nurse. My chosen field was Maternal and Child Health. My career took many turns but the core was always helping children and young adults. I taught nursing and later became an administrator in a community college, always focused on what was best for the students. My last job was President of Bismarck State College in Bismarck, North Dakota. My big question there was always how this decision affects the students. After retirement, my husband, Sloan and I returned to North Carolina to be near our family. We both worked in the Guardian ad Litem Program. This program works with children in foster care. We felt great satisfaction in advocating for these children.

Now, as I write this, I think back over my life and realize that relationships are the most important things in life. Our relationship with God is the most important one we have, followed by family, our friends, and those we touch in the course of our lives. When we form relationships they overlap each other and enrich our lives.

In Jerry's book, *The Family*, published in 2010, you were enlightened with stories told by children and staff in the children's home of my youth. This book, *Cousins*, that you have just read, enlightened you regarding residential child care through your readings from writings by professionals, and children and staff from more than a dozen children's homes across this country and Africa. You now have a knowledge base of residential care that will abet you while on your pathway finding opportunities to help children in care and the children homes charged with responsibility of caring for children.

At one time in my life I believed that children were better off in a foster home instead of an orphanage. My experience with Guardian ad Litem showed me the good and the bad side of foster care. My experience at the Free Will Baptist Children's Home showed me the positive side of residential care in a children's home. This is especially true when God is at the center of the home, and children are reared using Christian values. They are taught Love, responsibility, cooperation, and a strong work ethic. This home prepared them for their place in the world.

I am enjoying my retirement. I searched for a way to be a blessing to young people God put in my path. After much thought and prayer, God laid two verses from Titus on my heart. I work with young women in our church in a group I formed called The Yahweh Sisterhood. The purpose was set by Titus 2: 3-5:

[3] The aged women likewise, that they be in behavior as becomes holiness, not false accusers, not given to much wine, teachers of good things [4] that they may teach the young women to be sober, to love their husbands, to love their children [5] to be discreet, chaste, keepers at home, good, obedient to their own husbands, that the word of God not be blasphemed. (KJV)

This describes the role of older women in the church. We are to be a role model and a mentor to the young women. This added much joy to our lives.

My husband, Sloan, and I are surrogate grandparents, parents, counselors and confidants. These young people bring great joy to us when the little ones come running to us on Sunday morning saying, "mommy, mommy. Can I go home with Miss Donna?"

Dr. Donna S. Thigpen, President Emeritus
Bismarck State College, Bismarck, North Dakota

About Donna Thigpen

Donna Thigpen's professional and academic background is impressive: 1964–67, Public Health Nurse in the Pitt County Health Department, Greenville, North Carolina; 1968–72, Public Health Nurse in Richmond, Virginia; 1972–78, Director of Nursing Department for the James Sprunt Community College, Kenansville, North Carolina; 1978–89, Dean of Administrative Services for the James Sprunt Community College; 1990–95, Assistant Vice President of Student Services for Trident Technical College, Charleston South Carolina; 1995–2006, President of Bismarck State College, Bismarck, North Dakota; 2006, President Emiterus at Bismarck State College. In addition, she is President of D and D Consultant Services, a member of numerous boards and professional organizations at the state and local level, and she was appointed by Governor Jim Hunt to the North Carolina Board of Nursing from 1978 to 1986. Donna holds a BNS from East Carolina University (1964), an MSN from the University of Maryland (1968), and a Doctor of Education (EdD) from North Carolina State University (1993).

Acknowledgments

In July 2011, a year after publication of *The Family*, I attended homecoming at the Free Will Baptist Children's Home, the home of my youth. Throughout the day, people came up to me and asked when the sequel would be published. I said I wasn't sure. The truth is that I had never planned for a sequel, until these people began inquiring.

As a writer, I've learned you can waste a lot of time unless you follow your pen. You'll experience a lot of downtime with writer's block if you try to force the pen to write just to fill the pages. Knowing the subject material is vital. After deciding to produce a sequel, I wandered through the latter part of 2011 searching for a vision for it. I met several adults from childhood residential care facilities in different states. I wrote two columns that year about other adults associated with children's homes—one from North Carolina and the other from Tennessee. I looked back at columns I'd written prior to 2011 about children's homes other than Free Will Baptist. There were quite a few. This sealed my vision for the sequel, and *Cousins* became a reality.

While *The Family* helped me face unresolved issues from my childhood and heal from them, *Cousins* has taking me to the top of the mountain in helping me reach final resolution and acceptance of my journey along the many dirt paths I've traveled. Knowing all the writers who contributed to this book has been therapy for me. They have nurtured my subconscious, unlocking doors that I'd closed for so many years. Meeting these 'cousins' has enlarged my family, a family that's always been there. In addition, I maintain solid friendships with the child advocates who contributed to the book, and I know these relationships will continue into the future. Cousins and advocates, you have my heartfelt thanks for your willingness to get off the highways and onto the dirt path for this book. Without your readiness to share your life experiences and be vulnerable, this book could not have been born. Thank you.

I am also deeply indebted to the following people who assisted me in other ways to bring these stories to life. I am forever grateful to them.

Susan Smith. I am very grateful to my wife for her support and patience throughout the late evenings and early mornings required during this production phase. She endured my mood changes, and has been the steadiest force by my side during this journey. She deserves my utmost thanks.

Gary Fenton Barefoot, curator of the Free Will Baptist Historical Collection, University of Mount Olive, Mount Olive, North Carolina. Gary contributed a piece of writing, and provided invaluable factual verification on other aspects of the book. He saved me time and many miles of travel.

Gary Lee, president and CEO of the Free Will Baptist Children's Home, Middlesex, North Carolina. Gary was an ardent supporter of the project from the beginning and graciously provided valuable help when asked.

Lynna Mitchell, publisher and general manager of *Tazewell County Free Press*, Richlands, Virginia. Lynna has encouraged my writing as a columnist since 1996. My writing skills developed through the years thanks largely to this regular practice. Without her support and patience, this book could not have been possible.

Kathy Hoard, vice president of Human Resources, Holston United Methodist Home for Children, Greeneville, Tennessee. Kathy has been helpful through the years—especially with the fruition of this book. It always began with my eating her chocolate candy and continued with our wonderful conversations. As a member of the Home's CORE training team since 2000, Kathy always had my handouts prepared for my class. Some of the stories in this book are from these handouts passed out to new employees of the Home.

Carrie Brown, staff member, Free Will Baptist Children's Home. Among Carries many responsibilities is coordinating alumni activities for the home. She has been especially helpful to me in providing photos and information about alumni.

Attorney Allen Thomas, Wilson, North Carolina. Allen once again offered his solid support, legal advice, and encouragement. Thank you, Allen.

Christine Coleman. A special thanks to "Chris," who spoke at the Free Baptist Homecoming several years ago. She is also part of "the Family" after becoming a member of the Free Will Baptist staff in 2016 as Vice President for Programs and Services. Her contribution detailing her seventeen years in residential care is unique for this book. She brings professional and childhood experiences to the quality of care for children on campus and is a unique resource for administration. I'm happy our paths crossed.

Edith Hedgepeth. Edith was one of my houseparents at the Free Will Baptist Orphanage. I hadn't seen her since 1953 when she and her family left to pursue other employment. Then in 2012, she called me. She had read *The Family* and wanted to know if I was going to do a sequel. At that time she was in her 90s and taking regular flights in a two seater airplane with a friend! We had such a good time catching up on each other's lives that it was difficult to get off the phone. We have maintained contact since thn. She wrote her story by hand and mailed it to me, and I happily included in *Cousins*. Edith is a special woman, and I have a soft spot for her.

Mable Stevenson. A professional Social Worker, Mable and I worked together for many years at the Wilson County Department of Social Services in Wilson, North Carolina. She learned about this book and referred Archie Thomas Rahmaan to me. They were on a cruise together when she met him. I am thankful his story found its way into the pages of this book. My thanks to Mable for its fruition.

Maggie Powell, maggiepowelldesigns.com. Maggie is a good friend and professional graphic designer who helped me with the layout and production of this book. She nudged me quite a bit to keep things moving, and is part of the reason you're reading these words today. I am happy our paths crossed.

There were other writers who considered sharing their thoughts for this book, but ultimately decided it was not the right time. They each gave great thought to their decision, and I am grateful for the consideration they took in coming to it. They remain my friends and professional associates, and I have enormous respect for their support of children in care. They know who they are. I remain fortunate to have them share life's pathway with me.

Made in the USA
Middletown, DE
25 June 2017